外黒人

GAIKOKUJIN - THE STORY

III

Contributors

Edited by Joshua S. Yeley

Proofreading by Dynah Deborah D

Cover Art

Drawing: Griffin Reid

Calligrapher: Minori Ito

Note: Please make your contribution by leaving a review of the book here:
https://www.amazon.com/review/create-review?asin=B01AQT38V2&ie=UTF*&#

https://www.goodreads.com/book/show/28349177-gaikokujin---the-story

Thank you in advance!

Copyright

Publisher's Cataloging-In-Publication Data
(Prepared by The Donohue Group, Inc.)

Names: Amaru, Takuan.
Title: 外黒人 = Gaikokujin - the story. Book III, Quest for Christ consciousness / Takuan Amaru.
Other Titles: Gaikokujin - the story. Book III, Quest for Christ consciousness | Quest for Christ consciousness

Description: Nagoya, Japan : AfroAsiatic Books, [2018] |
    Book III of a trilogy. | Interest age level: 014-060. |
    Includes bibliographical references.
Identifiers: ISBN 978-4-908556-07-4 (set) | ISBN 978-4-
    908556-05-0 (print) | ISBN 978-4-908556-04-3 (ebook)
Subjects: LCSH: Racially mixed youth--United States--
    Fiction. | African American youth--United States--Fiction.
    | Asian American youth--Fiction. | Race--Fiction. |
    Christianity--Fiction. | American Dream--Fiction. |
    American literature--Japanese American authors. |
    LCGFT: Biographical fiction.
Classification: LCC PS3601.M37 G353 2016 (print) | LCC
    PS3601.M37 (ebook) | DDC 813/.6 [Fic]--dc23

Published by AfroAsiatic Books
www.afroasiatic.jp
www.gaikokujin-thestory.com

外黒人

GAIKOKUJIN - The Story

<u>Book III</u>: Quest for Christ Consciousness

Takuan Amaru

AfroAsiatic Books

Nagoya, Japan

Table of Contents

Preface

"True despair is a sense of hopelessness so impossible to deal with that a person will try anything to change his/her situation" ～ *Tak Amaru*

    In February 2014, I laid on the tatami floor of my house in Kagoshima, Japan. For nearly three years, I had been unable to walk. In spite of doctors continually insisting the injury was not serious, and following their rehabilitation instructions to a tee, I was still on crutches and living the life of a disabled person without receiving any type of disability financial assistance. At one point, I had to be admitted to a hospital and was relegated to using a wheelchair. So, as you can imagine, my savings were depleted. Unable to go to work, my wife had to become the primary bread-winner. This sudden, unexpected shift in our roles destabilized our relationship to a point from which it would not recover.

    "Godammit! What the fuck is wrong with me?" I screamed, tears of frustration flowing down my cheeks, falling onto the tatami. Following another rehab session, and not feeling any progress whatsoever, I was beyond depressed. Secluded way out in the countryside, I was free to vent my feelings out loud. And this I did often. "Nobody can help me…the doctors, my friends, even my wife! What the fuck am I gonna do? Dammit! Dammit! Dammit!" I yelled, slamming my hand against the floor.

This was a typical afternoon.

One evening as I lay on the tatami I asked myself a question. *Have I ever been in this type of dire situation before?* The obvious answer was 'no' because having been an athlete my body had always been strong. However, when I thought on a deeper level, I remembered the desperation I felt to find God back at Ft. Bragg. That was the only other time I can recall having doubts about my immediate future— meaning whether or not I might die soon. Had I not went to Jon & Curt's church that day, I cannot imagine how I could have continued living. Totally at my wits end, although I was not suicidal, I had contemplated every other insane tendency.

So maybe the answer is returning to Christianity?

Even in my woeful situation, the idea of singing and clapping my hands at a Sunday service brought a wry grin to my tear-stained cheeks. However, on a deeper level, I recognized it was at church where I had been brought into contact with my Higher Self—*and this is what I needed now!* Understanding the 'church' represents a body of believers, I realized that every member of our church taught me something about myself; they were like my brothers and sisters. *How did they do that?* I contemplated. Then the answer hit me like a lightning bolt. *By showing me different aspects of the 'human condition,'* I came to understand. And this carnal reflection allowed me to see the weaknesses in my own character. It was only after defining my problem was I able to piece-together a solution.

Upon reaching this conclusion I sat up in the darkness and, with an extreme effort, crawled across the floor and fumbled through a desk-drawer until I found what I was looking for: a candle and some matches. After placing the lit candle on an altar dedicated to my ancestors, I glanced through the flickering light at a clock mounted on the wall. Just as I thought it was almost 8:00. Knowing my wife would not be returning until after 10—totally exhausted as always—I lay back down to focus on my body. Having grasped that, like the members of a church, each muscle, nerve, and gland represented the members of my 'church-body,' I was determined to find out what they could show me.

Closing my eyes, I took a deep breath and moved my right leg from the hip until I felt a twinge of pain. *Hmmm*, not really pain but more a feeling of instability. At that point, I started moving my leg in various directions until I discovered the exact motion that seemed to work the damaged muscles in my lower-back. Following a short rest, I proceeded to do 100 repetitions of the same motion. Then I repeated the entire process with my knee.

Within a week, I felt some progress.

Day by day, I continued to add different movements and soon I had invented new exercises. Some I still do to this day, while others were scrapped for their lack of efficiency. After a long and winding road, in 2016, I was finally able to discard my crutches (and canes) for good.

Book III

Chapter 1: Which Way to the Lord?

The singing and hand clapping became much louder once I opened the first set of double-doors leading into the storefront building. After pausing to take a deep breath I opened the second set and entered the church, all the while bracing myself to be caught up in some sort of Holy Rapture. Nonetheless, after walking in and taking a look around, to say my first impression was disappointing would be a massive understatement. A choir consisting of eight adults, some wearing shirts and ties while others were clad in t-shirts and jeans, was standing on a retractable stage. Next to them, just off-stage, was a middle-aged white woman in a long-sleeved print dress seated behind a piano. As they butchered *Amazing Grace*, I stayed near the entrance and watched in a state of dismay.

In addition to my frustration, I now felt foolish for believing I might actually find the Almighty here—amongst a group of typical Christians in their cheap, off-the-rack suits and *Buster Brown* shoes. When one busta, who was wearing thick glasses and a cockamamie grin, stumbled on his way over to greet me, I was so disgusted I turned around to leave; but in that instant something caught my eye which froze me in my tracks. Scanning the sparse congregation, I spotted a familiar face. However what got my attention had nothing to do with human features, for it was much deeper. Once we made eye contact, I peeped through the window of his soul and glimpsed what could only be described as the Spirit of God. This was long before I knew anything about God being *'manifest in the flesh,'* as it is written in *First Timothy 3:16*; so at this point, the only thing I understood, or even cared about, was the possibility this person might hold the key to my salvation.

When the sharply-dressed man in a teal-colored suit stood up, I forgot my previous agenda to abandon ship and side-stepped past the clumsy usher just as he was extending his hand to welcome me. My skepticism now having been replaced with a sense of relief, this was underscored when the man spread his arms wide and crushed me in a brotherly bear hug. It was only after he had forcefully expelled the air from my lungs when we finally shook hands.

"Tak, it's really good to see you!" Curt roared with a firm grasp on my palm.

As dirty and despicable as I felt, to be wholeheartedly welcomed—not questioned or judged—this was indeed the greatest blessing. By far the most sincere greeting I had ever received, Curtis Crawley was radiating compassion from every fiber of his ebony being. And this was not a one-time thing. In fact, this was the vibe every time I was with Curt, Jon, or any of the men and women who I had the privilege of calling my brothers and sisters during my two-plus years at the Doorway of Christian Unity. Even as a teen, I was aware that humility was a characteristic which could only be faked in the short-term; so several weeks later, when their passion never wavered, I became a true believer. Being confronted by people with no ulterior motives—these self-proclaimed 'Soldiers of the Lord'—completely blew me away.

Personally, I believe Curtis Crawley, who everyone

called 'Craw-dad,' was delving deep within. The fact he never wanted anything from me, not even my friendship, hinted his quest was on the spiritual level. Although we did eventually become friends, the only relationship that mattered to either of us was a personal one with the true and living Christ. 'High on life' but not in a corny way, both he and Jon personified much of what I sought as a young man. In short, they commanded the respect of those around them while maintaining an air of coolness. Put another way, they were strong, intelligent black men who did not feel the need to sound or act like white boys.

The tears welling-up in my eyes revealed my emotional baggage. Curt, recognizing my challenge, walked away to greet some other people who just arrived. Two men with high-and-tight haircuts along with their wives were standing where I had been seconds ago. A tattoo of a maroon beret with a lightning bolt on one of the soldier's forearms looked familiar; so I imagined I ran into these guys before at the PX, or maybe somewhere around the barracks. After Curt led them to the visitors' seats, which were on the right side in the second and third rows, he returned.

"Tak, the sermon's about to start. Allow me to show you to your seat," Curt said, speaking in his usual cheerful voice. Once we started walking, he gave me a run-down of the itinerary. "You picked a great day to come because Jon's opening up for Pastor Bart this morning. He's going to tell us how he became a Soldier of the Lord." After saying this, he then gestured toward an attractive woman seated on the left side, in the first row. "I'm sitting over there with my fiancé, but if you have time later we can talk some more, okay?"

Once I assured him I had no plans after church, Curt left to greet another arriving visitor.

Seated on a hard metal chair, not only did I feel terribly uncomfortable but also extremely nervous because everyone, it seemed, was staring at me. Fortunately, about a minute later, Jon walked in the room. Entering from a back hallway, he emerged through a purple curtain draped from the ceiling. This magic show-like entrance caused everyone to focus their attention on his approach; which allowed me to relax and remove the phony smile from my face. As Jon, dressed in a charcoal-grey suit complemented by a black tie with white polka-dots, placed his notes on the lectern, and peeked over his round wire-framed spectacles, at his audience. When his gaze met mine he smiled. Happy he remembered me, I was eager to hear this charismatic preacher's message. It took Jon another couple seconds to find a passage in the Bible. His preparation complete, he closed his eyes and took a breath to ground himself.

"Praise the Lord!" he suddenly bellowed.

"*Praise the Lord!*" everyone around me shouted back, not surprised in the least.

"Good morning folks," Jon then greeted us in his usual voice. "Let's pray."

Hearing this, everyone bowed their head for the opening invocation.

"Lord Jesus Christ," Jon began, "you died on the cross so that we, through your divine sacrifice, could be made whole and thereby come to know God as our Father. Lord, please allow your words to penetrate deaf ears and hardened hearts...*blah, blah, blah.*"

Listening to him, I was disappointed to hear the same, generic phrases the TV evangelists used; and this continued even after the opening prayer. Just as I was getting drowsy, he

4

got my attention by switching topics.

"For those of y'all that don't know me, my name is Jon Coltier. Welcome to the Way! I'm looking forward to meeting and getting to know each one of you, so allow me to tell you a little bit about my childhood." Pausing here, the handsome pastor-in-training glanced around the room. "I grew up in Texas and am from a poor, black neighborhood in the Dallas - Fort Worth area. When I was a boy, lots of drugs were being sold on my street which in turn, as you can imagine, led to other types of crime and violence. At the age of thirteen, I was fortunate enough to win an academic scholarship to a private, boarding school out in the suburbs. This allowed me to escape the ghetto—and for that I'm eternally grateful. On the other hand, I was wholly unprepared for the new environment I found myself thrown into a world of privileged, Southern white kids who never met a black person before—correction," he emphasized with a raised index finger, "They never met a black person who wasn't either working for them, or in some other subservient position. Once I was away from my family, like most teenagers, I wanted to fit-in and make friends. With no knowledge of God, I quickly learned to compromise my values to be accepted. In return, my classmates allowed me to have a sort of 'mascot' status. But this new role also included being the target of racist jokes. Not to mention my designation by some of the bigger boys to be their human punching-bag."

As a few sympathetic murmurs were heard, Jon cleared his throat.

"But the story gets better," he insisted, "because all that changed on Easter Sunday, 1981. On that morning, I left for church as one person and returned home as someone entirely different. Suddenly, I no longer felt a need for acceptance because I *knew* my purpose. That day, Jesus resurrected my soul! And guess what? I don't think I ever confronted any of those bullies but, by the end of my sophomore year, they beat a hasty retreat whenever they saw me coming."

"Amen!" someone yelled from the crowd. "They're arms were too short to box with God!"

"Believe it or not," Jon resumed. "I likened my encounter with Christ to finding some good pot." As Jon takes a sip of water a few astonished whispers could be heard circulating through the audience. "Back in the day, whenever me or one of my friends had something good, the tendency was to share it because experiencing 'it' with others heightened the joy of having it. So, ladies and gentlemen, that's what I came here to do this morning—share."

When, at first, no one responded Jon realized the need to clarify.

"Folks, I'm talking about sharing the gospel with you, not smoking pot. What did y'all think? I was gonna promote a *Peter Tosh* 'Legalize it' campaign, right here from the pulpit?" As some people laughed, others just smiled seemingly exhaling a sigh of relief. "However at the same time," Jon continued, "I'm not ashamed to say I grew up in poverty and some of its trappings, because nowadays I live a clean life as a saved and sanctified Soldier of the Lord...hallelujah!"

"*Hallelujah!*" echoed the crowd in unison.

As Jon recounted the circumstances which had led him to getting saved, my attention was riveted on his words. Smoking pot. Feeling like a mascot. Being picked on. These

6

were experiences I could relate to. By the time Pastor Bartholomew approached the pulpit to relieve Jon, I really got excited. Since he was the main orator I naturally assumed his words would be even more inspirational than Jon's had been. Nonetheless, it took less than a minute to realize this was not the case.

Joining the Way allowed me to spend time with Curt and Jon. And believe it or not, I even befriended the 'corny folks' once I humbled myself and learned to view them differently. Being received and guided—i.e. shown true brotherhood—by these two, young ministers was more than I could've ever hoped for. Although I respected Pastor Bart as the leader of the church, he had little to do with my reason for showing up each Sunday. In fact, I had difficulty paying attention to his drab, redundant delivery.

"Please open your bibles to Genesis, chapter 12," the pastor instructed. *"Now the Lord said to Abram: 'Go from your country, your people, and your father's household to the land I will show you. I will make you into a great nation, and I will bless you. I will make your name great, and you will be a blessing. I will bless those who bless you, and whoever curses you I will curse. And all peoples on earth will be blessed through you."*

Although the leader of the Way wore reading glasses and held a Bible, he never looked at the book in his hand while reciting the scripture. Once finished, he removed his glasses and placed the 'good book' back on its stand. "Abraham, who was called Abram at the time," he explained, "was instructed to leave the comfort of familiarity." Pointing his finger at us, he then bellowed in a commanding tone. "Go to uncharted territory and build a great nation, and I will bless you!" After lowering his voice to its normal volume, he resumed. "Not only did God promise Abraham he would make his name great, he also vowed that people would be blessed *through* him!" Stopping here, he inserted a hand into his pants pocket. "Pastor Bart, what does that mean to us now, in the nineteen-eighties?"

As the pastor pretended to have a conversation with himself, I listened to the congregation giggle in such a sporadic and uncertain manner that I glanced around the room expecting to see 'Laugh Now!' placards being displayed.

"It means," Pastor Bart continued, "as a spiritual heir of Abraham *you* are a blessing to Fort Bragg and Fayetteville." Appearing confident he had us eating from his hand, the minister then began pointing into the audience. "It means *you*, Sergeant or Private, are the one who keeps the peace in your barracks. It means *you*, Missus Housewife or Ms. Office Worker, are the person who maintains it in the home or at work…and *you*, son or daughter, are the one who makes peace at school a reality…and *you*…" Descending the pulpit, he walked down the center aisle randomly pointing at people sitting on either side of the room. Upon reaching the end, which was the exit of the building, he turned around and retraced his steps. "Understand that wherever you are," the pastor insisted, "your mere presence allows God to do His work through you!"

While choruses of 'Amen' and 'Hallelujah' echoed around the room, the pastor climbed the steps to the stage and returned to the lectern. "Ladies and Gents, here at the Doorway of Christian Unity, we are committed to being living witnesses of the resurrection. That's why on Monday and Friday afternoons, we mobilize to uncharted territory to preach the gospel. Like Abraham, God sends us out there on faith alone. And like Abraham, if we do this God promises to bless us," the pastor passionately preached, swaying to and fro. Although his comments continued for several more minutes, I stopped listening.

Busily flipping through the pages of Genesis, I was mesmerized by the events in chapter 15. There, Abraham had a dream about a 'horror and great darkness' which descended on his people. It is written that Abraham and his seed were condemned as strangers in a foreign land. As slaves, they were forced to serve 'them' for four hundred years. Reading this scripture, I was reminded of our story—not only here in the Americas but the entire melanin-rich diaspora—so when it ended with God promising they 'shall come out with great possessions,' I was so excited all I wanted to do was share what I'd read with Curt and Jon. For this reason, when I looked up and found both of them staring at me I was shocked. Feeling confused and nervous again, I looked around the room, taking inventory of my surroundings while focusing on what the pastor was saying.

"*Who wants to be saved?*" Pastor Bart yelled like he was issuing a challenge. "If you're tired of running around the same sinful circles, like a gerbil running on its wheel going nowhere. If you're sick of being caught-up in a sticky web of lies and deceit. If you're looking for real answers, understand that Jesus is here and ready to embrace you. He's been watching you, waiting for this divine moment; so don't miss this chance because the fifth chapter of *First Thessalonians* tells us the Lord will return like a thief in the night!" By this point, the pastor was on a roll. "Folks, don't get left behind because when the saints go marching into that magnificent city paved with gold, believe me, you're gonna wanna be in that number!"

On that cue, the pianist began playing, '*When the Saints Go Marching in.*'

As the congregation rose to its feet with the choir, I looked back at Curt and Jon only to find both of them had disappeared. After searching the room, I spotted them standing on stage next to the pastor: one on each side of the frail man. The three of them were facing the audience and, as far as I could tell, seemed to be beckoning people to come forward. Watching in awe, I was amazed when a handful of people walked to the stage and knelt down—something about this scene jarred my memory. *Wait a minute, I know what they're doing!* Beyond confirming this was the same ritual Mick had mentioned on our way to Michigan, I vaguely remembered taking-part in one myself back in 6th grade. Well sort of. This occurred when my friend, Brian, invited me to his church for 'Kids Outreach Night.'

As a sheltered, military-brat who was investigating what it meant 'to be black,' an opportunity for a guided tour through the grimiest sections of North Philly was an offer I could not refuse; so of course I eagerly accepted. We arrived at the *Holy Temple* a few minutes before the scheduled 7 p.m. starting time. As Brian's friends, both boys and girls, came up to greet him they took a good look at his slant-eyed buddy. Looking around, I determined the congregation was 100% melanin-rich. For this reason, once the event started, I was aghast to discover the same-ol', tired white man messages streaming down from the pulpit. Shaking this off as a bad coincidence, I got excited when Brian reminded me the main event was a movie about street gangs back in the sixties. Hearing this, I reached into my pocket and pulled-out the flyer he had given me a week ago. Unfolding it, I glanced at the title and read it aloud: "Cross and the Switchblade."

In the opening scene, the camera focused on a switchblade being activated. This was followed by a group of teens chasing down a member of a rival gang and beating him to a pulp. Even though the acting and film quality were both sketchy, I was really getting into it. That is until *Pat Boone*, starring as the 'Great White Hope,' showed up. Supposedly based on a true account, when *Booney* began to single-handedly tame the crime-ridden streets with nothing but a Bible, I dismissed the movie as nonsense. At the conclusion of the low-budget flick, the pastor held an altar call. Although I had no idea where Brian was going when he said, "Come on Tak, let's go." I got up and followed him down the aisle. I did this mostly because of the way his mother was staring at me; she made me feel like I had no choice. Considering she was watching us, I must have gotten 'saved' that day. Honestly due to all the laughter—plus the terrible stench—I cannot really remember.

With over thirty children answering the call, we comprised three rows of kneeling youth. Seconds after the pastor started praying over us, the kid in front of Brian passed gas. It was such a loud, ear-piercing fart that many children began to snicker right away. Opening my eyes I looked at Brian and, together, we fought to suppress our emotion. Just when I was about to reclose my eyes, the same boy turned around to sniff the damage and suddenly—just before the smell hit me—he jumped up and ran toward the restroom. Seeing this everyone, even the adults, busted-out laughing. Judging by the soggy sound plus the foul odor, it was clear that homeboy needed to change into a clean pair of drawers.

"*Stand-up!*" screamed a voice inside my head. Once my daydream was interrupted, I turned my head just in time to see the last of the saints marching past my seat. Knowing it was now or never, before I had time to change my mind, I stood up and stepped into the aisle. Seconds later, I joined the group of people kneeling before Jon, Curt, and the pastor.

And just like that I got saved.

Chapter 2: Training the Spirit

Jumping out of the shower, I hurriedly toweled off in my area of the room. While I rushed to get dressed, the sound of a key being inserted into the door broke my concentration. As a result, I dropped my bar of Speedstick. "Who dat?" I asked, peeking around my locker. It was one of my roommates, Pvt. Guillermo Perez. Still in his BDUs, he was leisurely sauntering through the doorway toting a plastic bag from the PX. Instead of answering my question, he gave me a news bulletin.

"Yo Amaru, I just saw Crawley outside the chow-hall."

"Word? What'd he say?"

"Well actually, umm…"

"What? Come on spit it out," I said half-jokingly. "Don't tell me you ducked him again?"

"Man, you know any discussion with him turns into a three-hour rap session," Perez commented with a bashful grin. "No disrespect but I don't have time for that today. See Amaru, since you're already saved you don't have to worry about him anymore." My shy roommate then cracked a joke, which was rare for him. "Now I know what you're saved from: Crawley's long-ass conversations."

While chuckling at Perez's comment, I wondered how I missed seeing Curt on my way back from the gym. "Thanks for the info. That guy's punctual as he—" Realizing I was about to swear, I cut my sentence short.

"What was that?" Perez teased in a sarcastic tone. "Were you about to say 'hell?' You know that's a curse word, don't you? Be careful because a devout Christian like you could wind up in hell for saying bad words like 'hell.' And I heard 'damn' is even worse."

"Ha ha ha," I said without laughing. "Hey what's gotten into you? You're a regular ol' comedian these days, I see."

Hearing this caused *Chill* to smile.

Pvt. Guillermo Perez, a.k.a. 'Chill,' was a laid-back guy from the East-New York section of Brooklyn. Although we were the same age, due to his reserved mannerisms—Chill was quiet and shy—I had assumed the senior role in our relationship. Being a supply clerk who assisted the armorer, Perez had daily interaction with most of the soldiers in our company. Since he was cool with everyone, I started calling him 'Chill-Guill,' which eventually got shortened to 'Chill.'

"Yo Chill, all jokes aside, don't forget there's a better life waiting for you."

"Yeah I know. Thanks."

"A-right then, I gotta jet. So cool-out." Saying this, I shut my locker and hurried out the door to search for Crawley. Running down a flight of steps, I scolded myself for being late because one of the main targets for today's witnessing mission was Chill, himself.

Two days ago, when I informed Curt of some of the unique challenges my company was facing, he accused me of exaggerating—especially about the drugs. Realizing seeing was believing, I grabbed my jacket. "Let's go," I said, "we gotta make a quick stop before the evening service."

"What? Where to?"

Without another word, I walked out my door and led him down a flight of stairs. After walking around the building to the south entrance, we entered the company dayroom. There, he met two *crackheads* and some other shady characters up-close-and-personal. When Curt started witnessing I had to interrupt so we could make it to the service on time; hence, once we were in the car Curt vowed to return. For this reason, the next day at work I was not surprised to receive a phone call from him.

"I'm jumping tonight," Curt said. "So we gotta wait 'til tomorrow to deploy our special-op on your barracks. Just you and me."

That night, while Curt put his knees in the breeze, I followed his instructions to a tee by visiting each private on our 'hit list' to recite my 'Why I got saved' testimony. According to Curt, after laying this foundation, the Holy Spirit marinates in their soul. "Then, we go collect the fruits of the harvest for the glory of God!" he had told me.

Sprinting around the corner of Building #1303, I stumbled as the mess hall came into view. Luckily, I was able to regain my balance without falling; but Curt was nowhere in sight. "Amaru! Yo Amaru!" Hearing a familiar voice, I turned back and saw a group of guys walking toward me. One of them was waving his arms to get my attention. "What's up Money? Where you been?"

It had been a couple weeks since I had last spoken to Mr. Muhammad. Although his real surname was Jackson, I called him 'Mr. Muhammad' to highlight he was one of those fake practitioners of Islam—you know, the kind that eats pork chops and bacon sandwiches on the sneak-tip. Jackson was infamously known for his drunken dissertations about the

'Black Man's Natural Religion.' Normally his rants took place outside the lower-enlisted club in the wee hours of the morning. "We are the original, divine people of this planet...the white man, with his devilish ways, is nothing more than a lab experiment gone awry," he once stated before asking me a question that, for some reason, has always stayed in my mind. "Did you know the word 'Caucasian' means one whose evil effect is not confined to one's self alone, but affects others?"[1] Because I had written Jackson off as a fool, I was shocked years later to discover much of what he'd said in works by noted scholars and spiritual leaders. Perhaps had he not been so addicted to 'bony white women,' I might have taken his words more seriously.

Despite having no time to talk, I stopped to crack a few jokes.

"Ssup Mr. Muhammad?" I greeted my homie with a grin. Walking up to his six-man crew, I noticed some familiar faces so I gave pounds all around.

"You still lost in the white man's religion?" Jackson wasted no time before taunting me back.

Referencing the last time we met, I countered just as quickly. "You still hiding bottles of *Miller Lite* behind your back, trying to front like you don't drink? Hold up, what's that?" With a surprised expression, I pointed near his feet.

"What?" Looking down, Jackson took the bait.

"Oh my bad," I replied nonchalantly. "I thought I saw a white girl fall out your back pocket."

"*Bah ha ha ha ha!*"

When his buddies began laughing at his expense,

---

[1] Quote by Elijah Muhammad in *Message to the Blackman in America (p. 116)*

Jackson appeared irritated but he ignored them. "I saw your Christian homeboy walk by a couple minutes ago. That's who you're looking for, right?"

"Which way did he go?" Ready to resume my search, I began to jog in place.

"He went that way, toward my building." After pointing at a portion of the barracks situated behind the gym, he offered me a guided tour. "There's only one way in or out, and I didn't see him leave so take it easy slim, you can just roll over there with us."

With that, he and his friends started walking. Even after I fell in step with his crew, Jackson and I continued cracking jokes; however, once we entered his company area our attention was arrested by the all-too-familiar sounds of discord.

"*Pussy, I'll fuck you up!*" yelled an irate voice before strangely adding. "Where do you think you're going?"

"Oh shit! Looks like we got here just in time." Yelling this, Jackson jogged over to the building where the commotion was taking place. "What's going on Bradley?" he said to the guy making the threats. Although the dude he called 'Bradley' was wearing *civvies* like his companions, it was obvious by his haircut and demeanor he was a GI. When the four guys and two girls ignored Jackson, preferring instead to stare up at the second floor, he tilted his head to see what everyone was looking at.

Eventually Bradley acknowledged him.

"Ay Jackson," he said slapping hands with his buddy. "I'm about to fuck this joker up, that's what's going on." Following the handshake, Bradley returned his attention to the second-story terrace. "Muthafucka, bring your punk-ass back down here!"

We could not see the person Bradley was talking to but we could hear his feet climbing the steps. As soon as the unknown person reached the second floor and exited the stairwell, however, he would be visible on the terrace. Once I deduced this situation was not related to my goal, which was finding Curt, I began walking away, figuring I'd go check out the gym. By this time, I had to dodge the droves of soldiers, who were arriving on the scene, hoping to see a fight. Although I was not attracted to violence, I was curious to see how the guy climbing the steps would play the precarious cards he was being dealt; so just before exiting Jackson's company area, I stopped and leaned against a building. When the lone swordsman appeared on the terrace with both hands on his hips, an amused grin materialized onto my face.

"Who dareth speaketh unto me using such vulgar language?" Glaring down from the balcony with a stony snarl etched onto his features, Curt was pointing at his pursuers.

He can't be serious! This was my only thought as Curt, adorned in his battle-dress uniform, appeared to be auditioning for a role in *Othello*. Before anyone had a chance to wipe away their stunned expression, Curt grabbed the handrail and broke down in hysterical laughter.

"*Bahahahahahaha!*"

"That nigga's up there laughing at you." As one of the girls uttered this in disappointment, she moved away from Bradley, preferring to stand with the other young lady in the group. Once the two girls began whispering and giggling, the guys also made their opinions known.

"Someone's starting to smell like pussy…"

"And *he* ain't a female either!"

With his friends giving each other pounds behind his

18

back, Bradley quickly became frustrated. "What y'all talking about?" he fired at his buddies. "Ain't nothing changed, I'm about to whoop that muthafucka's ass. We'll see how funny he thinks this is after his jaw is broken!"

This was the only moment I stopped laughing—but it did not last for long.

"Hey, hey what're you so worked up about?" Curt likewise had stopped laughing but he was grinning even more than usual. With both of his elbows propped on the handrail, Crawley was now leaning forward with his head resting on his interlaced fingers. Clearly enjoying the moment, he looked very comfortable. "Nah, I'm just kidding dude, relax...besides I already apologized."

"*Fuck that!* You gots to pay, them's the rules!" Bradley shot back.

"The rules? What rules? What're you talking about? Man, are you listening to how stupid you sound?" Responding thus, Curt re-exploded into laughter.

Jackson, always looking to instigate trouble, jumped in when he saw his friend losing heart. "Brad, I don't give a fuck what he did, or didn't do. I don't like the fact that he's in our building poppin' shit, so if you're scared I'll handle this."

This proposal set off a fracas as the group discussed whether or not Curt should be taught a lesson. An interesting side-note is during their thirty-second dialogue with each other, Curt was busily involved in a sort of private monologue of his own. "Brad, Brad!" Crawley yelled down from his elevated platform. "Don't listen to them, they're not your friends, they don't have your best interest at heart. Look, the only reason I greeted the young lady was because we almost bumped into one another, I meant no disrespect. Brad...Bradley I'm talking to you. Are you ignoring me?

Listen to reason and stop the violence, *pleeease!"* By the time Curt completed his satirical skit, he was on his knees grasping the railing with one hand while pointing at Bradley through the bars with the other.

He was hilarious.

"So what's it gonna be, bitch? You coming down?" Bradley yelled threateningly. "Or do I have to go up there and throw your ass down?"

"You really wanna fight, huh?" Curt asked in a less mocking tone as he slowly rose to his feet.

"That's right, muthafucka!"

"And you want me to come down there?"

"I'm done talking!" Having made this declaration, Bradley, Jackson, and one of the other guys started walking toward the stairs. With Crawley being outnumbered, no one ever expected Curt to bring the fight to Bradley and his crew.

But that is exactly what happened.

Due to being doubled-over in laughter, I did not actually see Crawley leap over the balcony. By the time I opened my eyes, his body was already tumbling downward like a whirlwind. Bouncing off the ground, he executed a somersault before expertly landing in front of Jackson and Bradley. Standing there with both fists clenched, Curt personified the unstoppable force of 'Christ Energy.'

Word is bond, his stunt was straight out of a Kung-fu flick!

Before the dust had time to settle, Bradley, Jackson, and both of their crews took off running toward the parking lot. As bystanders jeered the fleeing cowards, I walked up to Curt. "Impressive!" I said clapping my hands. "All I wanna know is, when's Jesus gonna teach me to flip like that?"

Although I knew my one-liner was dry, I never expected a rude reply.

"Don't touch me!" Curt yelled right before I embraced him. "Back up!"

Stunned, I stopped in my tracks without replying. Other spectators who had arrived to talk to Curt walked away after witnessing his abrasiveness. As the crowd slowly dispersed, Curt and I both stood there stoically silent; the only sound was Curt's heavy breathing. Although I was intent on getting an explanation, once a minute or so had elapsed, I began to lose patience. "I'm outta here," I finally said, turning to leave. This is when I noticed his breathing was far more labored than it should have been, not to mention he was favoring his left leg.

"Tak, wait…" In spite of the beads of sweat dotting his brow, Curt spoke in a calm, cool manner. "I'm sorry for yelling at you but…" Pausing here he rocked back and forth in an unsteady manner. "Can you step closer?"

"What?"

"I think my ankle's broken." Having uttered this, Curt collapsed into my arms just as I was stepping forward; I almost missed him.

"You can't rest here," I said after ensuring he could stand-up with my assistance. "Can you make it to my room?" Once he nodded, we began limping away together. As I supported his left shoulder, I reflected on how he was going to fight both crews all by himself—even after sustaining the injury.

"You two need some help?"

Hearing a concerned voice, I turned my head and saw Chill running toward us.

"I was on my way to the mess hall—what happened?"

With a worried look etched on his face, Chill positioned himself under Curt's other arm.

Once Perez was in place, Crawley, who had been dealing with his pain in silence, suddenly beamed a grin my way. "God doesn't promise it'll always be pretty," Curt declared, "but He does always promise to make a way for us to complete our mission."

"Tak, I hear what you're saying but—" Before Chill completed his statement, Curt cut him off.

"But you're not convinced?"

"It's not that. I just don't know if religion's what I need right now," Chill honestly responded from his section of the room.

"The Word talks about the consequences for those who are lukewarm in spirit," Curt came back. "It says the Lord will spit them from his mouth!"

More than roommates, Chill and I had become friends over the last couple months. So, understanding his strong-willed character, I believed he had heard enough. Knowing if we pressured him too much he would distance himself, I tried to relay a 'cool out' hand signal to Crawley but he paid me no mind. Recalling Perez's previous comments about Crawley's long-winded discussions, I decided to interrupt. Just as I opened my mouth to speak another voice penetrated our gathering.

"*I want to get saved!*" Aware the voice was coming from outside our room, I whipped my head around just as two knocks rapped softly on the door.

"Come in," Chill and I chorused together.

"Ssup Bellamy," I said with a grin upon seeing our chocolate-complexioned neighbor enter the room. Then I noticed the normally smiling brother from Jacksonville was upset about something.

"Amaru," he said in a somber tone, "I could hear y'all through the wall…I hope I'm not interrupting."

"Not at all brother," replied Curt before adding an emphatic, "*Ouch!*" Seeing a soul ripe for the picking, Curt had forgotten about his injury and tried to stand. Once Chill and I helped the hard-charging sergeant back to his seat, he elevated his leg onto a chair and replaced the ice pack. "Tak, I'm gonna sit this one out," he said with a grin.

"Might be a good idea," I responded before approaching Bellamy. "Okay Reggie, what can we do for you?"

"Amaru," he muttered, "I've noticed you're different now that you're saved. You've really changed and I want to change my life too."

This was the point in the conversation when Curt would normally take over; so naturally, I looked back over my shoulder.

"You know what to do, right?" Curt spit this out before I could say anything.

"Who me?" I almost objected before realizing the need to appear calm. "Oh yeah, sure…sure I got it."

On that day, I was forced to take an enormous stride as a Christian. Realizing Chill and Bellamy had no idea this was my 'Cherry Blast,' even though I was nervous, I was determined pull it off like a veteran. "Let's pray," I said, laying a hand on Reggie's shoulder and bowing my head like

I had seen Curt and Jon do many times. "Lord Jesus Christ, we come to you on behalf of our brother, Reginald Bellamy. Lord, we know you died on the cross for our sins. It says in your Word, that whosoever should accept the Christ as his lord and savior shall be saved from the fires of hell…" *So far so good!* I was relieved everyone appeared to be taking me seriously as I repeated what I heard Curt and Jon say many times. Once I was out of memorized material I peeked over at Crawley hoping he would take over but, to my dismay, he was chanting a prayer under his breath with both eyes closed. With no one to assist me, I turned back to Bellamy and asked a simple question.

"Reggie, do you believe Jesus died on the cross for your sins?"

"Yes," he replied in a scratchy voice.

"And are you ready to accept Jesus as the lord of your life?"

"Yes, I am committed to changing my life!" Bellamy cried out. When tears burst from his eyes, Curt hopped over on one leg and put a hand on his other shoulder. As he did so, I dug into my memory bank and remembered what came next.

"Bellamy, repeat after me," I said in a grave tone. "I, Reggie Bellamy, am tired of living a dead-end life as a sinner."

"I, Reggie Bellamy…" he began in a tearful tone.

"I accept Jesus as my Lord and Savior…"

Since Reggie was weeping the entire time, it was easy to cut the ceremony short. "Lord, bathe me in the blood of righteousness forevermore. Amen."

Once Reggie completed his oath, we all opened our

eyes and took turns congratulating the newest member of the '144,000 Club.'

Finally Curt took over.

"Reggie, you did a great thing tonight!" Crawley's intense stare communicated the emotion in his message. Following another hug, he hopped over to my bed and replaced the icepack, which had fallen on the floor, back onto his leg. "Chill," he said, "I really hope you change your mind. Together, the three of us are gonna pray for you." Then he looked at me. "Tak, do me a favor: open your Bible to the 13th chapter of Matthew and hand it to your roommate."

As I reached in a drawer to grab my Bible, Chill and Reggie took a seat on Chill's bed. After finding the correct page, I handed the Bible to Reggie and he passed it to Chill.

"Perez," Curt began, "this is a story I want you and Reggie to read later when you have time. But for now I'll give you a quick summary. It's about a farmer—they call him a 'sower,' which just means 'planter.' This farmer went out to sow his seeds. Some of his seeds fell by the wayside and were devoured by hungry birds. Others fell on rocky places where there wasn't a lot of soil and it wasn't very rich. Although a few plants sprang up the sun's heat soon scorched them. The Bible also says a few buds sprang up amongst some thorns but the thorns strangled them to death. However a precious few—the scripture assures us—were planted in fertile soil. There the roots took hold and yielded plentiful crops, some even a hundredfold."

Mesmerized by his Biblical acumen, I watched Curt gesture in my direction.

"I'm confident Tak's one of those rare seeds that will yield a bountiful crop, and I'll tell you why. The first couple times I witnessed to him, just like you Chill, he wasn't convinced. By the way, do you guys know Mick?"

Chill nodded and Bellamy shook his head.

Turning toward Reggie, I explained. "Mick was a friend of mine who got saved one night in the shoppette parking lot."

"Just before Mick started praying with me and Jon," Curt said looking in my direction, "Tak went inside to buy some beer. "Before you went in, what did you say?" Following a quick chuckle, he replied to his own question. "Something like: 'No disrespect but I came here tonight to get drunk'." When Curt busted-out laughing, Chill was so startled he flinched and Bellamy actually jumped to his feet—this is what made me laugh.

"I don't know why everyone thinks that story's so funny," I said, still snickering.

"*Yeah right!*" Curt shot back with emphasis before continuing his narrative. "My man Mick's a good guy…and he seemed to be living right for a couple weeks. But in the end, he got choked by a thorn of lust, liquor, or whatever sinful vehicle it was that caused him to backslide." After readjusting the watery icepack, he drove the lecture home. "Gentlemen the point is, seeds don't become plants overnight. The truth is it usually takes longer for the roots of stronger plants to take hold." Having said this, he pointed at Bellamy. "If you have any questions ask Tak. If he doesn't know the answer, feel free to holla at me." Then he glanced at his watch before turning in my direction and barking: "Hallelujah! As the sowers of this crop, our seeds have been planted—let's go!"

With that Curt stood up and walked out—without a limp!

Although I was just as shocked as Chill and Reggie, by the time they looked at me I had already wiped away my astonished expression. Standing up, I walked toward the door like nothing was out of the ordinary.

King of the Weight Room

"Put on two more plates. I got this!" Feeling pumped up, I was determined to push myself.

"Aw shit, Amaru's movin' up with the big boys!" Carney encouraged and teased me at the same time.

By his own admission, Sergeant Jerome Carney became motivated to lift weights due to living the life of a 'ninety-eight-pound weakling' in the projects of Newark. Once he conceded an addiction to using weight-gainer supplements, I imagined he dabbled with illegal steroids too. This he never admitted.

While I was no stranger to the gym, after I got saved, my training regimen gradually began to reflect my ascetic lifestyle. Every morning, whether we had PT scheduled or not, I went for a run followed by sets of push-ups, flutter kicks, and pull-ups. Since it was important to test the limits of my endurance three times a day, after inhaling my food at lunchtime, I ran to the gym to do as many reps as possible until minutes before the afternoon formation. However, it was in the evening when I really 'made my money.' This was the idiom Curt chose to express making significant gains in any chosen endeavor.

For me, the numerous gyms on post were bastions of relief from the monotony of military life. Serving as my substitute for the courts, the gym was the only place I could relax. Similar to my fanatic devotion to improving my jump shot, lifting weights became both a means to ground myself and a way to channel aggression. For some reason, I felt being a soldier for God committed me to training like a warrior. This was probably because whenever I punished my body, I swear I could feel my ancestors smiling. Once I became a known-face at the facility on *Smoke Bomb Hill*, many of the weight-lifting elite began giving me pointers. Regularly spotting these veterans allowed me to study their technique. The guy who taught me the most was Carney.

"Tak, I didn't know you could bench two-twenty-five."

"*What?*" I exclaimed sounding insulted. "I'm maxing at two-fiddy cuz! Where you been?" After sneering at Carney in a joking manner, I laid down on the bench and took several deep breaths, I then whispered the mantra for clearing my mind. "Let there be strength in peace and peace in my heart...Amen."

"Ready, one, two, three, lift!" Carney barked like a drill instructor. Known for being a master at getting the most out of his training partners, on this particular evening, I was that lucky guy. "Looking good Amaru!" the master encouraged. "You're definitely getting stronger. Damn, when's the last time we worked out together? Looks like I'm gonna have to start checking my rear-view mirror. I like that! Come on, no pain - no gain!"

But sometimes he talked too much.

"Shut-up!" My voice was barely audible as I struggled to control the downward motion on my thirteenth rep. "Help me with these last two," I said while feeling the burning sensation serious weight-lifters learn to fall in love with. As the barbell touched my chest, my pectoral muscles quivered.

"Last two my foot!" Carney scolded mercilessly. "Tonight you're training with the best! Or have you forgotten? Cuz, you got *four* more plus ten negatives. Let's go!"

When Carney finally took the barbell out of my grasp, my arms and chest were on fire. Breathing deeply, I slowly sat up before excusing myself to the water fountain. This is when I realized my arms had ceased to function. "Move your arms, Amaru!" Jerome yelled across the fitness room before he busted-out laughing.

Happy the fountain was pedal-activated, while I gulped-down mouthfuls of water, I heard Carney talking about my recent development. "Y'all see that young-buck?" he said to four guys who were taking a break. "If he keeps puttin' in work like that, he'll blow-up in no time." Then Carney wrinkled his features into a frown. "But y'all…" Shaking his head in disgust, he trained his finger on the foursome. "Y'all ain't giving up that kind of effort. That's why you pogues'll never be nice like this!" Clenching his fists, Jerome majestically raised both arms and flexed his huge biceps.

Once I had quenched my thirst, I relaxed for a second and watched Carney posing for his fans. I imagined he could become a professional bodybuilder if he did not want to re-enlist. As Carney continued to admire his own physique in the mirror, I decided to stretch-out my back by doing some pull-ups.

"Man, if I was that diesel, I'd go to *Big P's* in just a pair of pants, with no shirt on!" exclaimed one of Jerome's dazzled followers.

"And you best believe, all the girlies would be on

you," replied another.

"Hell yeah!" chimed in a third guy.

Listening to their murmurs of agreement, I was disgusted to hear grown men fawning over another man like that. After dropping to the ground following my last rep, I was about to express my distaste but Carney beat me to it.

"Well, if y'all think I'm so diesel, instead of staring like a bunch of chickenheads, it should motivate you chumps to get to work. Then, one day, you too can be the man flexing in the mirror."

"Cock-a-doodle-doo," I said, returning to the bench to grab the towel I had forgotten. "Just another rooster passing through," I said before moving toward the leg-press machine.

"Amaru, what's that supposed to mean?" One of Carney's fans asked this defiantly, sensing my sarcasm.

"I get it!" Carney bellowed as he started laughing. "He's saying he's a rooster like me...not a chickenhead like y'all!"

When others nearby likewise began to chuckle, the same guy responded to his hero's punchline by attacking me. "Amaru, you're full of shit!" As he said this the surrounding area got quiet. "Just 'cause you spotted Carney tonight and he gave you a compliment doesn't mean you're in his class. You're just a beginner...an amateur. It takes years, not months, to get that diesel."

"Maybe for you average, run-of-the-mill types but I ain't no rubbernecking chickenhead...I'm dedicated to this." Blowing him off, I turned toward the center of the room. "Testing one-two, one-two," I said, pretending to speak into a microphone with a hand in front of my mouth while the other one was raised in the air to get the room's attention. "Here ye

30

one and all, I promise that I will catch Carney on the bench before my ETS."

"Stop dreaming!" one of them clucked as the other hens cackled right along with him.

"When you getting out Amaru?" Carney asked in a serious tone.

"Next September."

"September, huh? Well, I'll be leaving for Ranger School a couple months before that. Colonel Packer promised me by the summertime. And when I graduate, I'll be switching units, so y'all won't see me in here no more. In other words, baby-boy, if you want to use me as a measuring stick, you got a little less than a year because next June will probably be the cut-off."

"Well, in that case, June it is!" I declared without scarcely a thought.

After Carney started laughing again, I sealed the gentlemen's wager by shaking hands with him and several other witnesses. Having vowed to over-take him before he left for Ranger School, I must have been out of my mind. Honestly, I was just trying to create a goal worthy enough to focus my workouts. Well it worked. For the record, Jerome was maxing at over three-hundred-fifty pounds. More importantly, everyone knew he practically lived at the gym after work.

Similar, to my bet with Reed in Jump School, this 'macho man' wager once again placed me in the spotlight. And just like that time, just to be competitive, I had to create ways to train harder than my opponent. Taking my commitment to heart, I solicited Curt's assistance. Knowing his affinity for competing in triathlons, he often talked about alternative, training methods. Although I did not understand how it would help my bench press, I agreed to join him twice a week for his iron-man exercise regimen. Amounting to climbing ropes, various calisthenics, and lots of running, according to Curt, if we could run six miles in under thirty minutes, we qualified as 'world-class' athletes. He coined his latest challenge: 'Eclipsing the five-minute mile.'

Slippery as Ice

"No, don't do it!" Despite Curt's warning, I bounded over what minutes before had been a dirt path, meandering down a tree-lined hillside.

Prior to the first crack of thunder, we had been struggling up a steep hill. When warm raindrops began pelting our bodies, almost instantly, small ravines formed in the grooved terrain. This created such a difficult surface to run on that in order to maintain our balance, both of us at times, had to touch the ground with our hands. Following a strenuous effort, we eventually reached the summit. By this time, the rain was slicing down at us. While taking a quick breather, Curt warned me to adjust my erratic, running style on the way down.

"Tak, you know where we are?"

"Yeah…Area J, why?"

"Because these training areas are especially dangerous in bad weather." When I did not seem interested in his commentary, Curt became irritated. "Don't you want to know why? Ask me why."

"Okay, why?"

"Because this ain't dirt we're running on, it's clay.

Red Carolina clay. And it's as slippery as ice in the rain!"

'Slippery as Ice,' somehow that rang a bell.

Back in the Division, we were forced to participate in training-competitions. These events occurred whenever the commanders felt it was necessary to raise troop morale. The victors of these hoo-rah activities were usually given a three-day pass; not to mention all the pomp-and-circumstance which goes along with being singled-out in formation as a winner. One of these pursuits was the infamous Endurance Run. Try to imagine running / walking a marathon in full web-gear while holding an M-16. Now envision doing it in the heat and humidity of a North Carolina summer! The type of iron-man event guys like Curt relished but I hated, when I was forced to compete in one, it was never my intention to win. I just wanted to survive the ordeal in one piece.

A couple hours into the tiresome race, the muggy weather yielded torrential rain. This was a welcome change from the glaring sunshine just a few minutes ago. The water somehow rejuvenated me. Feeling inspired, I picked up my pace which prompted some of the soldiers I passed to encourage me to 'Go for the Gold!' Even as more and more soldiers cheered me on, my feelings about the race never changed; I merely wanted to hurry up and finish this foolishness. Nevertheless, when I glimpsed the guide-on coming into view, I realized I had caught up with the front-runners at just the right time—as we were nearing the home-stretch. Recalling hearing we reached the halfway mark some time ago, I deduced the finish-line had to be just over the hill we were approaching. Suddenly, out of nowhere, I began fiending for a three-day weekend at Myrtle Beach.

Looking ahead of me, I saw a soldier exchange his M-16 for the guide-on; he did this as he passed him. Now I understood what Top meant when he proclaimed that: "No soldier is permitted to run in front of the unit colors." As lightning bolts lit-up the western sky and rain poured down by the bucketful's, I laughed at the irony of my situation. In spite of my low opinion of holding the guide-on, I wanted that 'rag attached to a stick' more than ever because the guy crossing the finish-line with it got a three-day pass, starting on pay day.

"Boys, welcome to lovely Area J! If it ain't raining, it ain't training…watch your step." Seconds after Sgt. Quick yelled this, I caught up to him. "Private, did you not hear me? Slow down! The ground's slippery as ice," my platoon sergeant admonished.

Thinking he just didn't want me to win that three-day pass, I accelerated even more. "Gotcha Sergeant," I mumbled on my way by. Once I passed him, I looked ahead and counted only three bodies separating me from R&R in the sunshine. With a grin on my face, I charged up a large mound all the while imagining how nice it was going to be lounging on the beach—away from Sgt. Quick. After passing another soldier I reached the top; our unit colors were so close I could make out the winged panther swooping down from the heavens without squinting. I was ecstatic.

Then I slipped.

Hitting the ground flat on my back, I lost all control of my body, as a gushing mudslide cushioned my fall. Once I got swept into the reddish-brown current, I ended up sliding all the way down the hill, sort of like a novice skier who had unwisely dared to tangle with an expert slope. Eventually, I was deposited in a rust-colored lagoon at the bottom of the rocky sliding board. After clearing mud out of my eyes, ears, and mouth, the worst part—even beyond the humiliation of being laughed at by Sgt. Quick and the others—was the arduous task of climbing back up to search for my dropped weapon. With water pouring down the hill, as much as I tried, it was impossible to gain any footing. Therefore, you can imagine my relief, as I recognized my roommate slowly making his way down the treacherous slope with my muddy M-16 slung to his back. Needless to say, I spent that weekend in the barracks scrubbing clay off my equipment. For this reason, you would think my previous Area J gaffe should have prevented me from committing the same error again. But it didn't.

"*Tak!*"

Floating over a myriad of jagged boulders jutting from the now streaming flood, I could barely hear Curt's voice. Due to the steepness of the hill, I was afforded an extra millisecond to search for a suitable area to place my foot. In spite of this, the instant I touched the moist clay my body was swept backward into a horizontal position; I never had a chance to gain my balance. Once again airborne but now totally out of control, I clenched my eyes to brace myself for the imminent collision with the rapidly approaching trees. *It was at this precise moment—while in midair—that an angel reached out and grabbed me!*

As soon as I felt two hands on my shoulders, my forward momentum ceased, causing me to harmlessly splash down at the edge of the cascading current. I knew it had to be an angel so I quickly flipped over into the front-leaning rest position to see what my savior looked like…and was shocked to see Curt sitting in the water next to me. With a big grin on his face, Curt completed his previous statement. "Tak," he repeated now in a much calmer voice. "You can't jump like that on wet clay because it's dangerous."

"I know."

"You know?" Curt sarcastically replied with a chuckle. "Oh, I can see that!"

"Well, what I mean is, now I know."

Following my reply we shared a laugh before helping each other to our feet. The instant we stood up, an amazing thing happened. The rain suddenly stopped; and I mean it went from a violent downpour to absolutely no rain—not even a drizzle. Before we had time to step out of the current, the sun popped out from behind the clouds and muggy wisps of steam rose from the ground all around us. From our vantage point in the middle of the forest, I almost expected to see a silverback gorilla peering at us through the mist.

"By the way, how'd you do that?" I asked, taking my first steps.

"Do what?"

"Do what?" I repeated in a mocking tone. "Save my life, that's what. I heard you yell my name when I jumped but you were over there." Saying this, I pointed at the other side of the flooded path. "How did you teleport yourself here in time to grab me?"

"Honestly, I have no idea. God told me to jump, so I did. Next thing I know, we were both splashing down into the water. You sure you're okay?"

"Not a scratch. How about you?"

"Just a minor one," Curt reported as we sat down on a grayish-white boulder at the edge of the stream; the stone happened to be shaped perfectly to accommodate two human bodies. In spite of his choice of words, he showed me a softball-sized hole in his t-shirt. Located on his right shoulder, the laceration started getting red as I looked at it. Before any more attention could be focused on his injury, Curt scooped a handful of water from the river and rinsed the blood away, before bellowing in his best paratrooper voice. "Come on soldier, let's get outta here."

With that, we started walking the rest of the way down the hill.

For the next year, Reggie, Chill, and I rarely missed a service at the Doorway of Christian Unity. In spite of our rookie status we quickly became regarded as veterans when some of the senior members, who also happened to be soldiers, were transferred overseas. At the same time many of the people we were witnessing to were joining our congregation. One of these new converts, a kid named Darrel, took an instant liking to me.

Whenever I saw *D,* he always had his arms tightly crossed, with his legs slightly spread and his feet pointing outward. Add to this the hard frown and it sums up to the embodiment of a classic, b-boy stance. And I cannot forget the 'certified tough' profile he invented to impress his listening audience either. "That's right home-slice," Darrel claimed the first time I met him. "I'm from the Brooklyn-Bronx . My family just moved down here to country-ass Carolina two years ago."

"Word up? The 'Brooklyn-Bronx,' huh? That's a rough area, cuz." Assuming a more street-like pose, I even grabbed my crotch. "Yeah, I used to kick-it in the B&B with my cousin sometimes. You can take the X-train there from

Harlem, right?"

"That's the fastest way cuz!" Saying this, D thumbed his nose in an exaggerated fashion.

"What are you two babbling about? There ain't no X—"

"*Chill!* Lemme holla atchu real quick." Having interrupted my roommate, I then draped my arm around the native Brooklynite's shoulder to walk him away from the impressionable thirteen-year-old. "Yo D, we'll be right back." Understanding if Darrel's fabricated background was exposed here and now, he would be humiliated, I wanted to save that breakdown for a more appropriate forum.

The first time I saw Darrel and his little brother, Eugene, they were playing together in front of the Pine Grove apartment buildings. These were the projects in Fayetteville. Sporting brand-new, Run-DMC t-shirts and shell-toe Adidas, they seemed out of place amongst the broken glass, trash, and cigarette butts littering the sidewalk. D was a shade darker and two-inches-taller than *Gene*. With his sculpted chiseled jawline, I imagined Darrel favored his father, while Eugene, with his baby-faced features almost looked like a girl. Walking up to them, I asked the obvious to break the ice. "Y'all like Run-DMC?"

Following a long second of staring to determine if I was friend or foe, they suddenly began performing a song by the emcee duo. This answered my question better than a simple 'yes' ever could.

"My Adidas! Walk through concert doors, and roam all over coliseum floors,

We stepped on-stage, at Live-Aid, all the People gave, And the poor got paid..."

Delighted by their performance, I sat down on the steps leading up to their building and listened. A couple minutes later, Curt, Reggie, and Chill joined us. By this time, the Spirit had moved me to grab the mic.

"My friend Jesus! Is larger than any shoe, 'cause God loves me and He loves you,

I stepped in the Way, yes I prayed, And just like that, My Soul got Saved!"

Once Darrel and Eugene realized I was imitating the rhyme pattern in *My Adidas*, they began dancing behind me like we were filming a video. Soon, kids from the nearby basketball courts ran over to see what was going on. Although many just listened, some of them ended up kicking their own rhymes too. When the bright-eyed youth noticed I was rapping about God, they had the decency to clean up their own lyrics without having to be asked. Out of the twelve or so teens to bless the mic that evening, the best flow was by a kid named Tyrell. His verses highlighted the grim realities which accompany growing up as a melanin-rich kid in a poor environment.

"How many of y'all know about the projects? Original Man damned to whiteman's plans and profits. With sistas and bruthas, stacked on one another, dope-heads fiend in the form of pregnant mothers. Yo this stage is packed, with highly-volatile cats, like pimps, prostitutes, and shorties pushing crack..."

When his lyrical gem concluded, Tyrell saluted us for spending time with them. "I never met no Christians like y'all before. Y'all ain't from 'round here, huh?"

"They're in the Army," someone yelled out.

Before the conversation had a chance to digress into insignificance, Curt redirected it toward the gospel. "Being a

Christian doesn't mean you can't be cool too," he declared.

"Or have a good time," added Chill.

Hoping one of my spiritual brothers would say more—or grab the microphone—I looked their way and saw Curt point at his watch. Seeing this I realized it was time to wrap things up.

"So what's up?" I simply asked. "Who wants a fresh, new life in Christ?" And beyond my wildest expectations, many youngsters stepped forward. On that Friday evening we prayed with about fifteen kids; however, on Sunday morning, when we arrived to pick them up for church, only Darrel and Eugene were waiting for us.

"There were some other kids here too, but their mothers came and got 'em." With his eyes cast downward, Eugene seemed to be apologizing. The sincerity embedded in the words of the eleven-year-old warmed my heart.

"It ain't your fault man," I said, softly punching his chest. "Those dudes'll come around once they see the miraculous changes in your life. Yo Curt…" I said as we piled into his VW Jetta, "Tell 'em about the sower who went out to plant his seeds."

"I got a better idea," Curt replied. "Why don't *you* recite the parable written in Matthew." Replying thus with a smile, he handed me his tattered bible before starting the engine.

"Amaru, you've changed! What's up with you these days?"

Startled, I looked up from my desk to see Specialist Kevin Robertson staring down at me. Totally engrossed in my work, I had failed to notice the six-foot-four, chocolate-brown soldier enter my office. As teammates on our brigade basketball and football teams, Robertson and I had become good friends. Reminiscing on how we used to drink beer together after our games, I knew what he was talking about.

"Tak," Robertson continued, "you're probably the only E-3 in the Army lucky enough to have his own office. Man, I thought we were gonna be in here chillin'!"

"Whaddya mean? You know you're welcome to kick-it here anytime you want." Responding thus, I did not quite understand.

"Kick-it? Where? In here? With you playing Mozart?" Saying this, he gestured toward the cassette player sitting on a filing cabinet in the corner. "Or even worse, *James Cleveland!* Yo, what happened to all those mixtapes by DJ Red Alert and Mr. Magic?"

"For the record, that's Beethoven you're listening to, not Mozart," I corrected him with a grin. "And you know I'll always be Hip Hop, ock! I still listen to KRS, but I can't get with the sinful messages of most of these perpetrating emcees. Besides, classical music helps me concentrate when I'm working. But if you got a dope tape, bring it," I said with a grin. Noticing his disagreeable expression, I tried to merge our interests. "Check-it-out, we're about to collaborate with some kids from the projects in Fayetteville."

"And do what?"

"We're throwing a party at that skating rink on Raeford Road. It's gonna feature a talent show, not to mention yours truly spinning on the 1s and 2s."

"Word? You're the deejay?" he asked showing some

interest.

"Yeah," I replied with a grin. "And cuz, wait 'til you hear some of the funky-fresh lyrics these young boys are rockin' in the name of God!"

The moment Kevin heard the word 'God' any remnant of a smile he had disappeared. "No thanks," he mumbled on his way to the door.

Shocked at his cold response, I watched him leave in silence. This is when I realized being a Christian means I must lose my friends. *Why does it have to be like that?* I contemplated. When I brought this question to Jon and Curt, they both nodded their heads in agreement.

"It comes with the territory," Jon began. "Tak, you gotta remember something: your buddy, Robertson, is still living for the world. And you, as a Christian, know the truth."

"Which is?" I asked.

"Which is," Jon replied, "that his paradigm is based on ignorance."

"Paradigm? What's that mean?"

"Without making things too complicated, let's just say he's on Satan's team, and you're a soldier of the living Christ."

"So that makes Robertson my enemy?"

"Lemme answer this one Jon," Curt jumped in. "Since the devil's our adversary, no mere mortal is bad enough to be our enemy," he stressed. "But think about it, if Robertson pays too much attention to you, it could destroy the way he believes the world operates. That's what Jon meant by 'paradigm.'

"So wait a minute," I interrupted again. "You think if Robertson hangs around me, it'll change the way he sees the world? That sounds a little unrealistic don't you think?"

"Not at all," responded Curt in a flash, seeming pleased I had asked this question. "Tak, you gotta remember something: you're not the usual Christian he's accustomed to coming across—people see you as being 'cool.' What I mean is, for example, you use a lot of slang when you witness, so kids from the street can really hear your message. Didn't you say he's from the same neighborhood as Chill?"

"Nah, Robertson's from Coney Island—"

"That's not part of East-New York?"

"Nah," I replied. "Both of them are from Brooklyn but not the same area."

"New York is so big," Curt said sounding confused. "Let's just say if the brutha is from the streets, you're speaking his language. Plus, you two were teammates. So, he considers you a friend. If you think about it, it's almost impossible for you to *not* threaten the way he sees the world. Tak, you probably won't be hearing from Specialist Robertson any time soon." Following a brief glance in Jon's direction, he summed up his prognosis. "But don't worry. He'll be back. And when he comes calling… hit him hard— with the Word, of course!"

Chapter 3: The Midas Touch

"Welcome to the cockpit of a CH-47 twin-engine, tandem rotor, heavy-lift helicopter…also known as a *Chinook*," Captain Pearson announced in a robust voice.

"Thank you, sir."

After giving me the five-dollar tour of the 'bird,' the almond-complexioned pilot instructed me to strap myself in the co-pilot's chair. In preparation for takeoff, he began flipping various switches while he spoke through a radio to the controllers in the towers. Glancing around the cockpit, I was as thrilled as any private-first-class would be in my situation. Not only did I get to avoid the dreary motor pool this afternoon, but more importantly, I was chillin' in a chopper with my Company Commander!

Once we were in the air and the captain finished setting our course, he explained why I had been selected to accompany him on this grand excursion. "Amaru, as I'm sure you've noticed by now, many of our people lack the proper motivation to achieve success in today's world. That's why when you took the initiative to sign-up for classes at Fayetteville State, I was impressed. I hope you don't mind, but I exercised my right as your commanding officer to check your records."

"Of course not, sir," I responded, slightly nervous about where this conversation was headed.

"Other than your Airborne termination, which you've

already explained was due to an injury you incurred on a night-jump, you have no blemishes whatsoever."

Now that I was saved, I wanted to tell him the truth about why I terminated. "Well, actually sir—" I tried to interrupt.

"Just a minute, allow me to finish. Then I'll let you say your piece, okay?"

"Okay sir."

"When I spoke to your platoon sergeant last week, he informed me you were interested in attending university when you ETS. Is that right?"

"Yes sir."

"Good, good. So, I imagine you're currently in the application process, considering you ETS in just over a year from now."

"That's correct sir."

"What about the Army's early-out program? Are you applying to that as well?"

"Excuse me sir?"

Seeing I did not understand, he explained.

"Since you're scheduled to get out the second week of September, you'll miss the beginning of the fall semester. Of course, you could wait until January, but at most schools it's more difficult to be accepted in the spring semester. And I know you don't want to wait a whole year before beginning your studies."

"Oh, I hadn't thought about that sir," I admitted, embarrassed at my oversight.

"No worries," Cpt. Pearson uttered while waving a hand through the air. "Listen, the commander of Alpha Company, Captain Davenport, told me he has a specialist named Samuels who just applied for it. I'm sure Samuels can tell you everything you need to know."

"Yes sir. Thank you very much!" Grateful for his assistance, I showed my appreciation.

"Don't mention it," he replied as his hand stifled back a yawn. "Now, moving on, what universities are you applying to? And while we're on the subject, allow me to add I hope you'll consider attending my alma mater, Howard University. The ROTC program there has a great faculty. Are you planning to continue your career in the Army?"

Stunned by his question, I tried to avoid giving a direct response. "I haven't thought that far into the future, sir. So far, I've applied to Penn State, Rutgers, and UNC, as far as division-one schools go. In case I'm not accepted by any of those, I'm also sending applications to Trenton State and Glassboro College. They're smaller schools in New Jersey; that's where my parents live.

"In-state tuition is much cheaper, yes I understand. I heard you say, 'division one.' Are you interested in playing ball too?

"Yes sir."

"B-ball?"

"No sir. Football."

"What about the black colleges?" he then asked.

Although I knew little about Howard, Morehouse, or any of the traditional black schools, since I never heard them mentioned in any *Sports Center* highlights, they had never even crossed my mind.

"Well, umm—"

"PX-92, PX-92. Do you read me? Over."

Luckily, before I had a chance to reply, the radio interrupted our conversation.

"Hold onto that thought Amaru," said the captain as he picked up the intercom. "PX-92 here. Go ahead."

Taking advantage of this breather, I exited the cockpit and went to the cargo area. Fearful Captain Pearson might not be so helpful if I revealed the truth, which was: there was no way I was returning to the military, nor attending Howard; as I considered how best to respond to his questions, my imagination was suddenly arrested by the thought of what it was like to jump from one of these twin-propeller helicopters. Allow me to emphasize this detail: I never forgot how demanding EDREs were, so I did not want to jump myself, but rather, I was curious about what a jump out the rear door might look like—from the viewpoint of a bystander. Since all, of my jumps had been from the side of a C-130 or C-141, which are both jets, the idea of jumping from a helicopter's cargo-door intrigued me.

After a couple minutes, Captain Pearson called me back to the cockpit.

"It seems we're nearing our first destination. We have orders to pick-up some grunts from the Division and transport them over Sicily Drop Zone. Come to think of it, they might be some of your old buddies. Were you in the oh-four? Or the oh-five?"

"Third of the oh-five sir." Replying thus, I was happy he had forgotten our previous conversation.

"Yeah, you might see some familiar faces."

"Are they gonna jump sir?"

"What's that supposed to be? A joke?" The captain sneered like I'd asked a stupid question. "When you were in the Division, how many times did you *land* in a military aircraft?"

"You're right sir, dumb question," I replied. Recalling

how just seconds ago I had been imagining what a jump from a Chinook would look like, I reflected that whatever I thought about these days seemed to manifest almost instantly.

After we landed, I followed the CO out the rear cargo-door to greet an approaching soldier. After salutes were exchanged, Captain Pearson shook hands and spoke to the lieutenant. Within seconds, a stick consisting of about twenty paratroopers appeared. When I recognized the familiar gait of my former platoon sergeant amongst the group lugging their gear toward us. Just seeing him allowed me to appreciate the contrast between what life is like in the Division and my current situation: although we wore the same uniform and lived on the same post, we existed in two very different worlds. Before Cpt. Pearson could greet the oncoming soldiers, I stepped forward and boomed my salutations first.

"Good day troopers!" I bellowed with a grin before adding: "Sergeant Quick, fancy meeting you here." Due to the dimness of the evening plus I was wearing my glasses, it took the motor sergeant a couple seconds to recognize me. Once he did, he tried to express his displeasure, but my commander cut him off.

"What the fu--?"

"Good evening Staff Sergeant, I'm Captain Pearson. I'm the pilot transporting your stick. It seems you already know my co-pilot," he continued in a serious tone. "We'll be taking off in exactly two minutes, so order your men to strap in."

Forty minutes into our flight, Captain Pearson sent me to the cargo hold with a message. "Amaru," he yelled over the turbulence, "go back there and inform our visitors we expect to be above Sicily DZ at around twenty-three-hundred."

"Yes sir."

Stepping through the door separating the cockpit with the rear of the helicopter, I spied two rows of exhausted troopers taking up both sides of the cargo area. Seeing them slumped-over in their seats leaning against one another made me remember how exhausting jumping was. "All this for an extra hundred bucks just ain't worth it—and I'm broke!" I mumbled with a grin before clearing my throat. "*Ladies!*" I barked as loud as I could. "Please give me your undivided attention. Captain Pearson and I would like to welcome you on-board the USS Enterprise. Our ETA is approximately twenty-three-hundred hours, so try to catch some z's between now and then. Oh, and since I'll be manning the controls, I apologize for any air turbulence in advance. By the way, it's good to see you boys again." Then I pointed at them. "Especially since, unlike you, I ain't jumping!"

"Fuck you Amaru…nasty-ass LEG!" someone snapped but in a comical tone. Although the voice was familiar I could not quite put my finger on the person's name; however, I was confident he was someone I was cool with. At any rate since there were lots of chuckles I knew my antics were being received good-naturedly. Before leaving, I searched for Sgt. Q in the subdued light but was unable to find him. When I returned to the cockpit, Captain Pearson was smiling.

"It's your turn, *co-pilot*."

"Excuse me, sir?"

"Don't look at me all surprised," he shot back still wearing a grin. "I heard what you said back there, and you didn't lie…" Standing up, he then offered me his seat. "Tonight, you're gonna learn how to fly!"

With Christ in my corner, life was great. It seemed

everything I touched turned into gold. With two of my three-year Army commitment now under my belt, Jon, Curt, and the pastor—not to mention the re-enlistment NCO—were grilling me about my future. In spite of Pastor Bart's claim that God wanted me to remain in Fayetteville, I never forgot the two reasons I joined the military in the first place: the GI Bill plus the Army College Fund.

Radically Saved!

"You ready to roll?" Curt yelled from his car as he stopped in front of my barracks.

Because I had insisted on hitting the gym, I missed catching a ride to the skating rink with Reggie and Chill. Originally, I had planned on skipping my work-out, but once Sgt. Will gave me and Stock the afternoon off, I was craving to break a sweat.

"Thanks for the ride," I said jumping in the passenger seat. "Bellamy and Chill had to get there early because they're on crowd-control. Let's just hope they're needed."

"It's no trouble, your barracks are on the way to the church and I just got off. Remember, I ain't in no soft, LEG unit like you," Curt teased.

"Well, just so you know, Sergeant *Hardcore*, I got released early today as a reward for my, and I quote: 'superior performance' on the IG inspection, boyee!"

"Oh really?" Curt, replied with an impressed grin.

"Yes indeed," I said before changing subjects. "You brought the music, right?" Checking the back seat, I spied two crates of gospel albums—plus a few R&B favorites—

from Jon's and Curt's collections. Once I spotted records by *Tramaine Hawkins*, the *Winans*, and *Al Green*, I felt satisfied the rest of the albums I requested were present and accounted for. That task accomplished, I sat back and relaxed.

"Since we're going to Quincy's after the party, I skipped dinner." While mentioning this, Curt was rubbing his tummy. "Maybe I should've gotten a quick bite at the chow-hall. You're coming too, right?"

"Nah cuz, you know the deal. Gotta get my nightly run in."

"What!" Curt exclaimed. "You do know the skating rink is twice as far from post as the church, right? We've been driving for almost twenty minutes."

"Hold up, don't tell me you gettin' soft? Yo, next week's challenge is sneaking up fast and if we don't finish in under thirty minutes, I'll—"

"Watch it!" Curt interjected with a grin. "The Holy Spirit's listening so don't make any promises you can't keep." Activating his blinker, he then turned into the skating rink's parking lot. Even though both of us were in the business of seeing miracles, the scene which unfolded before our eyes astonished us. "Praise God!" Curt exclaimed.

There were people everywhere. The line, which started at the entrance, was jam-packed and wound its way around the circular building out of sight. Upon closer inspection, we spied our church brethren patiently waiting near the front. Checking out the packs of kids playing tag amongst the parked cars, I picked-out Darrel and Eugene. Noticing their upbeat group consisted exclusively of melanin-rich teens, I was pleased the projects had come out tonight.

Walking forward, Curt and I shook many hands before finally reaching our congregation members. Next to the pastor stood another Caucasian man; he appeared to be the manager and by the looks on their faces, it was obvious they were uncomfortable about something. Considering almost half of the crowd resembled a typical audience at the Apollo Theater, I had an idea of what it might be.

"Good evening pastor. Sir."

"Good evening."

After everyone greeted each other, the manager wasted no time before reading us the riot act. "I need to be clear about something: if anything gets damaged in here tonight, your church will be held liable. Understand?"

"Of course, sir, no problem," Curt interjected, replying in his usual, cool manner before Pastor B had a chance to speak.

"Good," said the brash man as if the pastor himself had replied. "And Pastor," he continued, "I'm going to need your signature on this damage waiver—just for precautionary measures."

"Yes I understand," replied the frail clergyman. After Pastor Bart scribbled on the form he handed it back. Then, before I could follow the manager inside the building he called my name.

"Takuan, can I have a word with you?" Saying this, Pastor Bart turned and started walking.

"Ah, sure," I said expressing my surprise.

After walking a few yards the pastor stopped and waited until I arrived. "Takuan, quite a turn-out tonight, huh?" he calmly stated while gesturing towards the crowd which was now filing through the entrance.

"All for the glory of God," I replied without hesitation.

Smiling, he placed a hand on my shoulder. When Curt walked over and tried to speak he was ignored. "It seems," the pastor continued speaking to me, "you're quite popular in some areas of Fayetteville, where we have not had much success, especially at the Pine Grove Apartments and along Murchison Road. Right now, isn't a good time, so next week let's sit down and have a little chat, okay?"

Something about Pastor B's demeanor was vexing me. Watching him stare at me through his horn-rimmed glasses reminded me of my elementary school principal, Mr. Tucker—the guy everyone accused of being gay. However, with my mind being so preoccupied with doing a sound-check as soon as possible, I dismissed the incident without further analysis. "Okay," I nodded before walking toward the entrance.

The party turned out to be quite a unique event. To label the crowd as 'mixed' did it no justice. Toward the middle of the rink, the middle-aged to elderly Caucasians skated or stood around with their arms folded having a discussion; while in the outside lanes their children and grandchildren raced alongside adolescent, hood rats. Considering the amount of the excitement, it was surprising to find an even bigger party occurring off the skating floor, in the seating areas. As toddlers and infants frolicked about in every nook and cranny, the arcade machines and pool tables commanded huge crowds. Once the young mothers designated the cafeteria as the area for women nursing their babies, in no time, these ladies began chatting together amiably. In a nutshell, there were lots of people—both black and white—having a ball.

To appease the more reserved attendees, I avoided most of the soulful records for the first half-hour. Instead, I opted to play white, gospel artists like *Amy Grant* and *Carman*. My efforts were not well-received by the melanin-rich contingent.

"*Booooo! Booooo!*"

"*Fire the DJ!*"

When some teens began to voice their displeasure, I spied the manager glaring in my direction. Unsure of what to do next, in a near panic, I decided to start the live showcase earlier than scheduled. "Ladies and gentlemen, we're about to start the talent show." By this time, I almost had to scream into the microphone, in order to be heard over the sporadic booing. "All contestants get ready. Everyone else, please stop skating and clear the center of the rink. For those remaining on the floor, have a seat so the people behind you can see the show. Thank you for your cooperation."

When Curt skated over to the DJ booth wearing a worried look, I grinned at him before grabbing my list and calling off the first name. "Lady Sunshine...Lady Sunshine, where're ya at?"

When a little, blonde-headed girl holding a flute stood up and bashfully skated to the center of the rink, I silently cursed myself for not screening the performers beforehand. Although I wanted to skip to another contestant, now that she had been announced and everyone saw her, I knew this was not an option. Taking a deep breath, I sat down fearing the worst. But to my surprise, Goldilocks' rendition of '*Hush Little Baby*' was actually pretty good. At any rate, since she did not get heckled in front of her grandparents, I was relieved. As the faint applause was ending, I scanned the crowd and found the second act on my list: The Gospel Glee Club of Northern Fayetteville. It was a nine-member choir consisting of eight whites and one token black guy. "Umm, I don't think so," I muttered, knowing if the next act did not move the crowd the party might be a bust. Putting the paper down, I made eye-contact with Darrel. Once I saw him tap Eugene's shoulder, I unmuted the microphone.

"Microphone check one, two…one, two." Satisfied I was being heard, I announced the next act. "A-ight everyone, put your hands together for Fayetteville's own…and Pine Grove's finest: The 'D and E' Emcees!"

Dozens of girls screamed when the lights suddenly went off. Seconds later, when I turned them back on, everyone grew silent. They were astonished to see the two brothers standing in the middle of the rink, back-to-back, in their best b-boy poses. Wearing black fedoras and fat gold chains under their leather blazers, they were statuesque in their white-on-white shell-toe Adidas—this time with no laces. Finally, Darrel pulled a hand out of his coat pocket: it was holding a microphone.

"JE- SUS are the letters of his name!" Darrel slowly spit into the microphone a-capella, emphasizing each syllable. As he spoke, I scratched-in 'J' behind him from the record: *'Jam Master Jay.'*

Then Eugene responded in the same drawn-out manner: *"Saving people's souls is the name of his game…"*

Abruptly, they both spit the next line with me scratching: 'So check out the master', behind them. *"So check out the master and his sacrifice…"*

"D"

"And E"

"Rockin' Christ on a Friday night!"

Only after they ended the verse together did I finally drop the beat. Once the music hit, the crowd surrounding them jumped to their feet and started dancing. So, before The D&E Emcees could even get to their first verse, the party was already 'all the way live!'

"It seems your church's skating party was quite a success!"

As I exited the mess hall on Monday evening, Captain Pearson's enthusiastic comment caught me off-guard. "Ah, yes sir," I said after saluting. "How'd you know? Did you speak to Chill or Bellamy?"

"Or Coleman, Crawford, or maybe even Howard? Come on, don't stop there; your brand of religion's so contagious I'm beginning to wonder what you're putting in the water."

"Pardon me sir?"

"Nothing Amaru. Lighten up, it's just a joke. Last Friday night, on our way home from the movies, I happened to be driving by the skating rink with my wife and kids. Out of nowhere, my son suddenly yelled out: 'Dad, look! I've never seen so many black people at the skating rink before!" the CO said between chuckles.

"Yes sir," I proudly concurred. "The Fayetteville community really came out and supported us on this one."

"Is that right?" the CO sounded impressed. "Well ya know what Amaru? I believe in God too, so the next time you schedule a party there, lemme know and I'll bring the kids…they love skating. But that's not what I came here to talk about." With that declaration the CO assumed a professional tone. "I got three points of business: first, I wanted to make sure you spoke to Samuels about the early-out program. Did you?"

"Yes sir, I did."

"And?"

"And he squared me away just like you said. I've already sent in my application. Sir, I can't thank you enough."

"Next, I wanted to personally inform you that you've been selected to attend Air-Assault School. So pack your bags PFC, because you're leaving tomorrow morning with Sgt. Peterson, Stockman, Buswell, and McGuiness."

"*What?* I mean, there must be some mistake, sir. Sergeant Will told me last week—"

"Your platoon sergeant doesn't know about this yet as it just became official a few minutes ago. He'll be informed shortly."

"Uh...yes sir."

"What's the matter? You don't sound like you want to go."

"No sir, it's not that. I'm just surprised, that's all."

"Well, I know Sergeant Will claims he can't afford to lose you and Stock at the same time but in this case, he'll have to. You put in for this way before the others did, and if anyone's deserving of it, it's you. Since the IG Inspection last week, the sergeant major has been raving about you. In his own words: 'Why don't we have more young soldiers around here like Amaru?'"

Feeling humiliation at his praise, I thanked him again. "Sir, I really appreciate both the assignment and the kind words. I promise to represent our unit and Fort Bragg to the best of my ability."

"I know you will."

As he turned to leave, I snapped to attention before realizing he only stated two of his reasons for coming. "Sir?" I called out.

"Don't worry. All of your questions will be answered tomorrow morning."

"Yes sir, it's not that."

"No? What then? And make it quick 'cause I have a meeting with the first sergeant in five minutes."

"Sir, you said you had *three* things to tell me."

"Oh yes, how could I forget the best part? At tomorrow's formation, before you leave, you and Stockman will both be promoted to the pay grade of E-4. Congratulations, Specialist Amaru."

"Thank you, sir!"

"No thanks necessary, you've earned this." After shaking my hand, the CO made one more comment as I saluted him. "When you get to Fort Campbell, give 'em hell! Oh, excuse the profanity—you know what I mean."

"Yes sir!"

A half hour later, when I told my buddies the good news, I was sitting in the passenger seat of Bellamy's pick-up with Chill squeezed between us.

"What? That's great Tak! Man, you're really making it happen."

"Thanks Rej, but it's not me, it's the Holy Spirit. All praise is due to God."

"Praise God!" Chill exclaimed.

Walking into the church, I was still floating on cloud nine. Eager to share my good fortune with Curt and Jon, I searched around the room but before I could spot either of them, the pastor walked to the pulpit. "Hallelujah!" he yelled.

"I love Jesus! I say I *love* Jesus, yes, I do. Before we commence the praise and worship segment, is there anyone else here tonight who loves our lord and savior? Say Amen!"

"Amen!" came the enthusiastic response from the forty-plus members.

Once the music began, I closed my eyes and allowed the Spirit to have its way. If a soulful bystander had been watching—without hearing the music—they may have surmised that *Shirley Caesar* and *Aretha Franklin* were collaborating with the *Clark Sisters* in that tiny store-front dwelling. Completely absorbed in the moment, when a warm presence drew near, I opened my eyes and saw Curt standing there wearing his best 'Colgate smile.'

"Tak, it's good to see you brother!"

"It's even better to see you!" As I was completing my enthusiastic response, Jon also appeared. "Both of you!" I added before embracing the two pastors-in-training.

"Listen," I began after releasing them, "I got lots to tell y'all after church. And it can't wait 'cause I'm rollin' to Kentucky tomorrow morning."

"Say what? Kentucky!" With the praise and worship segment concluding, the music was fading when Curt blurted this out. For this reason, it sounded like he was yelling at me. Looking around the room with a childlike grin, Curt waved at the startled faces. "Sorry folks, everything's fine…just got a little excited, that's all." As he shared a chuckle with some of the onlookers, Jon made a statement-like question.

"I take it you got the slot for Air-Assault School?"

"Yup."

"Praise God. Okay, let's talk after the service," Jon replied as Curt cut him off.

"Before you run back!" he said still beaming.

Once everyone finished welcoming each other, we took our seats. Following a few minutes of church business, Pastor Bart jumped into the main topic of that night's sermon: tithes and offerings. "Folks, I don't want to beat this subject in the ground, but there still seems to be some tight-fisted individuals amongst us. Please open your Bibles to Proverbs 3:9 and 10." Although the pastor turned the pages in his Bible, once he began reciting the scripture, he never glanced at the lectern. *"Honor the Lord with your wealth, and with the first fruits of all your produce. Then your barns will be filled with plenty, and your vats will be bursting with wine..."*

As I normally did whenever he was speaking, I leisurely flipped through my Bible. Since I had begun tithing several months ago, it never crossed my mind he was referring to me. For this reason, I was shocked after the service when the pastor made a beeline toward me before I could exit with Jon and Curt. "Good evening Takuan," he interrupted our conversation. "Ready for our chat?"

I had completely forgotten about the appointment the pastor had made at the skating rink, so it astonished me that Jon and Curt did not look surprised in the least. *Had the pastor mentioned something to them?* Anyway, with no other option available, I dejectedly agreed. "Umm...yes, of course."

"Tak, we'll catch up with you later." After Jon said this, Curt co-signed his sentiment with a raised fist before walking out the exit.

Struggling to not show any anxiety, I followed Pastor Bart into his office. Once he seated himself at his desk, I sat down in a chair as he opened a drawer and pulled out a stack of envelopes. When he came to one with my name written on it, he pulled it from the pile. "This is yours, right?" he asked, placing last month's tithes and offerings envelope on the desk in front of me. Since my name was in plain view, I did not respond.

As I waited for him to divulge the purpose of this meeting, I grew antsy.

"Takuan," Pastor Bart began, "in Second Corinthians, chapter 9, the Bible tells us: *'Each one must give as he has decided in his heart, not reluctantly or under compulsion…for God loves a cheerful giver.'*"

Since this was one of his favorite scriptures, I was very familiar with it. As I wondered if he used it earlier while I had been engaged in my own Bible study, he swiveled around in his chair and reached into a bookcase behind him. Following a couple seconds of searching, the pastor grabbed a black-and-white notebook and placed it on the desk next to the envelope. While carefully wiping his glasses with a handkerchief, he explained the notebook was a record of the funds collected from church members. After saying this, he flipped to the A section and ran his index finger down the page until he came to my name. "Takuan, I've heard you give some grand testimonies about your relationship with Jesus and the positive impact He's made in your life. This is correct, isn't it?"

"Oh, no doubt about it pastor," I concurred. "My life has made a one-hundred-eighty-degree turn since I got saved."

"So, if God has been fulfilling his end of the bargain, then what's the problem?" he said examining my countenance.

"Problem?" I responded, still completely in the dark. "There's no problem sir."

"No? Looking at these records, it seems you're one of the cheerless givers this passage is referring to. My question is: why?"

"Sir, there must be some mistake. Since I began tithing six months ago, I haven't skipped a month."

"Ah, there seems to be some confusion. Allow me to add some detail for clarity." Saying this, he pointed at the scribbled notations next to my name. "Let's see...March, twenty-three-dollars, April, seventeen-fifty, May, twenty-two dollars," he stated before pointing at the twenty-five-dollars written on the envelope in front of me. "It seems last month was the most you've given so far." Sitting back in his chair, he adjusted his spectacles with this hand. "When I first began receiving these staggering low amounts, I thought they were offerings, so I didn't approach you about it. But last month, I noticed you had checked the box next to tithe, not offering. Is this correct?"

"Yes."

"Is that all you have to say?"

Still confused, I nodded.

"Takuan, I don't understand," the pastor shook his head doubtfully. "I thought we all agreed to donate ten percent of our income as Moses instructed in Deuteronomy. If I'm to fulfill my destiny in Christ and become a full-time pastor, first, I'll have to quit my job. That means my family will be depending on our congregation to pay the bills...not to mention the plans to build a new church."

"Sir, perhaps I should clarify some things about my personal life," I interjected.

"Of course, go right ahead." Although the pastor said this in a relaxed tone, his face revealed irritation.

"I wholeheartedly agree the church needs a new building and a full-time pastor. But before I got saved, way back in basic training, I signed an allotment agreement which sends most of my monthly earnings to my brother. He's using the money to invest in a business he's getting off the ground. May I also add that he is a faithful Christian who has prayed for me relentlessly. Anyway, when I get out next year, he's going to return my salary to me with interest. This is part of the money I'm going to need next year at college." Naïve to the fact that modern religion was a business, I mistakenly believed once Pastor Bart understood the only reason I joined the Army was to raise money for college, he would see with my logic and stop hounding me. Therefore, when he chuckled condescendingly, I was offended.

"Takuan, the Bible doesn't say—"

"Just a minute sir, I wasn't finished." Now that I was teed off, I decided to tell him the truth. "I had some questions about tithing, so I asked Curt and Jon about it."

"Oh, did you? And what did they have to say?" The pastor seemed interested to hear this.

"Not much. Like the Word instructs us, we didn't lean on our own understanding. We pulled out a concordance and researched every scripture related to tithing."

"Really?" Pastor Bart asked in a patronizing tone. "And what did the three of you find?"

"A whole lot," I stated confidently, now more determined to speak my mind than ever. "We found the scriptures you like to use but there were several others I never hear in church. For example, in Second Corinthians, chapter 8:12, the apostle Paul wrote a letter from Macedonia to the Corinthians. In it, he said that whatever you give is acceptable, if you give it eagerly—I'm not quoting. He also said that a family's needs should not be affected by tithing, but rather, each person should give in proportion to what they have been given. Basically sir, it seems Paul is telling us to give according to what's in our hearts, as well as our pockets—so that's how I tithe."

Hearing this, Pastor Bart was livid. "I'll be sure to speak with those two—"

"Why? Didn't you hear anything I said?" I asked in amazement. "They didn't tell me this, *God's Word did!* This is what Jesus' disciple wrote. Sir, why are you so angry? These are the words in the Bible."

"Takuan, you do realize your future, just like Jon's and Curt's, lies in becoming a pastor of the Way, don't you?" Completely ignoring the information, I just offered, the pastor remained steadfast on this worn-out path.

"I guess so but—"

"You do? Then how do you explain this nonsense about leaving for college next year?"

Hearing him call my academic plans 'nonsense' almost made me snap; but instead I took a deep breath and reminded myself that I was talking to the pastor of our church. "First of all, sir, I don't regard my studies as being nonsense and, in my opinion, it's very irresponsible of you to label them as such. Second, I've heard it mentioned several times that we have branches of the Way all over the country, so I don't see what the problem is."

Realizing he had underestimated my resilience, the pastor attempted to mesmerize me with another scripture. "Takuan, the third chapter of Malachi specifically refers to people like you—"

"People like me? What's that supposed to mean?"

"It says, and I quote: *'Will man rob God? Yet you are robbing me. But you say: how have we robbed you? In your tithes and contributions! You are cursed with a curse, for you are robbing me, the whole nation of you! Blah blah blah...'*"

By the time he finished his ramble, I was no longer willing to argue; I was looking for an avenue of escape. So, when his wife entered unexpectedly, I did not miss my opportunity.

"Oh, excuse me honey. I didn't realize you two were back here. I'll come back later."

"No, no, Missus Bartholomew it's okay, I need to get going anyway." Saying this, I stood up and closed our discussion. "Pastor, I'll pray about it."

Hearing this, the pastor shot me a dirty look but kept his reply civil. "We'll pick this conversation up after this Sunday's service, okay?"

"Okay," I muttered back, just wanting to leave. After walking to the door, I opened it and was still nodding my head when I remembered my assignment the following day. "Oh, I almost forgot, I won't be here Sunday."

"*Why not?*" both, of them, chorused.

"Because I have a training assignment in Fort Campbell, Kentucky—good night!" Without another glance in their direction, I stepped out of the room and closed the door.

As I filed passed the few lingering members in the main room, I tried to appear like I was not in a hurry. Fearing the pastor might call me back, I barely acknowledged anyone while making my escape. Once outside, without stretching at all beforehand, I started running. By the time I broke a sweat, the disturbing meeting with the pastor was all but a forgotten memory as I devoted myself to the five-mile run back to post.

Having settled into my pace, my mind focused ahead to my next challenge.

Chapter 4: Air-Assault School

"Ready to go *Specialist* Stockton?"

"Yes, *Specialist* Amaru. How about you?" With our new, E-4 rank pinned to both collars, Stock and I were in the back seat of the hummer grinning like two Cheshire cats.

"Okay, enough already!" Sgt. Peterson yelled over his shoulder from the passenger seat. "I'm not gonna sit here and listen to the two of you jerk each other off all the way to Kentucky."

"Aw come on Sarge, just one more time," Stock joked, tapping the E-6 on his arm.

This caused everyone to laugh.

Once we hit the expressway, I closed my eyes to review what little I knew about our training assignment. Similar to how Ft. Bragg was famous for being the home of the Special Forces and the Division, we knew Ft. Campbell was the headquarters for the *101st Airborne*. Nicknamed the 'Screaming Eagles,' their sleeve insignia featured a bald eagle under an Airborne tab. In spite of this, when Sgt. Peterson explained the 101st was actually a light-infantry regiment which specialized in pathfinding missions, we decided since they lacked the grand experience of putting their knees in the breeze, they were really just glamorized LEGs—and we planned to let them know about it.

Normally, paratroopers who voluntarily terminate their jump-status are no longer allowed to wear jump wings.

But I was. I received my special authorization the day after telling my platoon sergeant I had terminated due to an injury incurred on a jump; I even showed him the keloid-scar on my elbow from a motorcycle accident. The next day, to my surprise, Captain Pearson and the first sergeant showed up at my PT test to see if my injured elbow had healed completely and, after watching me knock-out a hundred and twelve pushups in two minutes, Top told Sgt. Barnaby to bring me to his office.

Following breakfast, I met Sgt. Barnaby outside Top's office. Considering the last time, I had been escorted by my platoon sergeant to the company headquarters, it ended with my CO labeling me a 'sub-standard human being,' it was no surprise I felt nervous. For this reason, when Top greeted me politely before asking me to have a seat, I was thrilled.

"Amaru," Top stated from behind his desk as he took off his glasses. "Believe it or not, you're still in the Eighteenth Airborne Corp. Now, I'm just a first sergeant so I dunno when the brass'll make the decision but eventually we'll be jump-activated. What I do know is, if it becomes official at the opening ceremony in a few weeks, including you, we'll have twenty-seven soldiers who're jump-qualified." Leaning back in his chair, the Vietnam vet scratched his grey-flecked mane. "Which honestly ain't that bad to start with, but the catch is, me and you are the only ones with any real experience. The rest of 'em are a bunch of five-jump commandos."

In Airborne School, five successful jumps are required to earn the coveted jump wings. For those who graduate but afterwards get assigned to a LEG unit, they are condescendingly referred to as 5-jump chumps—or commandos in this case—by experienced paratroopers.

After giving Top my consent, he thanked me before dismissing us from his office. The point is: I was ordered to keep my Airborne wings stitched to my uniform.

During July and August, the heat-index on Ft. Campbell was extremely hot and humid. This resulted in everyone becoming irritated by the mugginess. On our second day, Stock and I were walking to the mess hall when a group of young trainees pointed at our jump-wings and mumbled something amongst themselves. Even though I was saved, any type of behavior which could be construed as disrespectful usually resulted in springing Billy into action.

Pointing back at the foursome, I imitated the braggadocios stance the SEALs had taken in Jump School. "How dare you LEGs stare at bona fide paratroopers like that!"

Although we were aware that paratroopers were rare commodities outside of Ft. Bragg, we never thought we would get so much attention; some of the young privates gawked at us like we were rock stars.

"That's right," Stock chimed in, pointing at the crowd of about twenty. "From now on, whenever we walk by, either stare at the ground or salute…is that understood?"

"Whatever," one of them responded with a sullen glare.

In spite of Billy's swagger, the Air-Assault experience proved to be more than I could handle. We arrived five-days before training commenced and left almost a week after the graduation ceremony; so, in all, our adventure along the Tennessee – Kentucky border, which is where Ft. Campbell is located, lasted over three weeks. As the only trainees who were not from Ft. Campbell, our assignment was much more difficult than the others. I remember Stock complaining to Sgt. Peterson saying it wasn't fair how, at the end of each day of training, everyone else either returned to their air-conditioned barracks, or drove to their homes, while we clocked-in at our second jobs; and this strenuous shift did not end until midnight!

Paint, nails, screwdrivers—we did some serious work. Being the sole occupants of the old, WWII barracks designated for off-post trainees, we were ordered to start repairing our living quarters from the moment we arrived. Along with the holes in the roof and ceiling, there were also missing floorboards and numerous cracks in the walls and windows. Very little paint remained and whatever was left was chipping off badly. Both Sgt. Peterson and Stock had experience building houses so they showed the rest of us what to do. If not, there is no way we could have completed such complex tasks. Although we were told this extra-duty would end once the training started, since we had only completed a third of the work when phase one got underway, each evening, following a back-breaking day of training, we returned to the barracks and continued renovating the decrepit building we lived in. Unbelievably, after completing both jobs and taking our showers, it was then we faced our most formidable challenge: trying to get quality sleep in a humid building sweltering with fresh paint fumes. Even with the windows open and three industrial-sized fans on full-blast, it was virtually impossible to get any sleep. And due to inhaling these toxins all night, every morning we woke up with a case of the *vapors*.

Although the Air-Assault course consisted of only eleven days of training, there was a lot of information packed into those blocks of instruction—especially in the second phase. In all honesty, I would have flunked the course had it not been for another surreal relationship with another NCO. Unlike my other experiences, Sgt. Rogers and I actually had a genuine rivalry; however, the rest of the story should sound familiar. The matchup ultimately imparted a tough, character-developing lesson to a hard-headed youth amidst some comical circumstances. Fittingly, my first encounter with the Irish NCO occurred on what was called 'Day Zero,' due to being the day we took the entry examination for the course. To be admitted into the Air-Assault School, applicants had to successfully complete a two-mile run, an obstacle course, and an initial TA-50 equipment inspection.

We introduced ourselves to each other at the end of the two-mile run.

"Is this what you roody-poo LEGs at Campbell call a run?" I yelled out, continuing my SEAL impersonation. As I did so, I scanned the faces of the soldiers jogging around me.

"Specialist, shut the hell up!" screamed an auburn-haired NCO. Running outside the ranks in his black, Air-Assault t-shirt, Sgt. Rogers glared at me. "The only time you open your mouth around here is to reply to a question from the cadre, or to sound off with the cadence. Are we clear Amaru?"

"Clear Sergeant, Air-Assault!" I roared back wearing an astonished grin. Thinking this type of competitive talk would be the norm—like it was in Jump School—I was surprised to get rebuked so harshly. *Guess this ain't a high-speed operation after all*, I thought to myself.

There were three phases comprising the Air-Assault course: combat assault, sling-load operations, and rappelling. While the first and third phases were no piece of cake, they posed no real threat to graduating. Sling-loading, on the other hand, was an entirely different animal altogether. For three days, we practiced hooking-up external loads of various shapes and sizes. The purpose of the exercises was to prepare heavy, Army equipment to be airlifted by a helicopter. On the hands-on segment of the test, the instructors purposely set-up rigging gigs on four types of equipment. In groups, we rotated to each load one at a time and were given two minutes to inspect that piece of equipment and identify three of the four deficiencies.

Sounds easy huh? That's what I thought too.

Although I aced the written exam on the first try, even after three attempts, I never passed the hands-on part of the test. After learning that all of my Ft. Bragg brethren received a 'Go' on the pre-test, which was our first stab at it, I took the second test very seriously. To the point, while everyone else went off-post over the weekend to watch *Eddie Murphy* in his stand-up comedy, *Raw*, I remained at the barracks to study. Although everyone knew why I was staying behind, Stock cracked-up laughing when I told him that, even had I passed, there was no way I would go to a town named 'Lynchburg,' (Tennessee) with a bunch of white boys.

In spite of my dedication, the results were the same. Considering we had practiced rigging everything from *Hummers* to huge anti-aircraft weapons called *Howitzers*, there were a countless number of gigs to memorize. Strangely, it was not until I was seated in the backseat of the jeep on our way back to Ft. Bragg when I learned the secret to passing. Sgt. Peterson and the others agreed the trick was to imitate how the Air-Assault instructors approached each hook-up.

"Amaru, I watched you on your third test. You ran around like a chicken with your head cut-off." As the NCO resumed his constructive critique, Stock and the others chuckled. "You had no strategy whatsoever, you just glanced around like the gigs were gonna jump up and wave at you. Had you paid more attention in class, you'd would've noticed the cadre checked each hook-up in a certain order. It didn't matter which of them did it, they always used the same methodology."

"And they always took their time too," added McGuiness.

"Yup, that's true," replied Sgt. Peterson. "They repeatedly showed us the sure-fire way to identify the gigs but you had to use *their* system."

"Yeah…you're right, I get it!" I concurred like it mattered. "That's what the Air-Assault instructors meant when they said: 'Slow is smooth and smooth is fast'."

"Exactly! And don't forget 'Attention to detail' because they ran that phrase into the ground too," replied the NCO in his mid-thirties before shooting me a suspicious look. "Wait a minute, if you didn't know any of this, how did you end up passing?"

"That's what I've been asking him for the past three days but he won't fess up," Stock revealed as he poked my arm with his finger. "Especially since Sergeant Rogers was the instructor who checked his answer sheet."

"*Really?* Sgt. Rogers was the instructor who gave you a 'Go?'" McGuinness was so surprised he adjusted the rearview mirror from the driver's seat so he could see me; his eyes were wide with astonishment. "Man, I can't believe he didn't get back at you for 'busting his balls' that day at lunch!"

Hearing this, everyone shared a laugh.

"So, what gives, Amaru?" Sgt. Peterson gave me another inquisitive look. "How'd ya do it?"

Staring back at my interrogators, I shrugged my shoulders. "Honestly, I don't know."

My and Sgt. Rogers' rivalry was well documented. As stated, it began on Day Zero. In addition to the colorful episode after our run, I immediately became in danger of failing the course at our TA-50 inspection.

"Specialist, what the hell do you call this?" As Sgt. Rogers asked his question he pointed at several pieces of my equipment. "You see all these silver scratches? Anything painted black is supposed to be subdued. That means 'black,' in case your dumb-ass doesn't know what 'subdued' means." Then he picked up my entrenching tool and resumed dressing-me-down in front of the company. "Look," he said, showing me the shiny marks. "In a fire-fight, these areas will reflect the sun. That makes your TA-50 not only dangerous to you but also to your entire unit. You didn't know that? Hmm," the Air-Assault instructor scratched his head, "I wonder what else they're *not* teaching you boys over at Bragg?"

Although the marks he was referring to were evident, the only thing I registered were his demeaning comments about Ft. Bragg. "Clear Sergeant and I apologize!" Billy baited him in a loud, booming voice.

"Apologies aren't necessary, just—"

"No Sergeant they are," I cut him off. "Because I just thought those scratches were normal wear and tear. You see Sergeant, at Bragg, we actually *use* our TA-50."

Following a brief moment, Stock started to chuckle in

a drawn out, deliberate manner; which of course led to the rest of my Ft. Bragg brethren following suit. From that moment, Sgt. Rogers made it no secret he was out to get me. Unlike my other run-ins with NCOs, this episode reached its climax rather quickly—at lunchtime on the final day of phase one.

The Air-Assault School did not have its own cafeteria. Therefore, at lunchtime, we were free to go anywhere provided we were standing in formation at thirteen-hundred—or 1 pm for you civilian-minded individuals. That said, almost all the trainees ate at the nearest mess hall which was around the corner from the school, just a couple hundred yards away. Once off the school grounds, we were able to ditch rigid codes like the 'no walking' rule. This, the most annoying of our training mandates, required us to jog—never walk—whenever we moved from one area to another. If that wasn't bad enough, we also had to yell 'Air-Assault!' each time our left foot struck the gravel. Since we did this all day long, just being able to walk and talk normally was a refreshing break. Like everyone, I relished our noontime, sixty-minute breathers.

In spite of dining at a neighboring unit's cafeteria, the Air-Assault cadre always sat together at the first table near the entrance, making them the central feature of the room. This was the exact location where I remembered the drills and black hats sitting too. And like my former instructors, the Air-Assault sergeants acted like they owned the place. The difference was: in basic and jump school, our supervisors *did* own the mess hall. With no one present but us and them, the drills' and black hats' word had been the law. Whereas here, the overwhelming majority of GIs in the huge cafeteria were 'permanent-party' soldiers; which means they were stationed at Ft. Campbell. Since the Air-Assault personnel comprised an insignificant minority, I found it amusing that the instructors felt the need to put on this grandiose performance by sitting in front of everyone. After a few days of watching this odd behavior, I deduced these instructors had developed a complex. On that note, back by popular demand, Billy showed up.

"Check out those cornballs sitting up-front with their wack t-shirts, doing their best imitation of a Sergeant-Airborne. Word is bond, they ain't nothing but a bunch of 'wanna-be black-hats'." Spying on them from about twenty feet away, I was slouched in my seat as I spoke. Once my paratrooper buddies finished laughing, I lowered my head again. "Man, how are we supposed to respect them if the Department of the Army won't even build them a cafeteria?"

"Amaru, keep your voice down!" warned Sgt. Peterson.

"Don't worry," I said with a cocky grin. "*Mr. Rogers* and them are way too busy over there in the *Land of Make Believe* to notice anything that's going on around them. Just look at 'em," I said. "It's disgusting to watch a group of grown men pretending to have their own chow-hall…what an inferiority complex." Once I heard soldiers at the tables near us starting to laugh, I dared to raise my voice a few decibels. "But check this out Sergeant, even if those pogues did hear me, they couldn't do anything about it because in here they don't have jurisdiction to do *jack!* And why not you ask? Because, once again, this ain't their cafeteria; and in here, we're no longer trainees: we're permanent-party personnel just like everyone else." Flashing a grin, Billy got an idea. "You know what we should do?"

"What?" Stock asked in a curious tone.

"We should go over there and sit at their table."

"And do what, Amaru?" McGuiness inquired with an incredulous expression.

"Just ignore them. You know, pretend like we didn't notice they were sitting there," I said chuckling, "just to see what they'll do."

"Amaru, you're insane!" This is what Buzz blurted-out right after he recovered from laughing so hard he nearly choked on his food. As we, along with soldiers at the nearby tables, continued to snicker a loud voice suddenly smashed through my cynical banter.

"Amaru, what was that? You wanna come over and sit with us?"

A silent hush fell over the populace as everyone turned toward the sound of the voice. It took me a second to spot the fuming image of Sgt. Rogers—a.k.a. Mr. Rogers—standing next to our table. As Stock and the others nearest to me squirmed in their seats, the surrounding tables roared in laughter.

"Hey guys!" Sgt. Rogers yelled after the laughter had quieted down some. Once he had his fellow cadre members' attention, he resumed: "Have you had the pleasure of meeting Specialist Amaru yet?" While asking this he pointed to confirm my identity. "He's the loud-mouth from Fort Bragg. Stand up!" he ordered. "Stand up and tell 'em what you just said about us."

Since Sgt. Rogers was an NCO, I had to stand up but there was no way I was going to condemn myself by confessing. Once it was evident I did not intend to say anything, Sgt. Rogers really poured it on. "Oh, don't get shy now!" he shouted wearing a scowl. "I heard your whole stand-up routine, you're a funny guy. Well since you seem to be tongue-tied, lemme help you out. You called us a 'bunch of wanna-be black hats...'"

Standing there listening to Sgt. Rogers repeat my comments word-for-word, I could not fathom how I missed noticing his approach. Now I understood why so many soldiers at other tables had been laughing: they were watching the whole scene as it developed. In other words, as they were listening to me, they were simultaneously watching Sgt. Rogers eavesdrop on our conversation. Considering how long they had been snickering, I deduced he must've been standing there for a while. Following his vivid remarks, Sgt. Rogers insisted I join him at their table. By this time the cafeteria was dead silent.

"Come on Amaru, this is what you want, right?" Holding his tray in his left hand, Sgt. Rogers gestured toward his fellow cadre members with his right. "Come on, I wanna introduce you to some of the other *cornballs*."

Realizing the situation was plummeting from bad to worse, Billy decided to get the most out of his buck. Reaching down, I picked up my tray. "Okay Sergeant, let's go," I coolly replied. My audacious response caused Sgt. Rogers to gasp; this gave me a degree of satisfaction so I grinned ever so slightly. Before things could get too far out of hand, however, a charcoal-black sergeant sporting an E-7 insignia took charge.

"Oh hell no! Specialist, sit your ass down."

"But—"

"But nothing, Sergeant Rogers. This incident is over...for now." Seated at the head of their table, the cock-diesel NCO then glared at me. "We'll see your smart-ass back on the grounds—believe that!"

"Clear Sergeant, Air-Assault," I declared, returning his stare as I sat down.

Understanding how much energy I was about to expend that afternoon, I focused on eating every morsel on my tray. As I munched away, I could not avoid overhearing comments from the soldiers seated behind me.

"Man, they're gonna smoke his ass the second he touches the school grounds!"

"Heck yeah, stick a fork in him 'cause he's done."

As each instructor finished his meal, to a man, they all made it a point to walk passed me. A few of them got real close—and one actually nudged me with his knee. Not wanting to add fuel to the fire, I never looked up but I could feel their piercing stares. Once the last cadre member filed passed, Stockman was beside himself in anticipation.

"Tak, what're you gonna do?"

"Umm, I don't know," I said blankly, not really understanding the question.

Sgt. Peterson likewise sounded as if he thought Stockman's question was stupid. "What's that supposed to mean? Stock, everybody here knows what Amaru's about to do: a whole bunch of push-ups and flutter kicks."

"Yeah, and he might even do some wind-sprints and low-crawls if they get real creative," added McGuiness as laughter was again heard all around us.

Barely paying any attention, I took my last bite, drained my glass, and excused myself from the table. As I stood up every head in the room turned; which consequently thrust me into the spotlight. The energy surge associated with hundreds of people suddenly focusing in my direction took me aback. Not knowing what else to do, I stretched my arms and grinned before picking up my tray; but I refrained from issuing my trademark wink because, after all, I was a Christian.

Exiting the building, I pulled my cap down to my ears, lowered my head, and pasted a frown onto my features. Recalling the technique, I used to avoid Stew back in Airborne School, I planned to hide in the latrine until five minutes before formation. Nonetheless, it soon became apparent that repeating my Jump School performance was not going to be easy. This is because at Ft. Benning, until word hit the grapevine, only one company knew what had occurred between me and Stew, and even then, most of the trainees did not know what I looked like; whereas in this fiasco everyone had witnessed the proceedings first-hand. As a result, even guys in other classes who I never met before were pointing me out.

"Here he comes now…that's Amaru, right?"

"How does everyone know my name?" I complained as wave after wave of trainees scurried out of my path, avoiding me like the plague.

Upon entering the school grounds, I made it to the latrine nearest our formation area without incident. After taking refuge in the foul-smelling outhouse which, from the outside, looked like a beat-up, lime-green shed, I proceeded to keep a sharp lookout for any approaching cadre. Every trainee who entered acknowledged my unique status in one way or another. While most dudes just stared or laughed, others approached to make a sly comment or two, with some even lending a helping hand. "Amaru don't worry," one guy said with a raised fist, "no Air-Assault Sergeants are coming. Good luck man!"

"Thanks," I replied to that sympathetic soul.

When the room began to thin out, I knew it was almost thirteen-hundred so I muttered a prayer under my breath and waited for the last soldier to leave before exiting myself. Filing behind the pack, I yelled "Air-Assault, Air-Assault" almost in unison with the others. Since we were all heading toward the same place, as much as they wanted to, these trainees could not run away from me. This slight subterfuge proved significant because when we scampered up to the formation area, I counted at least eight instructors patrolling my platoon; and they were staring hard at every approaching trainee.

Limping forward with my head down, I spotted Sgt. Rogers practically standing on top of my grounded equipment. *I guess it's on*, I thought to myself, seeing that a confrontation was unavoidable. Since he had every advantage, I wanted to throw him a curveball by sneaking up on him. With this in mind, I stopped yelling and accelerated toward the Air-Assault Instructor; however, seconds before reaching my destination, someone recognized me: "There he is—there's Amaru!"

Sgt. Rogers, hearing my name, turned toward the sound of the voice which exposed his backside to me. Smiling at a pair of instructors who happened to be in my path, I ran up behind Sgt. Rogers before either of them could shout a warning and screamed in his ears: *"Air-Assault!"*

Taken completely by surprise, the startled NCO nearly jumped out of his boots. This, as you can imagine, caused the entire formation area to erupt into laughter.

"At ease!" Sgt. Rogers screamed once he composed himself. "At ease all of you. Or we'll stay in the front-leaning rest 'til dinner!"

"At ease!"

"At ease!" yelled the other instructors.

It took almost fifteen seconds for the area to become completely silent.

When Sgt. Rogers finally turned toward me, although he appeared calm his face was still beet-red. "Amaru," then he paused for a breath. "Man, you really gotta set of balls on you, don't ya?" As he spoke, he stepped closer. "Okay Specialist *Airborne*, we're gonna see just what paratroopers are made of this afternoon. But not here," he stated, glancing at the soldiers surrounding us. "Too much shade, don't you agree?" Then he slowly pivoted in a circle to survey the area. "Let's go over there," he said, pointing at a concrete slab in front of us about a stone's throw away. "Over there, where the sun's sizzling nice and hot—move!"

As I ran toward the area Sgt. Rogers was pointing at I could not help but notice the heat waves radiating over the black asphalt—the kind that shimmer over a long stretch of desert road. Since the concreted area was designed for leading a PT session, not only was it the perfect size to accommodate the two of us, but it was also close enough to be viewed by the entire formation. Before getting into the front-leaning rest, I made sure to wipe both my hands on my sweaty t-shirt. This turned out to be a wise move because when I touched the ground they sizzled like two pieces of meat being thrown onto a grill.

Like Sgt. Peterson predicted, I did scores of push-ups, flutter kicks, and other assorted exercises that afternoon. After a couple minutes, my bodily fluids cooled down the concrete so the heat no longer mattered. As sweat drained from every pore, Sgt. Rogers taunted me from a crouching position…then a standing position…then back to crouching. I calculated he would never dare to delay the training schedule by more than fifteen to twenty minutes; and for this reason, I remained silent and kept up with his cadence no matter what the exercise was, feeling confident I could handle whatever punishment he could dish-out within this time span.

"Come on tough guy, don't tell me you're getting tired?"

Since my only concern was to endure the PT session I did not utter a word. Instead, I complied with my overseer's commands and, though he continued to eye-ball me, I refrained from looking at him. Twenty-five minutes later, while I was still doing flutter-kicks with Sgt. Rogers circling me with his hands behind his back, it occurred to me since I had insulted the *entire* cadre their collective reputation was on the line. With this in mind, I glanced at the formation; and sure, enough all of them were observing me and Sgt. Rogers like spectators at a boxing match, or some other live event. Put another way, it was clear every instructor was prepared to wait as long as it took for me to break.

So, I made them wait.

Eventually I began showing signs of fatigue. When Sgt. Rogers squatted down, I expected another round of insults but I was wrong. This time he sounded sort of friendly. "Just say you quit and it'll be over, I promise," he almost whispered.

After all his yelling and screaming, why had he suddenly switched to a cordial whisper? This is what my intuition wanted to know. The only possible conclusion was: he was starting to feel pressure to end this session. Once I understood this, I was determined to go back on offense again. "Not clear Sergeant. I will *not* quit because paratroopers fight 'til death!" I yelled before tilting my head to glare into his face. "I ain't no LEG—like you!"

This was the first time I had spoken; so, my words seemed to have taken the Air-Assault Sergeant off guard. At any rate, it took him a second to respond. "Specialist—" When he finally did, I drowned out his words out by singing an Airborne cadence everyone was familiar with.

"I'm Airborne! All the Way! Fit-to-fight! Dynamite! I say: A- All the Way, I- In the Sky, R- Rough and Tough, B- Born to die…" In this manner, I was spelling out A-I-R-B-O-R-N-E so loudly that Sgt. Rogers had to bend down closer to make his next order audible.

"Iron-Mikes[2]— move!"

As I stood up to follow Sgt. Rogers' command, I was pleased to hear voices and laughter coming from the formation area. Glancing over at the crowd, it now looked like a party was going on. "At ease!" yelled the instructors; and in the blink of an eye, law and order was restored.

When I had to stop singing in order to breathe, it became apparent the Iron-Mikes would be my undoing. Now, with my legs looking rubbery, it was eerily quiet so Sgt. Rogers decided to spit some trash-talk of his own.

"What's the matter Amaru? I can't hear you…come on, sing us another song!" he taunted.

Feeling dizzy from the heat, I thought I was going to pass out; this is when the crowd began getting rowdy again. However, this time the cadre did not silence them. Just as I was about to keel over, the image of Reed defying the black hats in Jump School sprang into my mind.

---

[2] For a detailed description of this exercise, check the *Glossary*

84

I refused to quit!

At this point, Sgt. Rogers spotted a curious trainee who had wandered too close to the action. "You!" he shouted, "commere." Once the private was standing ten feet to my right, Sgt. Rogers pointed at me. "Doesn't Amaru look pathetic?" he asked, chuckling cynically.

The private-in-question just looked without responding.

"Hey, I asked you a question—sound off Private!" snapped the Air-Assault instructor, now pissed. "Doesn't Amaru look like shit?"

This was the moment my reserve tank hit empty. Slouched over on one hand and one knee, I was barely able to keep from toppling over. In spite of this, he shook his head; this impressed me so much I made eye-contact with him. "Negative Sergeant," the blonde-haired trainee replied nonchalantly. "Specialist Amaru looks fine to me."

"Private, if you—"

"Hahahahaha!" Before the irate Air-Assault instructor could finish his threat, I busted-out laughing and, with a tremendous effort, struggled to my feet. Perhaps this caught Sgt. Rogers by surprise, I'm not sure; but for whatever reason he stopped yelling, which allowed me to speak. "You know what Sergeant?" Billy uttered through parched lips, determined to deliver his last punch line. "Even if I am done, it took an exercise named after a paratrooper to do it—I can live with that!" Once this comment reached the formation, a ripple of laughter spread through it like a blazing inferno and, just like the black hat who had given Reed a hard time, Sgt. Rogers conceded.

For the record: 'Iron Mike' is actually a de facto nickname for various U.S. military monuments. That being said, any Army personnel worth their salt should associate the name with a famous statue of a paratrooper.

"Next!"

Being the only trainee still remaining, stalling was no longer an option. Grasping my perspiration-stained answer sheet in my right hand and a pencil in my left, I reluctantly stepped forward. After failing the pre-test and the test, this third opportunity, dubbed the 're-test,' was my final chance to advance to the rappelling phase.

"Well, well, if ain't my favorite specialist from Fort Bragg. How ya feeling this afternoon Amaru?" Seated at a small table, Sgt. Rogers gestured for me to hand him my paper.

"Fine Sergeant, Air-Assault," I replied, trying my best not to look like a loser. In spite of my positive response, I was crestfallen. Since I had failed to even write the minimum number of answers, passing or failing was a foregone conclusion: one, two, three strikes—I was out.

"Okay," the Irish NCO spoke in his usual, upbeat manner. "I see you ran outta time, huh?" Staring at my paper, he rattled on. "I s'pose you got the rest of the answers in your head, right Specialist?"

I was sort of confused but I went along with him. "Umm...yeah, right Sergeant."

During the time I had been standing in line

brainstorming for the missing answers, I was tormented knowing Sgt. Rogers was going to get the last laugh. *How did I end up in his line anyway?* However, when he looked up from my paper it was clear that seeking revenge was the furthest thing from his mind.

"Well?" he snapped. "What're ya waiting for? You need one more gig for this jeep. Let's go Specialist, chop-chop," he said, looking impatient.

Shocked into action, I dipped into my memorized list of possible deficiencies. "Uh, umm...the light switch was on?" I said without an ounce of confidence.

He pretended not to notice. "No. Gimme something else," he barked.

"The emergency brake was engaged?"

"Good job. Let's move onto the *Howitzer*."

"Umm…the chain link number was incorrect?"

"Good job."

I ended up guessing three more times before Sgt. Rogers finally said 'good job' for the last time. Then he handed my answer sheet back to me. "Hurry up and write-in the answers," he murmured under his breath. As I was writing, the NCO sat back, laced his fingers behind his head, and exhaled sharply. "Amaru, what's your MOS?"

"76 Charlie, Sergeant."

"Whaddya know? It's true!" Pausing here, he chuckled. "When I checked your records and saw that, I swore it had to be a typo. My question is: what the heck is a guy who can do push-ups and flutter kicks from now until the middle of next week doing sitting behind a desk ordering vehicle parts? Now that's what I call a serious misappropriation of Army resources!"

Not knowing where his monologue was going, I remained silent.

"Amaru, I wanna share a secret with you," he said with a grin. "Last month, I turned down a slot to go to Airborne School. I figured, why jump out of a perfectly good airplane?"

"Because we *can* Sergeant," I emphasized, repeating the come-back I had heard Curt give so many times to whoever dared to question the elite status of paratroopers.

"Yeah, there he is!" Sgt. Rogers laughed and clapped his hands together. "I knew you couldn't keep your mouth shut for too long. Listen, what I wanted to tell you was, after our little encounter the other day—and I must admit you put on quite a performance—I told my first sergeant I'd changed my mind. So, guess what? I leave for Fort Benning the day after you graduate from here."

Wholly unprepared to receive not only kind words but actual praise, I was stumped for a response. "Th-thank you, Sergeant. I…I dunno what to say."

"That's the point big-mouth. For once in your life don't say anything—not to anyone about this, you hear me? Now get outta here."

In that shining moment, I considered revealing the actual definition of 'LEG' to Sgt. Rogers. Although many believe the acronym only pertains to a soldier's jump credentials, in reality, it also includes character. For example, Curt told me he arrived to Ft. Bragg before attending Airborne School—and in the same breath he also made sure to say: "But I ain't never been a LEG!" And I wholeheartedly agree because the Curtis Crawley I knew never 'Lacked Enough Guts' for any mission. So, as far as I am concerned, it is more about courage, discipline, and honor, rather than just whether or not a guy has jump wings.

There were a few interesting moments during the final phase. Among these the 'Aussie' rappel, which was done headfirst, along with a grueling twelve-mile ruck march on graduation day were probably the most memorable. In my relentless effort to finish the ruck march amongst the top ten, I nearly fainted from heat exhaustion. The entire Air-Assault experience—which included the extra duty and the horrid living conditions—was difficult; nevertheless, passing phase two was clearly the game-breaker. Once Sgt. Rogers scrawled 'Go' with his red pen on my answer sheet, it was all gravy after that.

A few of the guys, especially Stock, insisted I got the best of Sgt. Rogers. Obviously, the Air-Assault sergeant had to be aware that some might feel this way. *So why did he allow me to pass?* Over the past twenty years, I've had some time to ponder this question and the best I can come up with is: Sgt. Rogers must have felt obliged to uphold a principle which, he believed, superseded the standard protocol. For me, it was an opportunity to witness a "man's man" cast aside his pride for something more significant than winning a meaningless pissing contest. Considering Sgt. Rogers' had me dead in his sights but decided to let me off the hook demonstrates a profound level of integrity. In other words, his commitment to a certain code neutralized his ego to the point he no longer took what had occurred between us personally.

Chapter 5: A Change to Believe in

"Air-Assault!" Following this thunderous scream, the three booming knocks on the door identified exactly who my visitor was; for only Curtis Crawley walked around on a daily basis that charged up.

"Hold up a sec," I yelled from behind my locker as I donned a pair of shorts. That done, I hopped and skipped my way across the room, imitating a running back, dodging pursuers and opened the door just in time to see Chill and Reggie run up the stairs.

"Look who's back!" roared Crawley.

"And without an ounce of fat to spare," added Bellamy from behind Curt.

"What's up y'all?" I said, happy to see my friends. "Come on in."

Fresh out the shower, they caught me in the middle of getting dressed; so, I went back to my locker and reached into my still-unpacked duffel bag to grab a wife beater. As the three of them entered my room, Perez resumed critiquing me.

"Yeah, looking like a light-weight indeed," clamored Chill. "I told you they'd make you sweat. Cuz, your abs and chest are cut-up!" As the only Air-Assault graduate in our congregation, Chill had given me some pointers before I left.

"Chill, you were right about everything you said," I admitted. "But I wish you would've schooled me on sling-loading, cuz. That phase took me for a serious loop!"

"Yeah, yeah, yeah..." interrupted Crawley. By his tone and demeanor, he was making it clear he did not appreciate being left out of our member's only conversation. Still wearing his BDUs, Curt then pointed at the maroon beret sitting snugly on his head. "But just remember, this is where it's at."

Then Bellamy, despite only being a PFC, outranked everyone in the room. *"At ease!"* he yelled. Once Reggie had everyone's attention he continued. "I don't have an Air-Assault badge or Airborne wings, I'm just a LEG...and proud of it!" The sheer absurdity of his statement kept us quiet. "I'm **L**iving **E**very day for **G**od!" When no one immediately responded, he tried to explain the pun. "Get it, there's an L in living, an E in everyday—"

"We get it," Curt blurted out, "it was corny, that's all." Crawley's response made everyone laugh.

Formalities concluded, I exchanged hugs and pounds with my brothers before I got back to unpacking. Chill and Reggie sat on Chill's bed while Curt took a seat on mine. Once everyone was comfortable, Curt began rubbing his chin as if he were contemplating something. "Lord Amaru..." Using his old-man tone, Curt proceeded to act out a humorous skit. "We, the Dukes of the Fayetteville Estate, have come to inform you of the noteworthy events which transpired since you last stepped foot within the borders of the kingdom."

Always ready to play along, I dramatized my movements and voice with a 13th century, chivalrous air. "Greetings to the Triad," I replied. "And I thank you for taking the time to grace me with your royal presence." Although Bellamy and Chill were laughing, I soon had enough of this theatrical recreation. Closing my wall-locker, I beamed our conversation back to 1988. "So, what's the scoop? What I miss?"

So, did he.

"Nothing much. You know how-it-is down here in North Cackalackee…not a lot changes," Curt responded. "Check-it-out, I can tell you everything that happened in one sentence: Stan and Nancy PCSd last week to Ft. Bliss; two of Darrel and Eugene's friends joined the Way, so you know they can't wait to meet you. Oh yeah, and yesterday Pastor Bart left for Arkansas."

"That was two sentences!" Bellamy nit-picked but we ignored him.

"Really? The pastor's not here?" I asked in a curious voice. "Why did he go to Arkansas? Oh, wait a minute, that's where he's from, right?"

"Yeah but he didn't go for good. He'll be back."

Hearing this, I hid my disappointment.

"He went there to handle some business for the church as well as some personal stuff too; so, no one's sure when he'll return," Crawley stated before breaking the good news. "But while he's gone, Jon and I are taking turns giving sermons on alternate weeks. This Sunday, Jon's up."

"Now that's what I'm talking about!" I bellowed, shaking Curt's hand.

As happy as I was to hear Jon and Curt had been left in charge, for me, this turn of events had other implications too: it meant there would be no bothersome discussions on tithing any time soon.

"Wait a minute," interjected Chill. "Before we start celebrating, there was some news in the company about you."

"Sergeant Will didn't tell you?" asked Bellamy.

"Nah, I haven't seen him yet. I just got here like forty minutes ago. What happened?"

"You know what happened," Chill responded in a mocking tone. "The same thing that always seems to be happening around here: you got *another* award. This time it was an Army Achievement Medal, I think?"

"Yeah, it's an *AAM*," verified Bellamy. "Come down to *PAC* on Monday, I got it in my desk." Then he grinned broadly. "Tak, you really got it like that with Captain Pearson, huh? You gettin' awards in formations that you ain't even in! Man, stop hogging the spotlight…I'm tired of listening to the CO and sergeant-major talk about you."

"I hear ya Rej," Chill concurred. "Yo Amaru, can another brother get some of that shine?"

"Hold up," Curt said, sensing the onset of a low-vibrational exchange. "Don't tell me y'all getting jealous over our brother's success?"

"Nah, don't worry about that. Well, not from *us* at least."

In spite of disliking the dip this conversation was taking, I had to find out what Reggie meant. "Who're you talking about Bellamy?"

"You know who," Reggie shot back with a snicker, "the same two jokers that've been biting out your back since we merged with Alpha Company: Smith and Davis."

PFC Smith and PFC Davis worked on the other side of the vehicle bay, in the Alpha Company motor pool. Smith and I actually did the same job; this would factor heavily into the dynamics of our relationship. Although they functioned as a tag team, in actuality, the only problem-child was Smith. Davis was his dick-riding, set-up man. Everyone thought of him as Smith's own personal *Ed McMahon*; in other words: a real brown-noser.

On Ft. Bragg, during peace time, in order to calm the savage beast and keep the war-mongers focused, sports competitions between the various brigades were heavily promoted. Some of the brass took these contests seriously and, accordingly, rewarded athletic GIs for their participation. While Travis Smith, a light-skinned, handsome brother from Louisville, carved himself into the go-to-guy on our brigade's basketball team, I led Ft. Bragg in catching interceptions as the free-safety on our flag-football team. My motto was: 'There ain't a QB on Bragg I can't pick!' Smith was also a member of our football team, which went undefeated in the regular season; he played wide-receiver. In fact, he was the reason we lost in the championship.

The season began shortly after my return from Kentucky. Our offense was mediocre but our defence, led by the secondary, was exceptional. We averaged three interceptions a game—and I made it my business to swipe at least one in every contest. Less than a week before the Bragg Bowl, Sgt. Sampson, who was the cornerback who usually lined up on my side, got sent overseas. Because everyone knew he was cool with Smith, no one complained when Travis insisted on being his buddy's replacement. We only had one practice with Smith at cornerback. At that time, I realized he did not understand the fundamentals of playing a zone; so, I tried to give him some pointers but he was not open to anything I had to say.

"I got this, Amaru," Smith said with a condescending chuckle. "Instead of worrying about me, just make sure you got your shit together!"

On the first play of the championship, the opposing

quarterback threw a screen pass in Smith's zone. In the biggest game of the season, he knew we had a new cornerback; so, like any good strategist, he was testing the rookie. Once Smith got burnt badly, the quarterback continued to attack Smith wherever he was on the field. Since Smith did not understand how to play a zone-defence, I told everyone to switch to man-to-man. But even after the switch, he still could not manage. Long story made short, we got blown out. After the game, two of our lineman confronted Smith, wanting to know why he had lied about having experience playing cornerback—they also accused him of being selfish. When one of them shoved Smith hard in the chest, for a quick second, I thought he might have to knuckle-up.

In spite of the disappointing loss, I considered the season a huge success. As we mounted win-after-win—until the last game—I got a chance to practice various angles of pursuit and check speedy wide-outs. Getting these reps were invaluable considering they probably would be my last opportunity to compete on the gridiron before my try-outs. Having my sights set on football at the collegiate level, I had no interest in playing basketball again. However, a couple months later, my battalion commander requested I play on our brigade team as a 'personal favor.' Even after explaining my church held services on Wednesdays—which was the night designated for the games—he continued to badger me. This favor was difficult to refuse considering I too was asking him for a favor. In fact, I was the one who had requested this meeting with the lieutenant-colonel; I did this because I needed his signature on my early-out application.

After fifteen minutes of standing at his desk

answering questions, I watched the battalion commander select a pen from his breast pocket. He appeared poised to apply his *John Hancock* on the form when, instead, he launched into yet another round of requests. "Come on Amaru, you can go to church on Sunday. Wednesday nights are for b-ball, my man!"

Listening to his horrible impersonation of a 'home-boy accent' made it easier for me to stick to my guns. "Sir, with all due respect, praising God is a seven day-a-week activity for me—not just on Sunday." Pausing here, I shook my head. "If the games were played on Tuesday or Thursday perhaps; but I cannot barter my allegiance to the Creator…if that's what you're suggesting, sir."

The grey-haired aviator appeared surprised I took my religion so seriously. "Amaru, don't get me wrong," he said, adopting a more respectful tone. "When I was a boy, my mama raised me and my kid-brother, Troy, to be good Christians. Right there in downtown Montgomery, Alabama, at Saint John's Methodist Church. Specialist, you ever been to a church in Alabama?"

"No sir, I haven't."

"No?" When Col. Packer showed astonishment, I wondered why he was so surprised. "I only asked 'cause I believe your daddy's from Alabama too."

"That's right sir, he is."

"Well Specialist, no offense, but until you spend a Sunday between the pews of a chapel in *Alabummy*, you don't know squat about God. If you don't believe me, just ask yo' daddy." Saying this, he chuckled. "Listen, everyone knows I respect the institution of church as much as the next man," he paused here before suddenly erupting. "But dammit Amaru, with you flanking one wing and Smith on the other side..." Shaking his head, the veteran pilot leaned back and stared dreamy-eyed into space. "Add in Sergeant Powell's uncanny ability to penetrate and dish, and yessiree, I believe we could compete for the post-championship!"

Refusing to be swayed, I tried to change the subject. "That's nice of you to say, sir. But may I ask a question?"

"Sure Specialist, what's on your mind?" Saying this, he reached in a drawer for a black, tobacco pipe.

"Sir, what makes you so sure I'm any good at b-ball?" I inquired, making certain to use his preferred jargon for basketball. Seeing him exhale in an exaggerated, melodramatic manner made me smile. Pretending to be disgusted, the lite-colonel wore a frown as he flipped his Zippo lighter shut and took a puff.

"Come on son," he replied, exhaling smoke. "Don't insult my intelligence, I'm looking right at ya. Any idiot can see you're a stud. And you grew up in a colored neighborhood, didn't you? I bet y'all probably shot the ball damn-near everyday, right?" Like many white southerners, Col. Packer harbored a few out-dated phrases and mannerisms; and he was not shy about expressing his peculiar style of thinking. Ironically, I respected that about him. "Besides," he resumed after taking another puff. "Captain Pearson told me about the ass-whipping you handed him when y'all played one-on-one. I believe his exact words were: "The kid's got range." He claims you can drain the three with the best of 'em—*even better than Smith's jumper*," he added with a wink. With Smith and I both performing PLL duties on opposite sides of the same building, comparisons between the two athletic clerks were inevitable. "He said at one point, you dropped six in a row—right in his face. Is that true?"

As cool a character as Captain Pearson was, he definitely was not an athlete. While taller than me by a couple inches, the man did not know his right foot from his left; so, defeating him was nothing to brag about. Thinking back to my CO's friendly invitation to 'shoot some hoops' at his house, considering I ended up eating dinner and watching movies with his family, I now suspected the good-natured request had actually originated with his boss-man; i.e. the grey-haired guy sitting in front of me. With this in mind, I agreed to attend *one* practice.

"Just one, okay? Just to see if you change your mind. If you don't wanna play after that, no problem. Agreed?"

"Agreed sir," I stated smartly. After shaking hands with the colonel, I watched him ink his signature on the form. As he did so, I glanced to my right and smiled when my platoon sergeant gave me a thumbs-up.

Curt was not pleased to hear I was going to miss his sermon on Wednesday but I went to the basketball practice anyway, determined to get it over with. Having arrived at the gym, I walked in and sat on the floor with the others to stretch. Since I knew everyone on the team, I came in feeling relaxed. That is, until everyone stared at me like I was an infidel.

"Amaru, what the hell do you think you're doing?" yelled their coach, Staff Sgt. Woods.

Then the entire team stood up and surrounded me.

Seeing this, I surmised Col. Packer had not contacted the coach. "Umm," I hesitated uncertainly, looking up at the menacing faces all around me. "I take it no one told you I was coming?" I asked, not sure of what to say.

"No one told us you were coming?" snapped their team-captain. "Who're you supposed to be? Air Jordan?"

Once Sgt Jefferies expressed his contempt, the entire team busted-out laughing before they turned around and walked away to shoot lay-ups.

Even after dropping Col. Packer's name, I understood how pompous my actions must have appeared. The fact was: my presence was disturbing the dynamics of a team headed for the playoffs. Having gelled together all season, they were preparing to play this year's defending champs, the 27th Engineer Brigade. In other words, the last thing they needed was an unnecessary distraction.

So, there I was: sitting on the bench getting the cold-shoulder from the reserves while the first and second-teams sparred against one another. Just as I decided it might be a good idea to leave, the door swung open revealing Col. Packer, along with an entourage of two majors and one captain.

"Good evening, sergeant!" the lite-colonel boomed, creating an echo in the gymnasium.

"Good evening, sir," Sgt Woods replied cordially with a salute.

Even before the VIPs could remove their coats and take their seats in the stands, Sgt Woods pointed at me. "Amaru, sub for Taylor."

As you can imagine, putting me on the floor with the starting-squad ruffled a few feathers. This notwithstanding, just as Col. Packer had envisioned, each time Sgt Powell penetrated the second-string defence, he consistently found either me or Smith wide-open. Whenever one of us drained a three-pointer, the commander's rumbling, baritone voice could be overheard.

"What I tell ya?" What I tell ya?"

100

At the behest of the colonel, we ended practice with a scrimmage. He also had one more request: that Smith and I guard one another. Considering we played the same position, plus we were identical in size, this seemed to be a natural match-up. Until now, I was oblivious of any unfolding drama; I was just happy the practice was almost over so I could hang up my sneakers and get back to church. Before long, however, I realized not only was Smith taking the game more seriously than I was but, more importantly, he had a beef with me. Well, it became rather obvious on the second trip down the floor when he low-bridged me as I came down with a rebound.

"Say *'Kumbaya'* Christian boy," he stood over me, pointing in my face.

"Smith cut it out!" yelled Sgt Woods, running onto the floor from the side-line.

"You're out of line, PFC!" Stepping in front of Smith, Sgt Jeffries shoved him backward before squatting next to me as I winced in pain on the floor. "Amaru, you okay?" There was a look of concern on the captain's face.

After performing a brief function-check on my body, I determined I was not injured. "Yeah, I'm okay," I blurted in a gruff voice before sitting up and wiping my hands on my shorts. "Our ball on the side, let's go."

As Sgt Jeffries helped me up, it seemed he was amused by my aggressive tone. Well, that changed minutes later once Billy got in the game. Smith, mistakenly believing he was alone on a fast-break, tried to lay the ball up gingerly off the backboard. By the time he realized what his teammates were yelling, it was too late. After hawking Travis down from behind, I sprang into the air just in time to pin his shot against the lower-part of the backboard in dramatic fashion. Moreover, since the priority for my pursuit was to enact what the scriptures refer to as: 'an eye for an eye,' I made sure to slam my knee hard into his back—without looking like I kicked him.

"Flagrant foul!" Smith hollered while sprawling headfirst out of bounds.

I did not follow Smith to taunt him but I remained near the baseline long enough to see him nearly collide with some stacked tables and chairs. By the time his teammates arrived to defend their leading-scorer, I was already jogging back toward them. While I did so, I was singing an improvised tune. *"The baby's crying my lord, kumbaya..."*

"That's enough Amaru!" yelled the coach.

From this point there were no further reprisals; the game was close with both squads playing hard and the lead changing hands several times. In the closing seconds, with the score tied, I stole a pass intended for Smith and outraced him down the floor. Fearing he would try to duplicate what I had done to him, I erased the possibility by dunking the ball and hanging on the rim with two hands. I did this only to defend myself but it appeared to everyone that I was taking a parting shot at Smith. Following their final time-out, Smith ran through two screens and caught the ball at the top of the key. Turning toward the basket just as I arrived, we both leaped into the air and he pulled the trigger just over my outstretched hand.

I turned my head just in time to see the ball swish through the net. As soon as Smith drilled the game-winner, he proceeded to celebrate like he'd won the championship. "See! See! I told y'all he ain't shit!" Then he turned toward me and his rant really escalated. "Amaru, you ain't shit! And you ain't got nothing for this! So, get your losing ass outta here…or at least sit down on the bench, where you belong!"

Although I felt no personal rivalry with Smith, being a fierce competitor, there was no doubt I had done my best to help my team win the game. However, for me, this is where the competition both started and ended. Until I left the gym that evening, Smith was still prancing around in an effort to be irritating. What can I say, it worked; but I held my tongue because, after all, I was a Christian.

Recalling my initial visit to both motor pools, as a private, I remember being escorted by a very polite, PFC Smith. At the time, considering he was several years older than me, not to mention a rank higher, I never saw the potential for a rivalry. Nonetheless, it's funny how the Army chain-of-command functions sometimes. Two weeks after being promoted to E-4, Smith was demoted for missing a formation. Therefore, a year-and-a-half later, while he remained an E-3, I had moved up two pay-grades. In fact, Stock and I were the highest-ranking, non-NCOs in either motor-pool.

Considering the circumstances, it is surprising Smith and I never came to blows. Especially after our Battalion Maintenance Officer, minutes after declaring he had 'never seen a more organized supply room than mine,' placed Smith—who at the time outranked me—in my charge. His specific orders were: 'Smith needs to learn Amaru's system and dismantle his *ate-up* ways!' This became official at our dress-rehearsal for the IG inspection during a severe scolding which took place in front of the members of both motor-pools.

"*Smith!* What the hell is going on in your supply room? It looks like a tornado just ran through there!" Since

Smith remained quiet, he continued. "By any chance, have you had a look across the bay at PFC Amaru's neatly arranged shelves?" After Smith listlessly shook his head, the BMO pointed at him. "Well, allow me to inform you of some of the glaring differences between his supply room and that disaster you got going." As he spoke, he gestured back-and-forth between the opposite ends of the bay. "First of all, he has the national stock numbers and the part numbers clearly listed under each item. It's so shipshape over there anyone can easily find whatever they're looking for lickety-split." Then he pointed back toward Smith's room and raised his voice. "In that filthy heap, I couldn't even find my own dick!" Following a few more graphic comparisons which illustrated Smith's ineptitude, SFC Polkowlsky removed his finger from Smith's face and walked away in sheer disgust. This indicated the dress-down was over.

"Sergeant Will," the BMO bellowed over to our platoon.

"Whaddya need Sergeant?" replied my NCOIC.

"I apologize for the inconvenience beforehand, but can you spare Amaru for a couple hours each afternoon?"

"No. Why?" After everyone laughed, including the BMO himself, Sgt Will responded again. "What do you have in mind, Sergeant?"

"I want him to show *Messy Marvin* how to run a proper PLL room. Smith needs to learn Amaru's system and apply it as his own. Have you taken a look at the chaos going on over there?"

A couple weeks later, I got promoted.

As my candidacy for poster-boy of the seven-five-ninth gained momentum, some previously warm personas became icily frigid. Initially confused by this phenomenon, I then recalled Cpt Pearson telling me to expect this because people were intimidated by a black man who aspired to reach his potential. For the time being, considering Col. Packer had signed my early-out application, I rationalized everything was being orchestrated by the Holy Spirit.

For the next six months, right through the New Year, there was no doubt something special was percolating at our fledgling church. Our membership, which had tripled in this time-span, was more than five times its size from a year ago. That was when a frightened, embarrassed private, straight from the VD clinic, had humbly tiptoed through the store-front entrance. During the pastor's absence, as people continued to get saved, the need for a larger building became more evident than ever. Chill, Reggie, and I, flourishing under Jon's and Curt's street-preaching tutelage, were netting converts by the dozens as we swarmed through Ft. Bragg and the surrounding Fayetteville area like killer bees.

These days, with numerous religions pedalling their dogma door to door, many people are familiar with witnessing. However, unless you have actually witnessed yourself it is nearly impossible to fathom the degree of difficulty. First, try to consider how many ethnic, educational, and social backgrounds exist. Next, imagine spinning a roulette wheel and showing up randomly at people's homes but, here's the catch, not as their friend, co-worker, or even acquaintance. Instead you are an unknown, uninvited solicitor who, in many cases, is also unwanted. Now for the test: the reason you came is to convince this stranger to accept something they cannot see, hear, taste, nor smell—on the strength of your words alone. Not just show interest, mind you, but have faith that you are a messenger from Almighty

God. This is a unique challenge indeed and, it was not until years later, in the early nineties, when I came to appreciate what we had accomplished in our roles as: 'Fishers of Men and Women,' as Jon liked to call us.

As a university student, I needed part-time work to buy textbooks. The easiest jobs with the best pay were waiting tables and sales positions—if you could land a decent gig. Since working in an upper-echelon eatery required sacrificing evenings and weekends, I opted for the other end of the spectrum. In sales, my job was to convince folks they *needed* whatever I was selling. Once I was able to determine a person had some interest in my merchandise, I focused on connecting with them as individuals, understanding that just like in witnessing my goal was to get my customers to like me. Achieving this usually led to a feeling of trust…and after that, I found I could sell them almost anything. In my three summer positions, whether selling knock-off perfume, third-rate Rembrandt paintings, or expensive steak knives, my managers were amazed at how quickly I was able to master their systems. Although I never listed 'witnessing' on my resume, the truth is, my salesmanship hatched from preaching the gospel. The fact of the matter is, those sales positions were a stroll in the park compared to the beat I used to walk in the Bible-belt trenches of *Fayette-nam*.

World Class Christians

The night before Curt announced to the congregation that the pastor's mother suffered a stroke, he divulged the morbid news to Reggie, Chill, and me in private. Having also revealed that Pastor Bart was locked in a legal battle with the nursing home where she was living, together, we prayed God's light would reach his family in their time of need.

When the pastor's leave reached one month this raised a few eyebrows. A month later, although some whispers could be heard, no one said much publicly. However, when his absence stretched into the fourth month, we started to believe he might never return. At this point, the radical vibe which already existed jumped to a new level. Fresh, exciting, and ground breaking, it was a beautiful time to be at the Way!

In spite of Jon's stunning reports to Pastor Bart over the telephone concerning new converts, starting after the second month, we were paid regular visits by a series of visiting evangelists. These pastors, having their own churches, were being dispatched by our headquarters in Arkansas. Whenever a new one arrived, he always had the same question in mind: 'What's going on in Fayetteville?' Each of these traveling apostles came to understand that nothing could influence our unique style of worship. When some of them tried to make even minor changes in our agenda they were politely ignored. To us, they were visitors at best; but many saw them as intrusive outsiders who just slowed us down. Like Curt, we now understood that we were the heirs to the Kingdom of Christ; so, we were intent on claiming our birth-right. When I began speaking in tongues, which is one of the Fruits of the Spirit discussed in *First Corinthians 12*, at first, I thought it was just a bunch of babble. But then, other gifts mentioned in the Scriptures started to manifest throughout the congregation.

In late winter, Curt and Jon decided to hold a week-long vigil at five o'clock in the morning to pray for Pastor Bart. Each day, prior to the crack of dawn, soldiers and civilians alike abandoned the warmth of their cozy beds to attend these prayer sessions. At first, nothing out of the ordinary occurred. It took about five or six days before I can say with certainty that I was noticing something magical taking place. Looking back, if I had to point at one moment which propelled my spiritual growth beyond the 'fake-it-until-you-make-it' phase, perhaps it was the events which transpired on the final day.

As my voice merged with the prayers of other congregation members, I felt myself losing touch with all worldly concerns. Within seconds, I sensed something tingling in the lower-half of my body—perhaps as far down as my feet. This throbbing sensation gradually grew and intensified as it steadily moved upward. Until now, I had linked any such feelings to the uncontrollable rage of the Beast; and I suspected the Beast was evil, being it only manifested in times of extreme emotion such as anger. This however, not being a dire situation, marked the first time this happened in an environment free of strife. And since my actions were being directed by the purest of intentions, I knew whatever was taking place was not related to the 'devil.' Leaving behind this indoctrinated fear is what, I believe, allowed me to appreciate this heightened moment in its entirety. I say this because by the time this surge was passing my shoulders, I knew what it felt like to be a god.

As I exited the church, I noticed the side-effect of this euphoric state was that colors, angles, and movements of objects were visually enhanced to a psychedelic level. So, in order to compensate for how shiny the cars looked, and how the greenness of the trees seemed to be reaching out at me whenever the wind caused long branches to wave, I pretended

I was wearing 3-D glasses.

"Tak, we gotta hurry…" As Chill jogged passed me saying this, I watched trails of yellow and grey from his PT uniform gently float behind him. "Formation's in less than thirty minutes."

Once I inferred that Chill did not see anything unusual, I broke into a slow trot behind him. By the time I reached the parking lot, he and Reggie were already entering Reggie's pick-up. For a quick second I stopped to gawk at the thick, bluish hue surrounding the truck.

"How ya feeling this morning?" Bellamy asked while I strapped my seatbelt.

Unsure of who he was talking to, I responded anyway: "Like a bomb ready to explode!" I said, wiping beads of sweat from my face with a towel. "I'm glad we got PT this morning." Just as Reggie was about to respond, a loud voice boomed over from a car parked about ten yards away.

"Tak, I heard ya in there…and I agree one-hundred-percent!" ballyhooed Curt a split-second before his vehicle roared to life. While he drove toward us, Bellamy and Chill looked at me for an explanation but, seeing I too was clueless, they gave Curt their undivided attention when he pulled next to me.

"Praise God!" Craw-dad yelled through his window. "Ay, I know you guys gotta get going—me too but wait a second." Saying this, he hopped out of his car and approached. As Curt and I gave each other a pound, I tried to ignore the onyx-colored trails following our fists through the window. "Tak, you were speaking to my spirit loud and clear in there and I just wanted to tell you I agree. That's all."

Realizing Curt was referring to my speaking in tongues, I thought he was clowning until he explained further.

"Love, honor, creed of a warrior…you pretty much covered it all." Then Craw-dad blurted out his verdict. "I'll pick you up tomorrow morning. That is, if you're not on-duty this weekend."

"Curt, what're you talking about?" I asked, feeling self-conscious.

"What am I talking about? It's time to become world-class Christians, that's what!" When I did not respond right away, he stopped smiling and frowned. "Don't tell me you forgot?"

"Heck no, I've *been* ready!" I responded with some attitude, "ever since I got back from Fort Campbell. To tell the truth," I added half-jokingly, "I thought you'd lost your nerve."

"*What?* Lost my nerve?" The hard-charging sergeant did not get a chance to defend his honor before Reggie interrupted.

"Excuse me fellas," Bellamy said. "I don't wanna be rude, but we really gotta get going."

"Yeah me too," Crawley said before giving me another pound. "See ya tomorrow!"

Once we were on the road, Chill asked for an explanation. "Tak, what was Crawley talking about? I know about the six-miles-in-thirty-minutes—and by the way that's insane—but did he say you were talking to him in your prayers?"

"That's what it sounded like, huh?" Replying thus, I admitted I wasn't sure.

"But wait a minute, weren't you speaking in tongues?" Reggie asked.

"Yeah, at least I thought I was."

"You were," Bellamy quickly confirmed, "I was right in front of you. So, if Crawley was serious, I guess we can add 'interpretation of tongues' to the list.

"What list?" I asked.

"The list of spiritual gifts everyone's been receiving. First, Chill started speaking in tongues. Now you're doing it too. I wonder what the Spirit's got lined up for me?" Reggie asked, sounding a little disappointed.

"What're you talking about Reggie?" I came back. "Weren't you the one who predicted the pastor wouldn't return for at least six months, just two days after he left?"

"Yup, you did," concurred Chill, looking in Reggie's direction. "I was there when you said it, praise God!"

Once again, Chill's exclamation spoke for all of us.

Judging by the way the sun's golden rays were shooting down in torrents, it was hard to imagine Fayetteville had been covered by a snowstorm less than a week ago. Although piles of sparkling powder lingered here and there, the recent spring-like temperatures had dried most of the PT area designated for the *504ᵗʰ PIR*. Sitting on the grass with my legs straddled in a V-formation, I slowly leaned forward as Curt gently pushed-down on my back. As soon as my chest was resting evenly along the ground, I felt my hamstrings flex to their limit.

"That's cool, right there."

"What's up with you today, Tak? You kinda quiet. Don't tell me you're scared?"

"What?" I was slightly peeved Curt had interrupted

my mental preparation with this type of small-talk. "Nah man, it's time to perform so there's no longer any reason for talking." Standing up, we switched positions. "The time for talking is over."

"Amen." As Curt said this, he leaned forward. "Like I always say, we're halfway to our goal...we got the talking part done. Now comes the hard part: the *doing* part.

"Hoo-ahh!" Barking my grunt-call, I wiped the sweat from my brow as his words fused with my adrenaline rush. My body, understanding the physical hardship it was about to endure, was already sending large quantities of oxygen into my bloodstream. "Let's do this!" I exclaimed. "I'm ready to stomp a mud-hole in this six-mile-in-thirty-minute illusion...nah I mean?"

"Tak, wait a second. I wanna say something before we get started."

Knowing Curt's tendency to be long-winded, I tried to avoid his sermon. "Curt, hold that thought until we're done, okay? We gotta get moving. Don't forget, we gotta meet Sam, Ralph, and Dennis later—"

"Oh I get it," he cut me off with a chuckle. "You trying to say I talk too much, huh?" Without waiting for a reply, he resumed. "Don't worry, I wanna get started too so I promise it'll be short." When Curt stood up, I noticed he was teary-eyed. "Hey man, I really want to thank you." Saying this, he lightly punched my chest. "Not for taking this run with me. I mean, thanks for that too but that's not what I'm talking about. I'm talking about for being my brother in Christ. Since you, Chill, Reggie, Darrel, Eugene, and a few others joined the Way..." Shaking his head, Curt seemed at a loss for words. "Let's just say, there's nothing more pleasing than serving God, but over the past year it's been a special treat seeing brothers like yourself taking great strides in your walk with the Lord. Hallelujah!"

"Hallelujah," I repeated. "And brutha, you're more than welcome! Now, speaking of 'taking great strides,' let's—"

"Wait a minute, lemme finish!" Curt objected with a chuckle. "Last week, I was meditating on the different aspects of God's nature."

Realizing this was going to take a minute, I sat back down and continued stretching.

"Take your everyday housewife for instance," Curt continued. "Not only does she cook and clean like a professional, but she's also a seamstress, a counselor, a teacher, as well as a lover, companion, and a mother."

"True, true," I said without any strong conviction, not understanding where his speech was going.

"Obviously, she relies on different skill sets depending on what she's doing. Sometimes it's necessary to be stern, for example, when her children misbehave. But later that same evening, she might need to show compassion for her husband when he returns home from a long day at work."

"Curt, I don't mean to interrupt, but doesn't this apply to everyone?"

"You got it soldier!" Crawley emphasized, pointing at me. "And thanks for the alley-oop 'cause that's exactly where I'm going with this. Check-it-out Tak, I've been searching for scriptures which describe God's various signatures on the face of Creation."

"Whaddya mean?" I asked.

As the mouthpiece of God, Curt was literally 'the Word made into Flesh'—i.e. a modern day Moses—so whenever he spoke about the Bible I never ceased to be amazed.

"For example," Curt resumed, "Jon expresses the leadership qualities of the Almighty: I'd follow Jon anywhere because he's a natural-born leader."

"Yeah," I agreed. "He reminds me of King David."

"Exactly!" Curt responded excitedly. "If you study *first* and *second Chronicles*, you'll see that Jon bears a striking likeness to David.

Wanting him to expound further, I asked about my two buddies. "What about Chill and Reggie?"

"I dunno about Reggie," admitted Crawley scratching his head, "because we haven't spent a lot of time together. But Chill, no doubt about it, demonstrates the child-like innocence required to be Christ-like."

"Are you talking about in the eighteenth chapter of *Matthew* when Jesus said we must become as little children to enter into the kingdom of heaven?"

"That's right, Tak. I see you've been studying," the teacher complimented the student with a grin before raising the stakes. "Since you're familiar with the scripture, can you explain why Jesus called these children 'the greatest' in the kingdom?"

"No, but I'll take a guess. Maybe 'becoming little children' somehow symbolizes the purity of the Christ?"

"Wow! I never thought about it like that but I guess that's also correct. That is, if we understand that *everyone* must bear her or his own cross." Amazed at this new insight, it seemed Curt almost forgot what he was talking about. "But hold-up, where was I?" he asked more to himself than to me. "Oh yeah, what I was going to say is, children are honest and pure because they're still intimately attached to God. Think about it: kids don't know how to be any other way until society shows them that lies and deceit are a normal part of life. The fact Chill grew up in a rough section of Brooklyn but somehow managed to maintain his innocence is truly amazing. This is his shield against the world. I believe as long as he cultivates this side of himself, harm will never come his way. The question is: will Chill figure this out?"

"Hmm," was all I could say, having not yet fully digested the information.

"Don't you wanna know what you express?"

"Ahh, I guess so," I said somewhat reserved. Although I was curious, for some reason, I was embarrassed to admit it.

"Determination," Curt blurted it out with a grin.

"Determination?" I asked, contemplating his meaning.

"No doubt about it. I can see the same kind of resolve within you that Paul displays in *Corinthians*."

"Really?" I replied while rising to my feet, still thinking about what he meant. "What about you? I think you show a lot of determination too."

"Yeah," he agreed, nodding his head. "I get fixed on doing things as well—but not like you! A great example is the first time we ran together. The way you ended this run sums up your personality." Curt then laughed before slapping me on the shoulder. "Tak, I have a confession to make: until that day, I thought you were a soft guy. You know, a 'pretty boy'."

"A pretty boy?" I complained with disdain. Even though Curt was speaking about the past, my sensitive ego was easily bruised.

"Ay, the first time Jon and I met you and Mick at the shoppette, your physique wasn't nothing like it is now. Plus, a couple weeks after that, you terminated out of the Airborne-infantry and got transferred into that *roody-poo* Aviation unit. And let's face it: you are a light-skinned brother with curly hair…" His brow knitted together as he paused to examine my features. "You kinda got that *Debarge* appeal."

Following a couple seconds of chuckling at his witty analysis, I jokingly replied. "Curt, that was funny and all but if you ever repeat that Debarge joke again, I'ma sneak you."

After Curt finished laughing for a second time, he grabbed my arm. "Lemme finish! At that time, you still didn't know your way around Fort Bragg, right?"

"Yeah."

"That's what I figured, because about halfway through our run I remember thinking you wanted to pass me."

"I did, but I didn't know the way to your barracks."

"That's what it seemed like because whenever I stepped aside, you slowed down."

"Until we reached the PX," I replied. "From there, I knew it was just one right turn and then a long, straight shot down *Ardennes Street*. After I passed you, I left you in the dust," I teased. "Nah, I'm just kidding."

"No," Curt admitted, "that is basically what happened—until you started throwing up."

"More like dry-heaving, nothing came out."

"When I caught up and asked if you were alright, you gave me the dirtiest look. Now that was a time when I thought you were gonna sneak me."

Chuckling, I lightly punched him. "Sorry," I said, recalling the moment he was referring to. "I wasn't angry at you, I was mad at my body. I couldn't believe it was betraying me if that makes any sense."

"It does," Curt assured me. "But check this out. After you answered: 'Yeah,' you spit on the ground, wiped your mouth with your forearm, and then took off again—even faster than before! I couldn't believe it because I thought you were outta gas, like me. So, I figured we were going to take it easy for the last two miles and just jog but you were like, unh-unh. That's what I call determination."

While I soaked in his words, Curt reached into his back-pocket and pulled out a piece of paper. After he unfolded it, I realized it was a pencil-sketched map of a section of Ft. Bragg.

"Remember," he said gesturing at his sports wristwatch. "I'm making sure we stay on a world-class pace so I marked five landmarks about a mile apart along the way when I measured the route using the odometer in my car." Then he handed me the diagram.

Following a brief glance at his artwork, I had a basic understanding of the route but I did not pay any attention to the landmarks, thinking they would be an unnecessary distraction.

"The last couple miles are the same as the other run: so, we gotta go down Ardennes again. As a rehearsal, I ran the route while you were at Air-Assault School."

"Did you time yourself?" I asked, eager to hear the results.

"Yeah. Thirty-two-oh-seven."

Hearing this, I was astonished he had done so badly. "You weren't even close."

"I know. And the strangest part was: it wasn't because I was tired. It was because my pace just wasn't fast enough from the beginning."

"Guess it ain't called 'world class' for nothing," I

interjected.

"Right," he concurred with emphasis. "Well Tak, I said all of that to say this..." Walking in front of me he grabbed both of my shoulders and steadied his eyes on mine. "From the start, we gotta run like you did that time after you threw up."

"Dry-heaved," I repeated but he ignored me again.

"But we gotta maintain that pace the entire time." Having made his point, he released me and grabbed the small parchment from my hand. Refolding it, he put it in his pocket. "It'll be soaked by the time we get back here," he said with a grin.

"What you meant to say was: 'it'll be soaked in *less* than thirty minutes," I declared with confidence.

Still grinning, Curt did his final stretches while I closed my eyes to pray. Seconds later, I felt his hand on my shoulder. "Lord," he stated. "We pray that you find our endeavour pleasing this afternoon. We also ask that you keep us from injury, and if it be your divine will, we'll be back here in twenty-something minutes. In Christ's name we pray, Amen."

"Amen my brutha. No more talking, let's get to the 'doing' part!"

Beaming like two children at an amusement park, we stepped to the starting line. As Curt adjusted his *Casio*, I bounced on my toes.

"Get ready, set...go."

"Vaya con Dios!" I bellowed, exploding forward.

Convinced we had the blood of kings flowing through our veins, no matter the activity, we gave our very best effort. So, although we defined our quest as eclipsing a mark which

put us among a select group of thoroughbreds, the truth was,
we were just exploring ways to realize our ideal self.

Since Curt knew the route better than me, he assumed
the lead in the beginning. Nevertheless, to maintain the pace,
it became necessary for us to pass each other a few times.
Running at a near-sprint, we were moving almost as fast as
the 25-mph traffic. As we scampered across the road at a
traffic signal a sneering GI screamed at us from his red,
Chevy pick-up.

"Hey, where's the fire?"

Ignoring the hillbilly, I yelled ahead to Curt. "We
gotta cross intersections too? What do we do if the light's not
green?"

"We're on a timed-mission soldier," he replied
between breaths. "Be all you can be!"

After entering the *Hammond Hills* district, which was
an on-post housing area, Curt assured me there were no more
busy junctions lying ahead. Then he yelled out our first
progress report: "4:57!"

In spite of running like the wind, once I reflected we
only had three seconds to spare, for the first time, I started
having doubts. *Maybe we're not 'world class' after all.* The
moment this seed of doubt was planted, out of nowhere, I felt
a furious surge of energy so powerful it caused me to break
my stride and stumble. Having experienced a similar surge
just as intense but vastly different in its expression the
previous day at church, I was not afraid, now understanding
this energy did not always manifest as the Beast.

"Tak, we're slowing down, take the lead," Curt yelled
over his shoulder before adding: "you gotta push us!"

Beast or not, I knew the timing was perfect. Taking a
deep breath, I stretched my legs and picked-up the pace. As I

dipped by my elder brother in Christ, there was only a single thought occupying my mind: *cover the terrain...cover the ground!*

Even on our best day, it is unlikely Curt and I could've competed with Olympic runners. After all, we were soldiers not track stars. Nevertheless, on this particular morning in 1989, we transformed ourselves into athletes of the highest caliber. Not for fame, money, or even a gold medal, for we had evolved beyond craving the world's recognition. No, everything we did was an expression of our love for Christ—especially our physical exertions. Perhaps the purity of our sentiment was expressed best by *Eric Liddell* in the movie, *Chariots of Fire*, as he proclaimed: "When I run, I feel His pleasure!"

"24:50," Curt mumbled as he passed me.

His words, plus seeing his ragged appearance, had the effect of snapping me out of my trance. Crawley's t-shirt, now darkened by perspiration, was clinging to his frame. Considering Curt and I were training buddies, I had seen him sweat on many occasions but there was something different this time. It was his demeanor. The normally happy-go-lucky Curtis Crawley looked desperate—this I had never seen before. Likewise, once I became aware of his ordeal my own sense of weariness came to mind as I too was spent. As the growing pain in my arms, legs, and chest reached unbearable levels, I feared I might pass-out. Understanding I needed a distraction, I looked to my left and saw the building where my life on Ft. Bragg had begun: the *82nd Airborne Replacement Center.*

This image triggered the flow of forgotten memories to spew forth. As I considered where I came from and who I had become, I easily recognized the footprints of the Almighty—the clues were everywhere. It was no coincidence, I humbly acknowledged, that each time I strayed onto a path laden with traps, shady characters, and unwholesome situations some force had shielded me. By the time we reached the *505th PIR* barracks, which was my former home, I was choking back tears remembering all the guys I did dirt with who were chaptered-out, locked-up, or just nowhere to be found. *I did nothing special to avoid being on that list*, I admitted to myself. *But yet here I am*. Not only did I realize I had been the beneficiary of a succession of miracles—one right after another—I now understood why Drill Sergeant Sandoval called me an 'anomaly.'

As Curt and I staggered forward, my tears became indistinguishable from the other bodily fluids pouring down my torso. No longer able to feel my legs, I imagined my body was floating on its own by the time the words: *'Strike Hold!'* which was the motto on the 504th PIR headquarters, came into view.

"Tak, it's the final-stretch," Curt said, panting heavily as I pulled even with him. Take us home!"

Digging deep, I summoned the spirit of determination and accelerated but within seconds a blur appeared in my peripheral vision: *Curt was passing me back.*

"Make a hole!" a burly soldier yelled when he saw me and Curt barrelling toward him. Once he yelled this, the pedestrians, who were all GIs, respectfully cleared the sidewalk. Running neck-and-neck completely fatigued as we were, to the onlookers, it must have appeared we were racing against one another. At any rate, since the finish line was in front of Curt's barracks, naturally some of the spectators began cheering for him. "Come on Sergeant Crawley, you can catch him!"

"Sprint from here," Crawley cried out.

"I've been sprinting," I weakly muttered back, unable to shift to a higher gear. For this reason, I was impressed Curt demonstrated the wherewithal to catch up again.

Then, just like that, it was over.

With both hands on my head, I inhaled gobs of oxygen. It was a struggle to remain on my feet so, after a few seconds, I leaned over and placed my hands on both knees—I was dead tired. When Curt failed to offer any information about our final time, I figured we missed our mark. Still breathing deeply, I summoned the energy to look at Crawley. Seeing him down on one knee with his head drooped over, I was appalled.

Even if we did not reach our goal, I felt no shame whatsoever. We had trained diligently and performed to the best of our ability; therefore, I was proud of both myself and Curt. Surprisingly, it could be said my optimism superseded any feelings of disappointment. "It's not whether you win or lose but how you play the game." Realizing the old-fashioned sports adage which Coach D preached was actually true, I smiled, recalling how back in the day I told him it was complete bullshit. *Wow!* I reflected. It really was about your attitude and approach and not the final score. With this understanding I decided if I ever ran into my ex-basketball coach again, after apologizing, not only would I thank him for teaching me properly, I'd also inform him that his efforts had not been in vain.

Standing up, I shuffled over to Crawley. Even after saying his name, he kept staring at the ground in silence; this prompted me to make some sort of conciliatory statement about how we had performed like champions. "Curt," I said placing my hand on his drenched shoulder. When he tilted his head upward, to my astonishment, he was grinning from ear-to-ear.

"28:15," is all he said.

Chapter 6: Season for Miracles

"Good morning Takuan."

Although over six months had passed since I last heard that voice, I knew who it was even before I spun around. "Good morning! It's been a long time, Pastor." The instant we made eye contact I was honestly glad to see him. Then I took a deeper look into those dark orbs and caught sight of a spirit which disturbed me so much I had to avert his gaze.

I never divulged this to any of my Christian brothers but, from that moment, whenever Pastor Bart smiled, to me, he resembled a canine baring its fangs. More specifically, I imagined he was a snarling jackal or a vampire. If you think about it, jackals and vampires share much in common: both are parasitical scavengers who sleep in the daytime, only to emerge at nightfall to roam the darkness in search of prey. This is what I was thinking as three others joined us.

"Good morning!"

As everyone greeted one other, I was relieved to have an excuse to turn away from the pastor. "Praise God!" I said with a broad smile while giving Jon a pound. Then I addressed the latest visitor to Fayetteville. "Pastor Seager, I'm surprised to see you and Mrs. Seager still here this morning."

"You and me too," said the blond-haired, middle-aged man before playfully poking his wife's shoulder. "It was her fault," he added with a grin.

Laughing along, Mrs. Seager responded. "All right already! How many times do I have to say it?"

"At least once more, dear," Pastor Seager teased.

"Okay everyone, I admit it," said the smiling lady in her forties. "I'm the one who bungled our flight reservations, it wasn't Bill. I don't know what happened."

"Obviously it was the will of the Almighty for you two to be here this morning," interjected the Jackal. "Perhaps He wants you to give us another one of those dynamic sermons I've heard so much about?" Again flashing his fangs, he made his request official. "How 'bout it, Bill?"

"I'd be honored Kelly but," Pastor Seager looked doubtful, "considering you've been away so long, don't you think you should speak this morning?"

Scanning everyone's face, I wondered if anybody else was confused.

"Actually Bill, we returned from Arkansas six weeks ago," Pastor Bart responded. "But since then, I've had to go back three times for court appearances or something else related."

"Are you talking about the lawsuit against your mother's nursing home?" asked Mrs. Seager.

"Yes," Pastor Bart simply replied.

"Oh, I thought today was your first day back." Rubbing his head, Pastor Seager seemed relieved. "So you're saying before last Sunday when I preached, you were already here?"

"Exactly Bill. I gave the sermon on the Wednesday before you arrived. So with the exception of Takuan here," he said gesturing at me. "Everyone has heard me preach several times since our return."

"Oh really?" Hearing mention of my name, Pastor

Seager then threw me into the spotlight. "Tak, I was just about to tell Kelly how you and Jon, along with Curt, are really shaping up into fine, young pastors. Now I'm hearing you've been playing hooky. What gives?" asked the traveling clergyman.

"No, it's not like that," I began before explaining my temporary duty assignments in Ft. Lee and Ft. Campbell, plus a couple lengthy stays out in the field. "Seems like every time Pastor Bart comes back, I get sent somewhere else. Or vice-versa."

"To be completely honest," cut in Kelly, "until Chill and Reggie told me you were in Virginia, I thought you were avoiding me. So you say you've been in the field too, huh?"

Perhaps I had grown paranoid but it sounded like the pastor was suggesting my story might not be a hundred percent true. This, to me, was the same as calling me a liar; so my face expressed my displeasure. Seeing this, Pastor Seager and his wife emitted nervous laughter like bad gas; but fortunately, before I could respond the front door opened revealing several new faces. "Come on Tak, let's go greet the folks," Jon said, gently nudging me toward the door. Nodding my head, I turned around and spotted someone I had witnessed to three days ago. At any rate, I was happy to distance myself from Pastor Bart.

"What up *dun*, it's good to see you!" I stated as I approached a tall, beige-complexioned man.

"Ay Tak, I came out this morning just like I promised," he replied while we slapped hands before gripping each other's palm in a soulful handshake.

"Dave, I never doubted you were a man of your word," I said with a grin. "Lemme show you to your seat, please follow me." Walking down the crowded aisle, I saw my sisters and brothers greeting other first-timers. Feeling pride at our collective fishing efforts, little did I suspect that today would be my final Sunday at the Way. Since my ominous meeting with Pastor Bart about tithing, I suspected my days were numbered. Although I had been to church since his return from Arkansas, due to our hectic schedules, the pastor and I had not crossed paths. For some reason, the Spirit had deemed it necessary to delay the inevitable for almost seven months.

Recently, as part of my battalion commander's campaign to encourage me to re-enlist, I had been shipped back to Ft. Lee for a supplementary course to upgrade my MOS. Ten days after returning to North Carolina, I was sent out to the field to support / observe a team of Rangers from Ft. Lewis, Washington. Although Col. Packer was a LEG, being a pilot from the Vietnam era, he had strong ties with most of the Special-Ops commanders. Hence, when these Rangers were being airlifted to Bragg, it was easy for him to get his number one field-negro what he referred to as: "A privileged opportunity to watch the best."

"It'll be a great chance for you to introduce yourself and shoot the shit with some of the guys," explained *Col. Pack*. "Captain Pearson said you expressed a desire to go to Ranger School. Specialist, did you know there's an NCO in our brigade heading there in a couple months?"

"Yes sir," I said with pride. "Sergeant Carney's a friend of mine. Well actually, he's a weight-training buddy," I confessed. "He talks about the Rangers all the time, sir."

"Great to hear you two are working-out together," he said before adding another comment. "And Amaru, it's good to know you're keeping better company these days."

"Excuse me sir?" Even while I was pretending not to understand, I imagined he was referring to my boy, *Wile E.*

"Nothing," replied the colonel. "It's not important."

A couple weeks after I got saved, Wiley turned up AWOL. Since then, no one had seen hide nor hair of him. That is, except me. One evening after dinner, shortly after my return from Ft. Campbell, I got an unexpected knock on my door. When I opened it, I did not recognize the person so I figured he had mistakenly come to the wrong room. For this reason, when the bearded man just stood there, I was somewhat confused.

"Yes," I inquired, showing some impatience. "Who're you lookin' for?"

Then the stranger smiled.

"*Oh my god!*" I emphasized, pointing not only at his full beard but also his fuller gut. "Man, you've gained at least thirty pounds. Come in!"

Following a few minutes of listening to Wiley brag about the loot he was making, I explained my walk with the Lord. As I told him about how many people in our company had likewise changed their lives—guys he knew like Chill and Bellamy—he listened without interrupting. Staring with a blank expression, it seemed he understood I wasn't bullshitting. But just in case, as soon as I finished, he reached into a coat pocket and pulled out a vial of white powder. Once I refused to do any lines with him, he promptly put it back in his pocket, stood up, and shook my hand.

After I opened the door, Wiley walked through it and turned around. "Amaru think about it," he said with a penetrating stare. "There's a whole world going on out there…and you're *not* part of it."

"Exactly," I replied with a grin. "I couldn't have said it better myself, good night." Then I closed the door.

As I walked back to my bed where an opened-bible was laying on my pillow, I wondered if the super-genius comprehended my meaning.

At the following Wednesday evening service, I patiently waited until the 'requests for prayer' segment was about to conclude before rising to my feet. I wanted to ask my brothers and sisters to help make my collegiate dream a reality.

"Good evening everyone. On April ninth, which is in two weeks, I'll be celebrating my twenty-first birthday while I'm home on leave. As most of you know, my ETS date is coming up and hopefully, in the fall, I'll be studying at either Penn State or Rutgers. I know my birthday request is kind of early, but I wanted to make sure I got it in because I'm scheduled to hit the field again this weekend." As I added details to my appeal, cheers of 'Hallelujah!', 'Praise God!', or my favorite, 'Oh Lord, give the righteous favor!' could be heard coming from the crowd. Hearing this, I felt relieved, like this automatically meant my trip to New Jersey was destined to go well.

Two days after we came back from the woods, Stock gave me a lift to Fayetteville Airport. There, a ticket agent informed me I had to take a shuttle flight to Charlotte Douglass International to board a Boeing 747 bound for Philadelphia. Thirty minutes later, I was strapping my seatbelt in the second row of a prop plane when a young GI dressed in his Class-A uniform sat down next to me.

"How ya feelin on this fine, spring afternoon!" said the friendly guy. "Are you a soldier?"

Although I too planned to show-off my uniform at home, there was no way I would ever wear the cumbersome outfit on a cramped airplane. After nodding my head, I proceeded to answer the next questions I felt confident he would ask. "My name's Amaru and I'm an E-4 stationed at Fort Bragg, just like you…PFC Johnstone," I replied after reading his nametag.

"You Airborne?" Johnstone inquired.

"Yeah."

"Well alright then! I'd buy you a drink but the stewardess told me there ain't no alcohol being served on this *ate-up* flight."

Considering the private-first-class already appeared drunk, I was relieved to hear this. This sentiment was highlighted when the staff asked the inebriated soldier to be quiet during the pre-flight, safety demonstration. As soon as the flight attendants stopped talking Johnstone resumed his one-sided conversation.

"I'm headin' home to Oklahoma City, Oklahoma—so nice they had to name it twice!"

Saying nothing, I smiled at his corny alteration of the slogan made famous by proud New Yorkers. While the aircraft accelerated down the runway, I sat back and closed my eyes.

"So where you headed?" he asked.

"Philly." Speaking softly with my eyes shut, I hoped the gregarious GI would get the hint and be quiet.

Shortly after takeoff, the tiny plane hit an air pocket

and dropped three feet. Feeling queasy, I gripped the armrests and clenched my eyes tightly as the cabin bounced at the whim of every air current. While the chatterbox rattled-on non-stop, I tried to ignore the growing nausea in the pit of my stomach. This is when something occurred to me: for the first time in my life I had something to lose. *Please Lord, don't let me die now!*

For the second half of the thirty-five-minute flight, 'Jabber-Jaw' Johnstone was silent. This is why I was so surprised to find him looking at me when we landed in Charlotte. As I opened my eyes and saw the distasteful expression glued to his face, I imagined he had been staring the entire time.

"I thought you said you were a paratrooper," he mumbled in disgust.

"That's what I thought too," I replied without the slightest hint of embarrassment. "Guess I'm already back to being a civilian."

"Trust in the LORD with all your heart and lean not on your own understanding. In all your ways submit to Him, and He will make your paths straight."

On my next flight, in order to kill time, I decided to commit *Proverbs* 3:5-6 to memory. Being so excited, it required all my accumulated discipline to calm down and make myself repeat it over-and-over again. In between reciting the scripture, I reviewed my list of priorities for my ten-day stay in South Jersey. Believing it was God's will that I make the upcoming fall semester, I wanted to make the transition from soldier-to-student as smooth as possible. With four obstacles still remaining, I was poised to hurdle three of them this week. First on the agenda was purchasing a car. Considering Ken had assured me my money was present and accounted for, I figured this would be the easiest leg of the relay—this prediction was not accurate. Next I needed two documents. To complete my application for the early-out program, in addition to a standard, university letter of acceptance, the Department of Defense required a letter from an athletic director or head coach. This letter had to specifically state I *was a member* of the football team—not just a try-out candidate. If I failed to produce the latter authorization, I would not be able to attend the fall semester. As daunting as my tasks appeared I was confident in my time of need the Holy Spirit would 'make my paths straight.'

As *Anita Baker's 'Been So Long'* painted the mood in my headphones, I stared out the window at the cesspool known as the Delaware River. Seconds after the brown water gave way to dry land, I felt a soft tug on my earphone. Looking up, I made eye-contact with the prettiest of the three attendants on the airline staff. "Excuse me sir," said the gorgeous Jamaican in her early-twenties. Not only did her accent give it away but I knew she was Jamaican because I overheard her tell another passenger she was from Montego Bay. "The pilot has initiated landing procedures so all electrical devices must be turned off at this time." Having completed her statement, she gently released my headset. A slim woman with curvy hips, long legs, and full breasts, her copper-complected angular features were adorned with just a touch of magenta mascara; I imagined she would be perfect to play 'Cleopatra' in a Broadway musical.

With so much beauty beaming in my direction, it was easy to smile back. "Sorry, I completely forgot." Thus apologizing, I turned off the music while she stood up and pushed on the overhead compartments to ensure they were secure.

"Thank you," she replied cheerfully.

As I placed the Walkman inside my carry-on bag, I spied a Christian leaflet. Placed there for just such a spur-of-the-moment situation as this, I grinned before casting my rod. "Miss, just a minute please," I called out before she walked away.

"Yes, what can I do for you?" the voluptuous stewardess responded, wearing a toothy grin.

Rising to my feet, I extended the leaflet in my hand. "This is for you."

Walking around the familiar confines of Philadelphia International Airport, I should have felt comfortable but I didn't. This was because something felt weird. Although everything looked the same, I was aware something was different. *Did Philly change? Or did I?* Like any metropolitan area, the City of Brotherly Love had its own unique signature. Three years prior, I knew that handwriting better than anyone. Now, having returned to the scene of my delinquent undertakings, I felt like *Job* in the Old Testament. And just like in the biblical story, once the Lord's safety hedge was removed, Satan wasted no time before testing his quarry.

After collecting my luggage at the baggage claim, I pushed my cart passed several airport employees, in their

UPS-like uniforms. Like most baggage handlers, these young men were blacks and Latinos. Seeing them reminded me that I'd heard a few characters from high school had gotten a job here. Scrutinizing the lot with a discerning eye, I spotted a familiar face but it took me a couple seconds to match the mugshot with a name.

"Eddie...yo Ed, what's up homie? *Di me Loco!"* Having thus saluted the brother of the artist who had drawn the fliers for Herb's Cut Party, I started walking toward him and his buddies. When he failed to respond and just stared back with a blank expression—along with the six other guys—I was embarrassed. Taking a second look I was certain this was not a case of mistaken identity. "Yo Ed, it's me, Sev. I know it's been a while cuz but why you acting like you don't know me?"

Once I adopted my street moniker, this got his attention.

"*Sev?* You're Sev?" Looking stunned, Eddie took a few hesitant steps forward. "Oh my god, you *are* Sev!" Having uttered this in disbelief, he ran over and crushed me in such an emotional embrace I was lifted off the ground. After releasing me he stepped back for another look. "The only thing I got to say is," he exclaimed shaking his head, "you've definitely changed—and you look healthy as shit!"

That was enough to convince me of my spiritual growth. But like always, the irony was never-ending.

"Yo T...T! Come over here and check-out Sev!"

I turned around and looked in the direction Ed was yelling. Seeing one his coworkers walking toward us, I instantly identified him as a kid who had been in my grade. His name was Ted but we called him 'T-Rex.' For years, T-

Rex was one of my best customers. This is probably why, unlike Ed, he had little difficulty recognizing me. "My man Sev! What's happening ock?" T-Rex shouted over the airport noise. Once he jogged over, we exchanged pounds and hugged. While locked in an embrace, he whispered something in my ear. "You got that cuz?"

Eddie, understanding what had been said, burst out laughing. "Yo T, Sev don't get down like that no more. He don't even live out here…he's a military man now."

Hearing this, T-Rex looked me up-and-down in shock. "Oh, word?"

"Well actually, I'll be out in a few months. But yeah, I don't get high anymore."

"*What!* Get the fuck outta here—you serious? Cuz, back in school you *always* had the blazing-ass cheeba!" Saying this, T gave me another pound. "So you switched-up your game, huh? Good for you Sev, because they locking up bruthas by the boatload these days. Word is bond, since you left for the Marines—"

"Army," I interjected.

"My bad," he continued. "Right after we graduated, I got sent-up north. I just got out a couple weeks ago so I'm trying to put all that bullshit behind me."

"A-ight…sounds positive," I encouraged him. "And you already got a gig too." Saying this, I went into fishing mode. Digging in my bag, I extended two leaflets to them.

"What's this?" they chorused, eagerly reaching for the pamphlets. After checking out the image of *Moses* on the front cover kneeling in front of a burning bush, they glanced at each other before looking back at me.

"It's a story you should relate to," I simply replied. "It's about God."

Back in high school, some friends accused me of exaggerating whenever I emphasized the degree of frustration and anger my father carried around with him. My response to these skeptics was to invite them over when I knew the Serpent would be home. Once they knocked on the door, they became instant believers.

"Who is it?" snapped the ornery man from his couch like an angry drill sergeant.

"It's me," is all I said.

Unsure of how my family would receive their black sheep back into the fold, I made Ken promise to keep my visit a secret. Somehow I felt surprising them in my Class-A's was a better way to break the ice.

"Ara! Takuan? Takuan is that you?"

Hearing my mother's voice through her bedroom window, I cried out happily. *"Sou-dayo. Uchino musukoda!"*

"Uso! Chotto matte-ne," she replied in delight.

As I imagined my mother scampering through the living room, I heard my father's voice. "Who's that honey?"

"Eh? Can't you hear? It's your son. Get up and answer the door," she half-joked, half-scolded my sire.

Seconds later, I recognized two sets of footsteps approaching.

While my father unlocked the bolt and removed the chain, he was grumbling in a jovial manner. "Boy, why you comin' home now? You know you makin' me miss the ballgame, right?" Hearing this, I was relieved he was not in a bad mood. When the rectangular portal to my past finally swung open, it revealed two familiar, middle-aged faces.

"Mom, Dad, it's great to see you! I love both of you very much!"

At that moment, none of our previous disagreements mattered. While we embraced, I realized how much I loved my parents. Arrayed in my uniform, I never felt more welcome than I did on that afternoon. It was hard to believe I was finally home: the prodigal son had returned.

Within an hour, Kay arrived with her fiancé.

Following another round of hugs and handshakes, my mother announced it was time for dinner; so everyone except my father sat down in the dining room. My sire opted to return to watching the game. Prior to feasting on what my friends called 'Asian-Soul food' I went to the bathroom to wash my hands. On my way back, I stopped in the living room to get the scoop on the Phillies. However, instead of finding my pop watching the game, it seemed the TV was observing him as he loudly snored on the couch.

Before digging into the sushi, salad, cornbread, baked chicken, greens, and rice—*I love me some Japanese rice!*—I asked everyone to bow their heads. "Lord," I said. "Thank you for the nourishing food we're about to receive. But more importantly, we're grateful for simply being able to assemble here in peace and harmony. In Christ's name we pray, Amen."

"Amen," everyone echoed as one.

"Mark, give me your plate," my mother said, extending her hand.

"Tak, I heard you got saved…that's great news!" said the stocky guy next to Kay as he handed my mother his plate.

"Thanks Mark," I replied.

Having been provided this segue, I briefly rehashed my conversion process while everyone dug into the food.

Following a litany of questions by Kay and Mark, my mother ended the interview. "Are you telling us you don't smoke or drink anymore?" she inquired with a doubtful eye. "I don't believe it."

"You can believe it, mom," I proudly declared, surveying their astounded faces.

"I believe you, Tak," Mark declared. "Just by looking at you, it's obvious you've matured."

Listening to Mark's kind words made me remember that years ago I did not like him. "Oh yeah, I almost forgot. This is kind of embarrassing but…" Saying this, I averted his gaze. "Mark, I want to apologize for stealing your bike back-in-the-day."

"Don't sweat it, it's forgotten," he hurriedly replied.

"It was just that—" I added before Kay cut me off.

"He said it's okay. It's over with!"

Given the fact it was past midnight when I discovered Mark's Schwinn outside my sister's bedroom window, I understood why he and Kay would not want any of those details being disclosed—particularly with the King Cobra coiled in the next room. Later, Kay revealed my intuition had been correct. Six months ago, the Serpent caught her and Mark in her bedroom 'doin-the-do.' According to Kay, he barged in and snatched Mark out of bed—butt-naked! After slamming him against the wall a few times, he then proceeded to choke him. *Sounds familiar*. She said this lasted for about a minute—sixty brutal seconds. Afterwards, my father dragged Mark down the hallway like a sack of potatoes and threw him out the front door. "I had to take his clothes to the porch!" she added, still embarrassed at the memory. Well it comes as no surprise that following this incident Mark never snuck through her window again.

"So that's why y'all decided to shack-up together, huh?" I said with a chuckle.

My return home had turned out to be a blessing indeed. With no lingering feelings of animosity, peace reigned supreme. On the eve of my birthday, I reflected, it was truly a season for miracles.

"Ohayo!" I yelled, walking in the door the following morning. Although my mother was nowhere in sight, I could feel her presence.

"Eh? Did you see Ken?" she called out from the kitchen.

"No. Was I supposed to?"

"You just missed him," she responded. He stopped by on his way to work to see you. Where did you go?"

"For a jog," I said before getting back to the topic of my brother. "What did Ken say?" I asked, briskly toweling off.

"He wants you to have dinner at his house tonight."

Initially imagining a birthday celebration, I crossed-off this possibility when my mother revealed only I had been invited. While soaking in the bathtub, I concluded this appointment must be business rather than pleasure. After donning a pair of shorts and a t-shirt, I enjoyed a traditional Japanese breakfast of miso soup, fish, rice, and some pickles appropriately named *'Takuan.'*

With no other plans, I ended up spending a relaxing afternoon at the Cherry Hill Mall with my mother and her friend; this lady was like an aunt to me. We returned home about three. Soon afterward my eyelids felt heavy so I retired to my bedroom for a nap. Two hours later, my mother woke me as I had requested. Following another shower, I felt rejuvenated as I donned the white-and-gray *Christian Dior* matching set my mother bought me earlier.

Seconds after leaving the house, I had to jump out of the way of a brown *hoopty* that was veering its way into our driveway. Although I had been looking forward to the one-and-a-half mile stroll to my brother's house, since I was running late, I was glad he came to pick me up. Even more surprising than his unexpected arrival was the fact he was driving his wife's ramshackle VW Rabbit, instead of his sleek, sky-blue Camaro.

"Kensuke, what is the meaning of this outrage?" I bellowed with a grin. "I can't be seen in this rickety contraption, after all my good man, I do have a reputation to uphold!" Considering my voice was embellished by my terrible attempt to mimic a nineteenth century, British accent, I never dreamt this might strike a nerve. Particularly since his wife was known to joke about her car's unstable ride herself; she used to say the 'VW' stood for 'very wobbly.'

"I see you haven't learned much," he griped. "Well, since you don't know anything about cars, I'll let you in on a little secret: don't judge this book by its cover!"

When Ken rebuked my attempt to hug him, all the while lecturing on proper values, I stood by and watched in amusement. "Hey, hey, it's good to see you too, bro," I said once he was finished. It took a couple seconds but Ken finally allowed me to embrace him; nevertheless he still appeared up-tight about something. "Let's be out," I said after releasing him.

Once Ken backed out the driveway, he resumed his ramble about the rusty Rabbit. At this point I should have suspected something. "I just had the timing-belt and the spark plugs replaced," he said turning down the radio. "And while I was at it, I went ahead and had the tires rotated too. Many people don't realize how important regular tire rotations are for the longevity of a car—"

"So," I interrupted. "How're the Phillies predicted to do this year?" Just wanting to change the subject, it almost worked.

"Pretty good!" he exclaimed. "We're trying to get an all-star outfielder from the Mets named *Lenny Dykstra*. If we do, our next stop is the World Series." Then he abruptly returned to the previous conversation. "Tak, lemme show you a snazzy feature on this otherwise bland-looking radio. Check-it-out, I installed it a couple months back. Looks like a regular ol' radio, right?"

By the time we completed the ten-minute ride I was eager to end our conversation so even before Ken finished parking, I got out the car. Seeing the passenger side had a few more dents than I remembered, I imagined Katrina had gotten into a few fender-benders since I left for the Army. As Ken exited the vehicle, I was already walking along the small path leading to his porch. This was my first look at the brown, two-story cape-cod. "This is your new house, huh?" I yelled back over my shoulder. "Impressive!" Since his kids were not on the porch to greet us, I wondered if they were inside. "Are Cristina and Gordon home?"

"Your nephew's upstairs taking a nap but your niece went on a field-trip today to a museum in Philly. I forget which one but her school bus should arrive in about thirty minutes. Katrina's here though."

Hearing this, I stopped on the porch and waited.

It was no secret that my sister-in-law and I did not exactly get along; so I did not try to hide my disappointment. My feelings for Katrina had little to do with her personality. Due to Ken being so much older than me, in many ways, he was a father figure. When he left for the Air Force, this had been bad enough. However, once he fell in love with Katrina, I felt abandoned. Lacking space in their love nest for a confused, younger brother needing direction, after Ken got married, we became complete strangers.

Once Ken caught up, I moved aside so he could enter the house first.

"Katrina? Katrina? Where are you? I'm back, honey…and Tak's here."

"I'm right here," replied a feminine voice as the kitchen door swung open. "Hey Tak," she greeted me with a hug. "Welcome back. And welcome to our humble home. This is your first time visiting us here, right?"

"Yeah. Before I left, y'all still lived in that apartment complex across from K-Mart." After receiving a glass of iced tea, I sat down on a beige, L-shaped sofa.

"Yeah, the good ol' days," added Ken.

"Good ol' days, my foot! I can't believe we lived in that cramped, bachelor-studio for three-and-a-half years. I couldn't wait to get out of there." Although emphatic, Katrina delivered her response with a grin. Katrina was average height and build with straight brown hair that hung just passed her shoulders. The first time I met Katrina she told me her father was a Special Forces soldier who had been killed in Vietnam. A week before I left for basic, she showed me a photo of a dark-skinned man wearing a green beret. Her mother being German, Katrina was a shade lighter than Ken's tawny complexion. Before Ken and Katrina could further debate on whose account of the past was more accurate, the telephone rang. Once Katrina grabbed the cordless receiver and retreated into the kitchen, I decided to initiate the business side of my visit.

"Ken, congrats on becoming a homeowner. You really got a nice house!" Saying this, I surveyed the chestnut-colored interior along with the splashy-colored prints decorating his couch, armchairs, and window treatments.

"Thanks, li'l bro. Still needs a little work here and there but it's definitely a step in the right direction." Replying thus, he proudly admired his own handiwork. "When Gordon was born we definitely needed more space."

"I hear you," I jumped back in before the conversation could digress too far. "Now that you're a homeowner, I'm ready to become an owner myself—a car owner. You're coming to the Volkswagen dealer tomorrow to help me pick out a Jetta, right?"

"Actually, that's what I wanted to talk to you about," Ken replied in a somber tone.

Puzzled he did not share my excitement, my anxiety mounted when Katrina returned to the living room and I caught the two of them exchanging an uncomfortable glance. When Ken averted her eyes by gazing out a window, Katrina suddenly became upset.

"You didn't tell him yet, did you?" she asked, placing both hands on her hips.

"I was about to. I was waiting for the right moment!" Ken snapped, likewise sounding irritated.

The only thing I understood from their back-and-forth

bickering was the commotion concerned me. Standing up, I interrupted them. "Tell me what Ken?"

Looking at me, my brother tried to calm himself. "Tak, there's no easy way to say this. Umm, I wanted to wait until the right time. As I said—"

"Ken, if you can't do it, I will." As Katrina spoke, she pivoted toward me.

Before she could divulge whatever information, she was holding, I decided I'd rather hear it from my brother. "Ken, spit it out," I said, starting to lose patience.

"Okay. But first, please sit back down. Katrina, you too."

Once everyone took their seats, I watched Ken take a deep breath before shooting another hostile look at his wife. Then he briskly ran both hands over his short afro. "Might as well get to the point—"

"He lost your money," Katrina uttered, unwilling to hold it in any longer.

"*What?* What's she talking about?" I asked, referring to Katrina like she was not in the room. "You lost my money?"

"Tak, let me explain—" Ken weakly replied before I cut him off.

"Hold up, in every letter you sent me, you said everything was cool. When I wrote you a couple weeks ago and asked you to withdraw my funds by the end of the month, you said okay. So you're saying you were lying all that time?"

"Of course not. I—"

"We made this agreement three years ago!" As I grasped the notion that my savings were gone, I grew

144

agitated.

"Yeah I know but—"

"It's 1989 and I need my cash not a bunch of excuses—what's going on?" Although I said this in a menacing tone, I could not bring myself to yell at Kensuke.

"Tak, you have every right to be angry but—"

"He got greedy at the end…that's how your money got lost."

"Katrina be quiet!" Ken snapped. "Let me tell him what happened."

"Then tell him the truth and stop beating around the bush!" she yelled back at him. "Takuan's your brother and he deserves, to hear the truth. Do you want to tell it to him? Or do you need me to do it?"

Ken, appearing frustrated, sat there for a second before responding. "I'll tell him." Looking back at me, he began to explain. "No Tak, I wasn't lying. Up until the end of March, your money was still accumulating interest but…" When he stopped talking in mid-sentence and just stared at the ground, it appeared he was too embarrassed to narrate any further.

"The bottom line is he got greedy!" Katrina, ignoring her fuming husband, repeated her earlier comment before providing details. "He decided our cut wasn't big enough so he asked me if I thought it was a good idea to reinvest the money."

"Wait a minute!" Ken exploded.

Everyone was now standing. With the two of them at each other's throat, the only reason I stood up was to be close enough to break up a fight should this become necessary.

"No! I've been waiting!" Katrina yelled back. "Now it's your turn to be quiet and wait!" Without another word, she dismissed Ken like a stepchild and turned toward me. "Tak, to be honest, I wasn't comfortable with this from the beginning because I don't know anything about stocks, bonds, or mutual funds. But as I watched the interest steadily grow, I slowly became a believer. In February, when I last checked, our share had risen to almost seven-hundred dollars. I was more than happy with that."

"Not even a thousand frickin' dollars," Ken griped before Katrina again silenced him with a wave of her hand.

"So, when Ken first mentioned reinvesting the money—promising it was a sure-thing—I encouraged him. That is, until he claimed we could triple our money in thirty days. That's when I told him he was crazy."

"Okay folks, I think I understand what happened." With this declaration, like a referee, I stepped between the two combatants. "Ken didn't make as much loot as he expected so he gambled on a get-rich-overnight scheme. Am I close?"

"Exactly," confirmed my sister-in-law.

Although Ken also mumbled something, I was unable to hear it over Katrina's emphatic response. "What was that Ken?" I asked.

"I said, it wasn't a get-rich-overnight scheme," he murmured under his breath with his eyes cast downward.

"*What!*" Whipping her head toward Ken, Katrina was livid. "Yes, it was! And I told you that's what it was once you started tripping over your own words trying to explain how it worked."

As round two of their argument escalated, I escaped to the bathroom to mull things over. Unfortunately, my birthday dinner was not shaping itself into a festive event after all.

Taking a seat on the closed toilet lid, I grabbed a copy of *Sports Illustrated* from the magazine rack. The infamous baseball legend, Pete Rose, was featured on the front cover with these words written next to him: *Under Siege*. Reading this, I imagined me and 'Charlie Hustle' had a few things in common.

Right then and there, I closed my eyes to pray.

"Lord, give me the power to release any feelings of bitterness or regret. I know through you there is nothing I cannot achieve so if it's not your divine will for me to go to college or buy a car make it known because I only want to do your will…*so what is it?* In Christ's name I pray, Amen." Opening my eyes, I stood up and gazed into the mirror. It was then I imagined hearing a flowing voice as the sound of many waters. "Don't worry," it said, "you're gonna get a car, go to college, and be on the football team." Having affirmed this, I returned the magazine to its place on the rack before washing my hands and face. After drying off with a towel hanging below the sink, I checked out my reflection and grinned when *He* winked at me.

Feeling much more confident, I went downstairs and returned to a living room now bathed in silence. "Okay Ken," I said, having decided to take the lead in the conversation. "Where do we go from here? The money's gone—that's in the past. Let's concentrate on the present-slash-future."

Hearing this, Ken excitedly jumped up from the chair he'd been sitting in. "That's why I was talking about Katrina's car earlier," he explained. "Why don't you just take the Rabbit?" Pausing to clear his throat, he then gathered himself before approaching me. "I'm no expert but after all the repairs and other additions I've personally made," he stated in a coaxing voice, "it's probably worth about the same amount of money I lost. So, I was thinking, why don't we just make it an even swap?" Gesturing to a set of drawers on the far-side of the room, Ken completed his sucker's proposition. "I got the title right over there."

Until this moment I was not angry. Although I had no backup plan, I had decided to let Ken off the hook. I mean what was I going to do? Kick his ass? Rob him? After all, he was my brother. However, as I watched him continue his sheisty, double-dealing approach, I got pissed off.

"Please tell me you're not being serious right now. Ken, you lost almost ten G's! Even if that hunk-of-junk on your driveway was all kitted-up with rims and a funky sound system, it still wouldn't be worth half that much."

"Here you go again, judging a book by its cov—"

"*Shut up Ken!*" shouted his better half. And before I had the chance to say anything, Katrina glanced my way. "You too!" she said before lowering her voice. "This is what's going to happen..." By the forthright manner in which Katrina conducted her family's business that afternoon, she earned my deepest respect. Appearing different from any other time I had ever seen her, her words were simple, steely in composure, and spoken with the authority of a queen. "Ken, you're going to take off from work tomorrow—"

"I can't take off tomorrow!"

"*Then...*" she continued, "you're going to take Takuan to the Volkswagen dealer out on Route 73." Having explained this, she turned back in my direction and spoke in a calmer tone. "Tak, tomorrow morning when Ken takes you there, feel free to choose any car you like up to ten thousand dollars." Following an uneasy pause, she added the missing piece to the puzzle. "And we'll pay for it."

"*What!?* Woman have you lost your mind?" Ken inquired in a not-so-pleasant tone. "Excuse me Ms. Mastermind but where's this ten-grand going to magically spring forth from?"

"Ken," Katrina wiped her tears with a *Kleenex* before resuming. "I have some money saved-up that you don't know about." Staring at the ground, she smiled through her frustration. "You know, the funny thing is, since I put it aside in case of an emergency, I guess I shouldn't be upset about spending it." While pausing to drop the tissue in a garbage can, she took a deep breath to compose herself. "For the rest, we'll take out a car-loan. I already spoke to the lady who owns the flower shop near Cris's school and she's agreed to give me part-time work."

"But you already have a job at the bank," complained Ken.

"That's right…and now I have *two* jobs," she snapped sarcastically. As she tilted her head to glare at Ken, I noticed her eyes were once again streaming tears. "Oh, and from now on, you have to pick Gordon up from daycare."

"No way!" objected Ken like a whining child.

Just then, the front door opened revealing the snaggle-toothed face of my six-year-old niece. "I'm home!" she screamed in glee. "Happy Birthday Uncle Tak!"

Seeing the beautiful princess, I rushed over to give her a hug. As her parents verbally slugged it out, Cris and I dipped outside for a stroll around the block.

"Good morning, Mr. Amaru." When I did not respond

right away, the salesman continued. "You have good taste—that's the GLI, the top-of-the-line Jetta," he said, pointing at the black car on display. "By the way, my name's Bill."

"Mornin' Bill," I replied with a yawn before returning my eyes to the Jetta. "Is it an '89?"

"Yup, that car's brand new," said the brown-haired Caucasian with a puffy moustache and receding hairline. "And I'm afraid she's a bit beyond the price range your brother mentioned." Saying this, Bill looked over his shoulder at Ken's receding image before gesturing in the direction of an adjacent lot. "Allow me to show you some of our best bargains. Your brother said—"

"Just a minute Bill," I interrupted, detecting a troubling bud which required snipping. "I'm the customer. My brother's only here to observe so from now on please speak directly to me."

"Understood," Bill responded.

For the next ten minutes, I strolled through the lot and checked-out many attractive cars; nonetheless nothing caught my eye more than the black masterpiece on display. Even though I could not afford it, I wanted to experience a test-drive. Making my way back to the front of the lot, I was surprised to find Bill standing there by himself.

"Did my brother come back yet?" I asked, thinking Ken might be looking for me.

Before answering my question, Bill glanced toward the restrooms. "I don't think so." Then he looked at me and smiled. "Did you see anything you like?"

"Not more than this one," I replied pointing at the sleek, shadowy vehicle. "Can I take her for a drive?"

"Of course."

Just sitting in the driver's seat was exhilarating enough. Following a cursory check of the interior, Bill showed me some of the features which distinguished the GLI from the standard model. Turning the ignition, I listened to the sixteen valves rumble like a purring tiger. After adjusting the seat and mirrors, I flipped on the radio and was pleased to find it already set to 105.3. As soon as the vibrant sounds of *Soul to Soul* penetrated mine, I was ready to hit the road.

"I wonder if Ken's okay?"

"My brother's a big boy, he'll be alright." With that, I engaged the clutch and shifted into gear. Once we were on the highway, I wanted to see what those additional eight valves had to offer so I pushed hard on the gas pedal. As the car exploded forward, I marveled at how easily we moved passed the other vehicles. By the time I shifted into fifth gear, I was more than impressed by the GLI's power but I also knew having a car this fast would only result in me getting pulled over on a regular basis.

As I was cornering the state-of-the-art Jetta back into the parking lot, Bill spotted Ken returning from the restroom. "There's your brother," he said, pointing his finger.

"Ay, where you been?" I hollered out the window. "You missed the test-drive, you feelin' okay?"

After Bill and I exited the car, Ken approached us

"Sorry I took so long," Ken said still wiping his hands with a handkerchief. "I'm okay now. Too much birthday cake last night, I guess. How was the ride?"

"Nice but a little bit over the top." Replying thus, I shut the door and followed the salesman. "Come on, Bill says he has something in the next lot that I'll like."

After passing a fleet of *Golfs* shaded in a variety of colors, we entered the used-car section.

"This is what I wanted to show you," clamored Bill, pointing at a navy-blue sedan. "It's the 1987 version of the car you just test-drove. And the best part is it's almost half the price—*think fast!*"

Even before snatching the keys Bill tossed out of the air, I had calculated that 'almost half the price' meant it was within my budget.

"Why don't you two take her for a spin?" the salesman asked, putting his dazzling smile on display.

Before Ken started the engine, we realized Bill was mistaken. The car was not the upgraded model, but instead, just the standard Jetta. For the next forty minutes, we took turns operating the 5-speed. What this car lacked in power it made up for by having a good feel to it: the car had personality. By the time we returned I had pretty much decided to buy it; nevertheless, we checked out a nearby *Nissan* dealer to test-drive a *Sentra*. We did this just to have another car in the same price range to compare. The Sentra was nice too but both of us preferred the Jetta.

Before returning to the VW dealer, Ken and I broke for lunch at a Jamaican restaurant we spotted during our busy morning of driving. Although the name of the joint escapes my memory, I cannot forget this place entirely because it had the best 'jerk' chicken I ever tasted. Following a few servings of ackee, fried plantains, rice and pigeon peas—plus the savory chicken—I had to stand up to keep from nodding off.

"Come on, let's go before I fall asleep!"

"Welcome back, gentlemen," Bill greeted us upon our arrival. "Like I said earlier Mr. Amaru, you have good taste so I knew you'd be back…please step into my office."

Following two hours signing various documents, Ken

and I finally put our pens down. Although I had to wait until the following morning to receive my car, I felt a sense of satisfaction. Not only did I get the car I wanted, more importantly, Ken was no longer acting squeamish. In fact, he even managed to congratulate me on my purchase.

"So, we gonna roll up to 'the Banks' tomorrow in your new ride?" Ken asked as he pulled into my parent's driveway.

Astonished by Ken's proposal, I was also surprised to hear him say 'the Banks' instead of Rutgers. Then I recalled this pseudonym was written on many of the pamphlets scattered all over my parent's house. "Are you taking me to pick up the Jetta in the morning?"

"Of course, how else are you going to get there? Since I gotta take another day off anyway, I might as well make a trip to New Brunswick. I've attended events on the Camden campus before but I've never had an opportunity to set foot on the main campus. This is a great excuse to."

Minutes after leaving the New Jersey Turnpike, Ken and I were rolling down College Avenue in my sparkling, blue Jetta with its white racing stripe. So many people were staring it reminded me of the time Mick and I were in Wiley's BMW. And likewise, once again, I felt like a superstar; however, 'Jesus Christ Superstar' might be more appropriate. Another notable contrast between then and now was my musical selection. Instead of *Eric B and Rakim* pumping out my speakers it was *Bebe and Cece Winans*.

Over a third of the students walking around the sprawling campus represented the international community.

This, in and of itself, was amazing; but what really had me in awe was the fact that over half of these pedestrians were females. Having been sequestered on male-dominated Army installations, this was a sight for sore eyes. After circling the block a few times, I parallel-parked near a campus bus stop. As I was inserting quarters into the meter Ken shut the door and put on his shades.

"Okay, what's our objective for today?"

"I wanna walk in there, tell them who I am, and hear them say: 'Congratulations Mr. Amaru, you've been accepted. Welcome to Rutgers University!' That would make my birthday week something to remember."

"Wait a minute, I thought you already got accepted?"

"Nah, I never said that."

"If not, why are we here? Until you get accepted, a counselor can't do anything for you."

In order to prevent Ken's skepticism from slowing my flow, I quickly explained the 'glass is half-full' perspective. "I have an appointment with an *EOP* counselor. According to the catalogue, the applications for this fall's incoming class are being reviewed this month. If I'm lucky, it'll be done in either alphabetical or chronological order. In either case, mine should be near the top considering 'Amaru' starts with an 'A', and I mailed-in my app last December."

"I see," is all Ken replied.

"No matter what," I continued, "I have to send a letter of acceptance to the Department of Defense by the twenty-fifth of this month."

"That's in two weeks. But I thought you mailed that application months ago?"

"I did. The submission deadline was back in January.

But I can send additional, supporting documents until the twenty-fifth."

"I see," he again responded.

As mentioned, Rutgers was a heavenly paradise compared to the dress-right-dress, olive-drab monotony of Ft. Bragg. Just as I was thinking this, a beautiful dark-skinned sista with long, natural locks smiled at me. Since she was walking in the opposite direction, I returned her smile. More than tantalized by her seductive aura, I couldn't stop thinking this is how Monie's hair would look if she had never gotten a perm. Just as I was about to ask her for directions she beat me to the punch.

"You two look lost," she said in a friendly voice. "Can I help you find something?" In spite of her offer she immediately reversed the conversation by interviewing me. Asking my name and student status was reasonable; but homegirl took it a step further by inquiring whether or not I had a girlfriend. After I answered 'No,' she smiled before adding: "Are you looking for one?"

If this is anything like what I can expect this fall, my celibate stance is in serious jeopardy, I thought to myself.

Eventually I got the information I needed. After thanking Lucille, we followed her instructions and rode the standing-room-only 'L' bus to Livingston Campus. Although it was a short fifteen-minute ride, it was actually located in the next town, Piscataway. The entire trip was pleasant indeed. Intoxicated by the sights and scents which naturally accompany a group of beautiful women, despite my commitment not to lust *Jimmy* was hard as a rock! When Ken and I got off at the student center, to avoid an embarrassing situation, I removed my jacket and folded it over my arm so it draped down over my waist.

"She mentioned this bookstore," I said as we approached a small building next to the bus stop.

Seconds later, Ken spotted our destination.

"Tak, you said we're looking for *Lucy Stone Hall*, right?" Looking where he was pointing, I saw students exiting a handsome, brown edifice. Next to the door was a sign bearing the name of the building. "These look like the classrooms on this side," Ken surmised. "Let's enter here and walk through the building to the offices. Maybe we can peek inside one of the lecture halls. I heard some of them seat over three-hundred students."

"Guess you weren't paying much attention to our travel guide."

"You mean Lucille? Not like you were, remember I'm a married man."

Playing off his insinuation, I resumed. "She said Lucy Stone Hall was built right after thousands of college students, nation-wide, made 'Anti-Vietnam War' sit-ins famous."

"I heard that part. Something about since Livingston was built to house us indigenous folks—I believe 'indigenous' was the phrase she used—Lucy Stone Hall had been intentionally designed with winding corridors and multiple exits. Something I didn't understand was: did she say this was done so the white faculty could escape if any violence kicked-off?"

"Yeah, what part don't you understand?" I asked sarcastically. "That white people are afraid of angry black folks?"

"No not that. Remember, I participated in some of those demonstrations. There was no blood being shed by *us*. That was the whole point. The military was committing brutal, terrorist acts overseas. Since we were anti-government, it was important for us to demonstrate peaceful solutions."

"What about *Kent State?*" I challenged his historical perspective.

"That was the pigs, they did that!"

"Of course, they did but you know how the media spins the story. They blame the victims for their own demise on camera—"

"While behind the scenes the bad-guys get away with murder." The former-panther seemed to recall some of his militancy.

Before I lost my train of thought, I returned to our mission. "Lucille also said most of the lower-level doesn't connect to the administrative side of the building so we have to walk around to the main entrance. Come on, I don't want to be late. The classrooms ain't going nowhere…we'll come back and check them out later, cool?"

"Sounds good to me."

After circumventing the outside of the structure, we still got lost when we entered. Feeling trapped in a maze, I stopped a male student for more directions. Seconds after thanking Simon, who turned out to be a cool guy from Trinidad, we climbed some stairs and used an elevator before finally arriving at the EOP Department. The Equal Opportunity Program was one of the controversial affirmative-action programs created for so-called 'minorities.' Walking by two doors, I knocked on the third one, right under the name 'Clifford P. Coleman, EOP Counselor.'

"Please come in," said a friendly voice.

Opening the door, I was greeted by a slim, chestnut-complexioned man wearing silver-framed spectacles. His bushy moustache and eyebrows made him look like a light-skinned Groucho Marx. "Good morning…Mr. Amaru may I presume?"

"Yes, yes," I replied, pleased he had not forgotten our appointment. "Actually, both of us are but I'm the one hoping to attend Rutgers in the fall. Sir, my name's Takuan and this is my brother, Kensuke," I said gesturing to my left.

As he stood up three folders fell onto the floor from the cluttered pile on his desk. After shaking both of our hands, he offered us a seat and told us to call him 'Cliff.' While Cliff made a futile attempt to straighten-up the mess, I scanned his office and found the standard African-American décor: a black history calendar, a poster of Dr. Martin Luther King Jr. giving his "I have a Dream" speech, slave footage, two Dogon ceremonial masks, and an African bushmen painting. The only piece I was unfamiliar with was a poster of a dancer in tights named *Alvin Ailey.*

Once the formalities had concluded Cliff opened our discussion on a sour note. "Allow me to apologize to both of you. Takuan, I tried to catch you at home before you left this morning. I see you're quite the early-bird."

"We did some car-shopping before coming here. Is there a problem Cliff?" I asked with concern.

"Yes I'm afraid." As he spoke, Cliff was putting files and other items from his desk into various drawers and onto nearby shelves. Eventually he finally found what he was looking for: a memo pad. "After our conversation yesterday, I went to the admissions office to check the status of your application but was unable to find it." Saying this, he flipped through the pages in the pad. "Ah yes, here's the information. It wasn't until this morning that something you mentioned on the phone registered."

"What's that?"

"You said you took some courses at Fayetteville State University, right?"

"Yes why?"

"Although you assured me it was less than twelve credits worth, it seems you've accumulated fourteen credits."

"Is that bad?" Asking this, I was confused thinking the more credits the better.

"No of course not. The problem is you have too many credits to be considered a true-freshman."

"And the only apps being reviewed are those of incoming freshman. Is that it Cliff?" asked my brother.

"You hit the nail right on the head Ken," Cliff replied. "Students with over twelve credits are designated as 'transfer students'," he stated with a grim expression. "And admissions won't be looking at those applications until June."

"*June!*" I blurted out.

"I'm afraid so. I hate to be the bearer of bad news but it seems you came all the way out here this morning for nothing." While contemplating this unfavorable turn of events in silence, I stared into the stoic face of Harriet Tubman as she gazed back from the wall. After a few seconds, Cliff snapped me out of my daydream. "Is June too late? When do you need—"

"In two weeks," I replied before he could finish. Unwilling to give up so easily, I put all my cards on the table. "Cliff, is there anyone else here I can explain my situation to?"

"Takuan, believe me, I already made those phone calls before you arrived. Everyone keeps saying the same thing. 'Tell him he's gotta wait until June'."

Nodding my head, I acknowledged his efforts. "Well at least I tried. Like the bible says: *'you have not because you ask not.'* So, I always make sure to ask."

"Really? The bible says that? Where? That is, if you don't mind me asking."

"Young Jedi," I spoke in my old, wise man voice before folding my arms to round-out the *Obi-wan Kenobi* routine. "I see you haven't been reading your scripture lately."

"How'd you know that?" Cliff replied wearing a sheepish grin.

"Because this sentiment is expressed all over the New Testament," interjected Ken. "For example, in John 14, verse 13 it says: *'And whatsoever ye shall ask in my name, that will I do, that the Father may be glorified in the Son. If ye shall ask anything in my name, I will do it'.*"

Now caught up in the Spirit, I added my two cents. "My favorite scripture on this is Matthew 7:7: *Ask and it shall be given you; seek and ye shall find; knock and it shall be opened unto you. For everyone that asketh receiveth, and he that seeketh findeth, and to him that knocketh it shall be opened.*"

"*Or what man is there of you,*" Ken continued the Shakespearean verse, "*whom if his son ask for bread, will he give him a stone? Or if he ask for a fish, will he give him a serpent? If ye then, being evil, know how to give good gifts unto your children, how much more shall your Father which is in heaven give good things to them that ask him?*"

"Wow that was impressive!" Rising to his feet, Cliff gave us a standing ovation. "You two must recite scripture together all the time."

160

"Actually, we never have—this was a first," Ken replied beaming in my direction. "But we'll have to do this again before you go back."

"I second that motion," I declared.

I was in third grade when Ken joined the service. By the time I was in fifth grade he had become a Christian. This was about a year or so before he met Katrina. Back then, I thought Ken's conversion was something weird.

Startled by a knock at the door, our attention was returned to the mundane world of schedules, and appointments. "Cliff, sorry to interrupt," stated a plump, older woman in a friendly but earnest tone. "But there's a young lady named Delta Martinez here to see you. She's your twelve o'clock appointment."

Hearing this, the three of us glanced at the *Benjamin Banneker* clock on the wall. Noticing it was ten past noon, we all stood up.

"Well Cliff, thank you for your help," I said shaking his hand.

"Takuan, this doesn't mean you're not going to be accepted."

"Don't worry about me Cliff," I declared with confidence. "I'm the son of the living God—where I come from there's no such thing as failure."

"What do you mean?" Cliff asked in a quizzical tone.

Once I saw the counselor patiently waiting for an explanation, I realized this was an opportunity to witness. "Cliff, what the human mind paints as failing is actually just the process of being redirected by the Holy Spirit," I revealed. The bottom line is: if I'm supposed to be here in September, nothing can stop me. I'll be here no matter what."

"That's right," Ken concurred.

"And with that sir," I shook Cliff's hand one last time. "I bid you farewell until we meet again—and I pray it'll be sooner than you think."

On the ride back to South Jersey, Ken's attitude adjustment surprised me. About five minutes after we entered the Turnpike, he turned the music down.

"Tak, here's another scripture that comes to mind about your situation. You know this one? *The LORD said: People of Jerusalem, when you stumble and fall, you get back up, and if you take a wrong road, you turn around and go back. So why do you refuse to come back to me? Why do you hold so tightly to your false gods?"*

"Ahh, you got me on that one," I admitted. "I know it's in the Old Testament but I don't know where."

"Jeremiah," he stated, "in the eighth chapter."

"Interesting last sentence," I said. *"Why do you hold so tightly to your false gods?* What do you think it means?" This question spurred a bible discussion which lasted for the remainder of the ride.

It was great to see Ken back to normal. Appearing much different from the clammy-palmed, shyster who was trying to unload a lemon two days ago, as I listened to him recite archaic verse, I was reminded of another form of timeless scripture—lyrics by the *Mighty O'Jays*:

For the love of money, people will steal from their mother; for the love of money, people will rob their own brother.

"Welcome to Trenton State College—I can't wait to see you in a Lions uniform!" This is what Coach Hamill roared after our trip to the admissions office revealed I had been accepted. Following a peek inside the football stadium, we walked back to his office. As we seated ourselves, the coach did not try to hide his excitement. "I been so caught up with recruiting I haven't had a chance to request any film on you but if you played for the *G-men* in '86—the year they took the states—you gotta have some talent!" Really revved up, the former offensive lineman completed his twenty-second evaluation. "What's your time in the forty?"

"I'm not sure but—"

"How close are you to four-point-five seconds?"

"Definitely faster than that," I declared with confidence.

"How much can you bench-press?"

"About three hundred pounds." In spite of never having attempted anything over two-eighty, I was confident I could lift much more.

Grinning from ear to ear in his Nike sportswear, the coach shook my hand again. "It's too early to pencil you in as a starter," he admitted. "But considering our top three receivers just graduated, you couldn't have come at a better time, son."

"Thank you, Coach. But I still have to wait on a few other schools before making my final decision."

"Yes of course," he said.

Minutes later, a graduate-assistant coach and a female student arrived to give me a tour. Shaking hands with Coach Hamilton one last time, I then exited his office with my escorts. As the three of us were walking, they pointed out various buildings such as the main library, the cafeteria, and some of the dormitories. Even though the campus was nice, I wasn't interested in anything they were saying. Right then and there I knew *TSC* was not for me.

That night, I reflected on both trips and decided Trenton State could not compare with Rutgers. Penn State was too far to visit on a ten-day leave; therefore, my only remaining appointment was the following morning at Glassboro State College. Kneeling next to my bed, I recited the proverb I had committed to memory when feelings of doubt tried to afflict my spirit. *"Trust in the LORD with all your heart and lean not on your own understanding. In all your ways submit to him and he will make your paths straight."*

After scolding myself for being weak, I climbed onto my mattress. "Lord, I submit," I whispered, "I trust you with all my heart."

With a smile etched on my face, I then drifted into a peaceful slumber.

"Takuan! Takuan, *denwa-dayo!*"

The next morning, I heard my mother screaming about a telephone call. Then she opened my door and her voice became so loud I sat right up, understanding this was no dream. *"Hai, hai...*who is it?"

Since I was expecting to hear the name of one of my high-school buddies, I had no idea what she was saying. *"Ra-to-ga-zu."*

"What?" I asked, rubbing my eyes and yawning.

"*Daigaku no namae-dayo?*" my mother explained, extending the phone toward me.

"It's someone from Rutgers?" I verified.

"*Sou-sou.*"

Hearing this, I eagerly grabbed the phone expecting to hear something good in spite of the sullen news I had received just two days before. "Good morning Mr. Coleman! I mean Cliff—is this you?" I greeted the caller excitedly.

Although the person was not Cliff, the cheerful lady greeted me like we had met before. "Good morning, Takuan. No, sorry I'm not Mr. Coleman. I am however, calling on behalf of the Livingston EOP Program. And forgive me for calling so early, hope I didn't wake you."

Glancing at the clock, I noticed I had overslept ten minutes. "No not at all, I have an appointment this morning. Ma'am, what can I do for you?"

"Takuan allow me to be the first to congratulate you. We just got notification from the Office of Admissions that you've been accepted for the 1989 fall semester. Welcome to Rutgers!"

"*What!*" I screamed while jumping out of bed. Not knowing what else to do I shouted down the hall at my mother's still receding figure. "*Oka-san, yoku dekita-yo!* I'm going to Rutgers!"

"Hello, hello...Takuan? Are you still there?"

"*Gomen nasai*...I mean, sorry ma'am," I said, replacing the phone to my ear. "I got a little carried away. Praise God!"

"Oh, are you a Christian?"

"And you know that—all praise is due!"

After giggling at my youthful exuberance, she asked me to come to the campus. "Can you visit the EOP office today to pick-up your letter of acceptance?"

"Sure, I can come right after my other appoint—"
Suddenly realizing Glassboro was three hours in the opposite direction caused me to reconsider my options. "Hold-up, if I'm already accepted at Rutgers I don't need to go there anymore, right?" After babbling my thoughts aloud, I came to a decision. "Yes ma'am, I can come right now—I mean after I shower, eat breakfast, and drive over there…you know what I mean."

"Takuan, please calm down," the lady advised amidst her laughter. "Take your time and don't hurt yourself—or anyone else for that matter," she joked. "We'll be expecting you sometime this afternoon. Is that okay?"

"Perfect. See you soon, bye." As I was hanging up the phone it occurred to me I didn't know her name. "Excuse me ma'am, one more thing."

But all I heard was a dial tone.

All Hail the Dean!

"Tak, it's good to see you again too. What's up?"
Because Cliff was wearing a broad smile, I thought he was joking. Nonetheless after we took our seats, he continued staring as if waiting for an explanation. Only then did I realize he had no idea why I was here. "My letter of acceptance arrived, right?"

Appearing confused, Cliff began rehashing old news. "Takuan, I thought you understood. Your application won't be reviewed until—"

"June, I know. I'm not talking about that."

166

"No? What then?" he asked dumbfounded.

"You really don't know, huh?" I asked, still scrutinizing his face for a hint he was putting me on. "This morning I got a call from a different EOP counselor."

"Really? What did he say?"

"The caller was a woman and she congratulated me on being accepted to Rutgers."

"*Are you serious?*"

"Yes. And she also told me to come here to pick up my letter of acceptance."

"Really? This morning? What's her name?"

As Cliff rattled-off his questions, I remembered the lady had hung up on me. "I was so excited I forgot to ask her name but I'm sure the call came from this office."

"No worries," he replied scratching his head. "Lemme walk over and talk to Jen." At that moment, the door opened revealing a slim Latina in her late-twenties; she was holding a folder in her hand. The woman, tawny-brown with shoulder-length curly hair, possessed both a cute face and a pleasant aura.

"Cliff," she said before noticing me. "Oh, I apologize for interrupting." Then she pointed. "You must be Tak."

"And you must be Jen," I likewise responded.

"Takuan Amaru, allow me to introduce you to my coworker, Jeanette Santiago," Cliff declared in a formal tone. Although this was our first time seeing each other, I had spoken with Jen several times on the telephone from Ft. Bragg.

"I heard I missed you and your brother the other day. It's nice to finally meet you in person," she said before adding in the same breath: "Cliff told me the news, June, so what brings you back so soon?"

"It's nice to meet you too," I said, rising from my chair to shake her hand. "And I was hoping you were about to tell me, Jen."

"Huh? Whaddya mean?"

Following Cliff's brief summary of the situation, Jen revealed she knew nothing about any phone calls. Moreover, she stated in her seven years working at Rutgers she had never heard of a transfer-student having their application reviewed before June.

"It's highly unlikely Tak but I'll ask around and see what turns up."

"Thanks Jen," Cliff and I both chorused as she placed the folder she was holding on his desk.

"This is Otto Garcia's file," she said before walking out the door and closing it behind her.

Once Jen was gone, I looked at Cliff. "Well somebody called me this morning so someone's gotta know something."

"I hope you're right," Cliff responded sounding doubtful. "Tak, do me a favor. Have a seat in the hallway while I round up our student volunteers. Maybe one of them made the call. Even if they didn't, they always seem to know more about what's going on around here than I do," Cliff admitted with a chuckle.

"Okay, take your time," I said rising to my feet.

Leaving his office, I strolled around the corner like a curious kid in a new neighborhood. Having the opportunity to talk to students instead of soldiers, I had crazy-fun walking around the EOP department. Everyone, even the staff it seemed, was brimming with joy. Instead of asking people questions about their ethnicity, I made a game of it by checking out their appearance and listening to their accent before positing a guess. Since there were many Asians and Caribbean islanders—cultures I was familiar with—I was correct more times than not. Every twenty-minutes or so, I went back to see if either Jen or Cliff had returned. Seeing they had not, I resumed my pleasant conversations with students, office workers, as well as janitors. Being in-tune with the Spirit allowed my best side to illuminate as I shared the details of my visit over and over again.

It was after one o'clock when Cliff finally called me. "Takuan come here please."

Hearing my name, I rushed to his office and was eager until I saw his face.

"I'm sorry Tak." Shaking his head solemnly, Cliff gestured for me to sit down. "I spoke with every member of the EOP staff and I just ran into the last student-volunteer outside the cafeteria. None of the counselors called you and no one knows anything about a phone call placed to your house this morning."

"*Really?* That's odd," I responded with the only words to describe this bizarre scenario. "I know someone called me this morning." In spite of the less-than-satisfactory results, I was appreciative of the time and effort Cliff had devoted to my case; after all I wasn't even a registered student. With this in mind, I recalled seeing two girls waiting in the hall and realized Cliff needed to get back to work. "I apologize for taking up your time." Saying this, I stood up and shook Cliff's hand. As I walked toward the door, Cliff remained standing behind his desk.

"No problem. And Takuan if anything turns up I'll call you, okay?"

"Okay." As I reached for the door it swung open—just missing my face by inches.

"Is Tak still here?" asked Jen as she ran in completely out of breath. Before either of us had time to respond, she recognized I was the person holding her by the shoulders. "Great! I thought I was too late." Without any further information, the petite counselor grabbed my hand. "Come on, we gotta hurry or we might miss him—you too Cliff!"

When the elevator door closed in our faces, we dashed down two flights of stairs. It was not until we exited the staircase when Jen began explaining. "Talk about good luck, I ran into Dean Reed and his secretary on my way to the financial aid office. They're here to clean out his office for retirement."

"Wow! I thought the old man retired years ago," said Cliff sounding amazed.

"Basically, he did but not officially. Since he was hospitalized three years ago, including today, he's only been here twice." Once we neared a receptionist, Jen stopped walking to finish her story. "Anyway, I remembered hearing Dean Reed fought in World War II, so I took a chance and told him about Takuan's situation."

"And?" inquired Cliff.

"Whaddya mean 'and?' We're standing outside his office, aren't we?"

Once the middle-aged lady seated behind the desk finished her phone conversation, she gestured for us to approach. "Hello Jen, nice to see you again. What can I help with you?"

"Judy, this is Takuan Amaru" Jen said, gesturing in my direction. "He's the young man I told Dean Reed about."

"Oh yes, the soldier," she confirmed looking me up and down. "The dean is eager to meet you. However," she resumed looking back toward the counselors, "he's only interested in speaking to Mr. Amaru."

Hearing this, I graciously thanked Jen and Cliff, assuring them I would be fine from here. "I'll come up to see you before I leave."

The brunette receptionist led me down a hall adorned with paintings of former deans on both sides. As we walked, I scanned the scholarly faces from yesteryear adorned in their argyle sweaters and three-piece suits. "Here we are," the friendly lady said, stopping at the last door on the right, "please enjoy your visit." As she knocked, I examined the gold nameplate affixed to the mahogany portal: *Dr. Edward J. Reed, Dean of Livingston College, Rutgers University.* Without waiting for a reply, the lady turned the knob and pushed the door open. "Sir, your one-thirty appointment, Mr. Takuan Amaru, is here."

"Great!" came a robust voice from inside. "Send him in. I wanna have a look at the soldier."

Once given permission to enter, I cautiously stepped inside. Scanning the dimly lit room, I discovered the dean seated in a recliner about fifteen feet from his desk. His shortly cropped hair was nearly all white and it sparkled on his head like freshly driven snow. For several seconds, he continued staring at the documents in his hand before finally tearing his attention away and looking at me. Upon making eye contact, I detected not only a certain strength of character but also the spirit of a leader. Seeing the half-packed, cardboard boxes on the carpet, I recalled Jen saying he was retiring due to illness. Nonetheless I was astonished a man exhibiting such vitality could simultaneously be losing a battle with prostate cancer.

"Greetings soldier!" boomed the dean enthusiastically.

"Good afternoon sir," I responded using my best paratrooper voice. Before I could cover the distance between us thereby preventing him from having to stand, he popped out of his chair like a gymnast and met me halfway.

"Specialist Amaru, having served as a Naval officer in World War II, it's a pleasure to shake the hand of a modern defender of our great nation!"

Once I felt his firm grip, I knew this meeting had been arranged by the Holy Spirit.

"The pleasure's mine, sir. And please call me 'Tak,' it's short for 'Takuan'." Stating this deferentially, I was surprised he knew my rank. After releasing my hand, he gestured me toward his desk. As I sat down in a chair, I noticed the worn, yellowish sheet of paper in his left hand bore the same governmental seal as my Army awards. At that moment, the secretary re-appeared with a tray holding two steaming cups. From one whiff, I knew it was Japanese green tea.

"Your afternoon tea, sir"

"Thank you, Judy."

Upon entering the room, Judy's smile vanished when she looked behind the recliner and saw the boxes. "Sir, I hope you're not packing yourself. The doctor's orders were for you to—"

"Judy, I'm perfectly aware of what Dr. Holliday said. Don't worry, I'm not packing. I just wanted to show Takuan my Medal of Honor but I can't find it. Do you know where it is?"

"Yes. You gave it to your grandson last year. Remember?"

"No but if you say I did, I know it's true." Then he

172

turned toward me and whined in a pleasant tone. "Dammit, I'm getting old!"

"Sir," his secretary continued, "if you're not going to need anything else, I'll take my lunch break now."

"Fine Judy, see ya later." Although their relationship was a professional one, Judy addressed the dean more like a concerned daughter than a faithful employee. Once she left, the dean confirmed my hunch. "That woman has been through hell-and-high-water with me," he said before chuckling. "My wife used to think we had something going on." Without ever confirming whether Mrs. Reed's intuition was correct or not, he sat behind his desk and put the weathered documents down. "Sorry I don't have the actual medal to show you but these are the orders for my award. I got it as a bright-eyed lieutenant back in 1944," he explained before asking a question. "You're in the Army, right?"

"Yes sir, that's correct."

"Takuan, do me a favor and relax. I dunno if you know but they're telling me I'm dying. So please lighten-up on the 'sirs' okay. I wanna enjoy myself."

"Understood." Although I agreed, I did not know exactly how he expected me to address him. Unsure of my next move, I played it cool and waited for him to speak again.

"It was a different world back then..." As the dean spoke, he gazed off into the distance. "It was a time when men opened doors for women and everyone, even teens and children, understood the value of proper manners. Nothing like it is today."

Not particularly liking the direction our conversation was taking, I tried to change the subject. "I heard you fought in World War II. If you don't mind talking about it, what ship did you serve on?"

Hearing my question, Dean Reed's eyes sparkled. "I served on what many historians claim was the most important ship in either world war: the *USS Texas*. You ever heard of her?"

"Yes," I lied. However, since it was only a 'little white lie,' I figured it was okay.

"Of course, you have—you're no civilian!" he bellowed. "By the way, where're you stationed at?"

Listening to the dean speak now, I was aware of a military swagger which had not been present just seconds ago. "Fort Bragg, North Carolina, sir."

"Bragg!" he roared, standing up in a rush. No sooner had the dean's leg hit the desk when I instinctively grabbed the tray with the tea cups, preventing them from spilling. "Nice hands," he praised. "And forgive me for getting so excited but I knew some good men from Bragg." Without further ado, he gestured toward the tray in my hand. "That's—"

"Japanese green tea," I blurted out.

"Yes, how'd you know?" The expression on the senior citizen's face resembled that of a boy who had just witnessed a nifty card trick.

"Because I'm Japanese...well my mother's Japanese. And if I'm correct," I paused to inhale its rich aroma, "this brew is from *Uji*. Uji's in—"

"Kyoto! Yes, that's remarkable! Takuan, do you consider yourself a connoisseur of Japanese tea?"

"No, no, of course not but since it's a staple of my culture I drink it whenever I'm at home."

While this was also untrue, I rationalized it likewise fell into the 'white lie' category. The truth was my mother

174

loved Uji tea, claiming it was far superior to other blends. As a child, I recalled her making a fuss whenever it was out-of-stock at the Asian food market. Being the *only* green tea, I knew, I mentioned it simply because I had been taught that socializing was more about making the other person feel good than being honest—especially when it came to white people. In other words: even had the tea turned out to be a different blend, say from Shizuoka or Kagoshima, it still would have appeared to the dean we shared a mutual interest.

"I never saw any action in the Pacific Theater but my buddies brought plenty of green tea back with them. After my first sip I was hooked; never had another cup of coffee again. It seems we have an awful lot in common, Takuan."

"Yes, we do," I agreed.

"By any chance are you Airborne?"

"Yes I am."

"Figures," he replied with a pompous air before adding: "I knew you couldn't be a dirty, nasty LEG."

Hearing this, I chuckled in astonishment. "How do you know about LEGs?"

Appearing very pleased, the Dean of Livingston College walked over and picked up a couple photo albums from the mess he left on the floor. "These are my pictures from the Navy," he said, wiping dust off the covers. Returning to the desk, he placed the albums between our teacups and opened the one on top. Pointing at a black-and-white photo of a young, handsome cadet, he smiled a thousand memories. "That's me when I was twenty-one. How old are you now?" he asked.

"Twenty-one," I replied.

"Like I said, we got a lot in common."

Flipping through the pages of his album was like

turning back the hands of time. As Dean Reed pointed at people and places from four decades ago he teleported us into the past. Using loads of military jargon—some of which I was unfamiliar—he talked about everything like it was happening now. Before long we turned to a page with a photo of a huge battleship. Smiling from ear-to-ear, the dean slid the album closer so I could get a better look.

"I used to love this boat!" he exclaimed with that far-off, nostalgic look of someone gazing at a picture of their high-school sweetheart. "The Mighty T—that's what we called the USS Texas—was my home for just over two years. How long you been at Bragg?"

"Just over two years."

Following another 'I told you so' facial expression, he began to narrate a fascinating story. "The reason I asked if you were Airborne was because it was our responsibility to provide cover for the paratrooper landing at Normandy. We did this by shelling the hell outta the Axis-held beaches." Stating this with pride, he waved his fist in the air. "But," he stopped his hand and raised one finger to emphasize his point, "it was rumored that one brigade in the 82nd Airborne had lost communication and jumped-in early by mistake—"

I was so surprised to hear the dean reciting the same 'hoo-rah' propaganda Sgt. Quick had forced me to study that I unwittingly interrupted him. "To this day, the oh-five's motto is 'H-Minus' because on D-day they had to fight the Nazis for an hour by themselves with no ground assistance."

"Yes, yes, exactly! An hour before D-day got underway," shouted the former lieutenant. "Tak, I imagine H-Minus means 'minus one hour' but what's the *oh-five*?"

"Oh, I'm sorry," I apologized before explaining.

176

"Some years back the regiment you know of as the 508th merged with the 505th. On Fort Bragg, we call the 505th the oh-five."

By the time both of us finished recounting the historical facts we knew about D-day, Normandy, H-Minus, etc., Dean Reed was feeling mighty good indeed. Honestly, I was afraid the old man might have a heart attack.

"Tak, you seem to know a lot about the oh-five. Is that your unit?"

"Used to be...I'm basically out of the Army now." Saying this in a joking manner, I avoided giving a direct answer. Here is another prime example where the truth would have killed the conversation. *Can you imagine how disappointed he would have been had I told him I terminated?*

"Tak, for their bravery and dedication those paratroopers were awarded a Presidential Unit Citation." As the dean spoke he showed me a photo of him in his Navy uniform with his arms draped around the shoulders of two soldiers. "These are two of the paratroopers I had the pleasure of getting drunk with one night. Captain Johns and Lieutenant Michaels were real stand-up guys. I'll never forget when we were leaving Europe how much everyone respected their battalion. The Nazi POW's downright feared paratroopers— they called them a 'bloodthirsty pack of jackals'."

"Really? Jackals?" I inquired in disbelief.

"Hell yeah!" he bellowed with the force of a company commander at morning formation. "And Tak, since you're one of the heirs of this outstanding legacy, I'd say we have that in common too."

"That's awfully nice of you to say but perhaps, in this case, there might be a slight difference because you're a war hero and I'm just a peacetime soldier."

In spite of my appeal the dean had heard enough. While I was still talking he picked up his telephone and started to dial. Unaware of whom he was calling, I returned my attention to the photos and flipped back to the first page. Once there I compared the eyes of the young lieutenant in the picture with the pair lodged in the wrinkled face speaking into the phone. Now, in the winter of his life, I wondered if the dean was satisfied with his list of accomplishments.

"Takuan, what's your social security number?"

His question caught me so off-guard I almost asked him why he wanted to know. "Umm, it's oh-five-seven..." After rattling-off the nine-digit *straw-man* code, although I looked back down at the album, I was intently listening to his conversation.

"That's right, last name Amaru, first name Takuan and he's a transfer student...you found it? Good. Listen to me carefully because this is important. I want you to take that application and put it in the 'Accepted Students' pile. Yes, you heard me correctly. And if anyone has any questions about this have them call me at the hospital, you understand? Thanks again, Rachel." After hanging up, Dean Reed looked at me with a self-satisfied expression for a split-second before murmuring in a low, scratchy voice. "There are a few privileges that come along with being the dean!" Then he snickered unlike any other time he had laughed up to this point. Witnessing this, I was reminded of an *Eddie Murphy* skit on *Saturday Night Live*.

Like Richard Pryor before him, Eddie did not apologize to the ruling class for being black. Quite to the contrary, he confronted many of society's ills—especially racism—by making fun of white people. In his behind-the-

178

scenes probe to experience life as a white man, Eddie wore make-up so he would appear Caucasian. In one scene Eddie tries to buy a newspaper at a convenience store and is surprised by the white shopkeeper's refusal to accept his money. "There's nobody around—go ahead take it." With a smile on his face, the man persuades Eddie to take the newspaper for free. What did Eddie conclude from this experience? In his own words: "When white people are alone they give things to each other for free."

If this is true I was feeling mighty white!

Overcome with joy, I rose from my chair to shake the dean's hand but, once again, he ignored me. I deduced this could only mean there were still blessings to come. Standing there, I watched him draw a crude map on a piece of scrap paper.

"You want to play football, right?"

"Yessir."

"There's a practice session about to get under way in an hour. Actually, it's the annual intrasquad scrimmage and Coach Anderson's expecting me; so, I'm afraid I have to end our meeting. Why don't you get some lunch then meet me at the football stadium on Busch Campus? Don't s'pose you know where Busch is, do you?" Asking this, he handed me the drawing.

In addition to the football field, his sketch also included the location of the nearest cafeteria.

"I saw signs for it on my way over here," saying this I glanced at his artwork. "But armed with this, I'm sure I'll have no trouble—remember I'm a soldier," I joked. "Thank you sir and I look forward to seeing you again at the field."

I was way too excited to enjoy my meal. After toying with my food at the brand-new cafeteria I moseyed over to the Hale Center, which was a state-of-the-art sports complex that appeared even newer than the dining hall.

When I arrived at the entrance of the football stadium, a campus police officer manning the gate emphasized this was a closed-practice. "Sorry buddy, no walk-ons allowed in today." By the humdrum way he said this, I surmised more than a few hopefuls for next season's team had already been turned away. Even after I explained my situation the officer was still reluctant to look into the matter; it seemed he did not believe me. "You were invited by Dean Reed, huh? Well nobody told us anything about the dean having any guests. You got any ID?" Once he saw I was in the military, he assumed a more respectful tone. "Specialist Amaru," he said reading the card, "you're gonna have to wait here until someone inside can verify your story, okay?"

"Okay," I agreed like I had an option.

It took almost an hour for a graduate-assistant coach to finally appear.

"I'm here for 'Takuan Amaru'," he declared to the guards. Before any of them could respond, he looked in my direction.

"That's me Coach."

After we walked inside, he escorted me to the sideline where a group of high school players and their coaches were observing the intrasquad game. "Don't stray beyond the forty-yard line either way and enjoy the remainder of the scrimmage," the young assistant blurted out before hurrying back onto the field. Left there alone, everyone wanted to know the identity of the newest candidate for a starting position. By the time an overzealous 'blue-chipper' ambled over to greet me, it seemed the fifty or so individuals had ceased watching the action on the field in favor of scrutinizing me.

"So," the stocky teen said before examining me from head to toe, "who are you?"

The brown-skinned youth was an inch shorter than me. Scanning the dark-green hoodie with "LB" written across his chest in white letters, I wondered if he played inside or outside linebacker. The indented-line running across his forehead explained his wavy hair; he was the type who wore a doo-rag all the time.

Smiling, I replied in a friendly tone. "Good afternoon to you too, my name's Takuan."

He just stood there looking unimpressed.

"And you are?"

"Still a junior at Pemberton High but I've been playing varsity since last year," he explained, demonstrating how he wanted me to respond: by listing my football credentials.

"Junior from Pemberton, huh?" I said, patting him on the back since he was not inclined to shake my hand. "Nice to meet you, Junior."

Ignoring my sarcasm, he pointed at two people standing along the sideline: an older white man and a teen who was wearing a green and white Pemberton t-shirt. "That's my coach over there and next to him is Julian Blackstone." By the way he emphasized the boy's name it was obvious he expected me to be familiar with him. Seeing I was not, he exhaled in disgust. "Julian Blackstone is the All-State halfback who broke the group four, single-game rushing record two years in a row, *hello?*" Following a patronizing snicker, he continued his commentary. "And the dude next to Julian in the black and yellow jacket…" Junior ended up giving me the run-down on most of the players present—high school, stats, and all. He finished his scouting report with a huge, monolithic-looking brother who reminded me of *Grimace*. "That's Malik Jamison. He's a second-team All-American that turned down scholarships at Florida State and Notre Dame to play close to home."

Even though I did not care, I humored the youth with a question. "Where's he from?"

Upon hearing my naïve inquiry, several bystanders turned to glare like I was stupid. Seeing their reactions made me realize just how much I was out-of-the-loop.

"E-liz-a-beth," Junior replied, stressing each syllable. "Dude, where you been the last few years? Living in a closet somewhere?" His snooty comments drew laughter from the bystanders.

Once the commotion had subsided, the crowd commenced their interrogation.

"Takuan, what's your last name and where'd you graduate from?" asked a man who I assumed was a sports writer.

"Are you All-State?" inquired one of the scholarship recipients Junior had mentioned earlier.

"Are you at least All-County?" Junior wanted to know.

When I failed to provide any blue-chip credentials, I heard the term 'walk-on' being mumbled like it was a dirty

182

word; it reminded me of the disdain paratroopers have for LEGs. With the mystery of my identity now revealed, everyone returned their attention to the field. It was clear the entire group was collectively snubbing their nose at me.

"So lemme make sure I understand," the boy from Pemberton resumed, not appearing satisfied. "You're just a 'nobody' from the Army? You don't even have a scholarship?"

"Nope," I simply replied.

"So why are you over here with us? This area is only for recruited players and their coaches."

"Not true," I replied with a grin. "What about you?"

"Me? I'm not here alone; I'm with a scholarship recipient. And my coach just so happens to be…" He was half done explaining when he realized I was only teasing him. Once he did, he promptly returned to the same line of questions. "No seriously, how'd you get in here? Walk-on's aren't allowed inside today. The campus police should've stopped you from entering because this is a *closed* practice. You didn't know that?"

By this point Junior was getting on my nerves. Since I wanted to be on my best behavior I tried to ignore him but as I returned to my attention to the scrimmage, it occurred to me this pest was only expressing what most of these snobbish jocks were thinking. With this in mind, I pivoted back in his direction. "Hey Junior," I said in a loud voice to address all the naysayers at once. "Obviously I'm an exception to the rule because, as you can see, they let *me* in."

"Yeah, I know that," he replied sounding bored. "But why?"

"Because young boy," looking around with a confident grin Billy put every negative spirit in-check. "I'm the Son of the Living God—that's why!"

"What? What's that supposed to mean?"

CRACK!

As he finished his question a loud collision occurred on the field. This was followed by a chorus of low moans and boos emanating from the crowd. "That's a late hit!" I griped in response to a wide-receiver nearly getting decapitated by the free-safety seconds after the whistle had blown. Although I had witnessed a couple running backs get tackled late this was the only time I complained, knowing WR was my future position.

"No shit Sherlock!"

Looking toward the sound of the voice, I was surprised to see the big monolithic brother, Malik Jamison, addressing me.

"That guy's a freshman," Malik continued, "just like you'll be real soon—better get used to it."

Everyone on the sideline became quiet when thirty people appeared in the end zone and began walking across the field. The group, consisting of older men in suits along with a few women and children, was strolling toward the fifty-yard, line where the coaches and players were also assembling. Seconds later, I noticed the entourage was being led by Dean Reed, himself. As the gathering was passing before us, a graduate-assistant started waving his hands to get someone's attention on the sideline. Since it was not the same guy who brought me inside the stadium I never imagined he was waving at me.

"Hey Nobody—Joe-nobody from the Army!" Junior yelled. "I think that coach wants you." Having returned to his place next to Julian Blackstone, his loud remark spurred the

184

blue-chippers to snicker again.

After making my way to the front of the group, I was standing between Junior and Malik Jamison when the assistant-coach reached the sideline.

"Are you Takuan Amaru?" he asked, looking irritated; it seemed he did not appreciate being tasked with retrieving the lowly walk-on.

"Yes sir," I replied in an earnest tone.

"Dean Reed wants you—come with me."

"Yessir." Prior to taking a step onto the field, I turned to make eye contact with the All-American before pivoting the other way to pat Junior on the back for the second time that afternoon.

When the graduate-assistant and I neared the center of the field, I took a knee behind the players while my chaperon walked over to stand with his fellow coaches. After Coach Anderson summed-up the highlights of the practice he allowed Dean Reed to address the team.

"Defense, great job out there today!" the dean roared. "I know the offense doesn't want to hear this but they got outplayed this afternoon." With this, the players wearing black jerseys slapped hands with one another while the red-garbed jocks remained silent. "But Ernie and Ty, you two hooked up on a couple nice completions."

To show his appreciation for the dean's kind words, Ty McQueen stood up and pointed at his quarterback with both index fingers before taking a bow; this resulted in a few seconds of laughter. Following some cat-calls by players on both sides, the elder statesman cleared his throat.

"Elnardo, it's good to see you're back to All-American form. I can't wait to see that on *ESPN* this season!"

"Thank you, sir, I'll do my best," promised the

handsome, almond-complexioned behemoth of a player. Then he stood up with his helmet under his arm and continued addressing the dean. "And sir, I'm speaking on behalf of the entire team when I say it's great to see you out here today!" Once the defensive captain made this heartfelt proclamation, every player, coach, and staff member gave the dean a hearty round of applause.

As the ovation faded Dean Reed appeared genuinely touched.

"Thanks, El, and all you guys," the dean expressed his gratitude. "Hey Coach, before I hand the floor back to you there's someone here I want to introduce." *Then he pointed at me.* "Tak, stand up."

As every player, coach, scout, and journalist turned in my direction, I felt my anxiety mounting.

"This is Takuan Amaru. He's the young man I was telling you about. Coach, you think we can get him into summer camp?"

Before the head coach could respond, the grumpy graduate-assistant who brought me onto the field decided to express his opinion. "Excuse me sir, but no way!" he whined, sounding frustrated. "We already have three redshirt freshmen who might not be able to attend because we can't find housing for *them*, and that's not even to mention—" As soon as the young assistant noticed that Coach Anderson and Dean Reed were both glaring at him he stopped talking and disappeared from view by dropping down on a knee like the players.

"But Coach, we can get Takuan in, can't we? As a favor to me?"

Although the dean phrased this as a request,

considering the circumstances, what choice did Coach Anderson have?

"Of course, we can. You have my word on it, sir." Then my new coach looked in my direction. "Takuan come over here."

After jogging over, I shook hands with both men before taking a knee next to the captains. Then I bowed my head—along with my teammates—and together we thanked God for a good scrimmage.

Chapter 7: Ye are Gods!

"For many are called but few are chosen…"

Two days after returning from New Jersey, still drunk off the Spirit, I could not wait to get to Wednesday's service to thank everyone who prayed for me. Opening my testimony with a classic phrase from the Book of Matthew resulted in the room becoming so quiet you could hear a pin drop. The next day, Chill and Bellamy agreed it sounded like the opening of a sermon.

"It's seems like just yesterday when I got saved," I resumed. "At that time, Curt and Jon said I had been chosen to do great things. Since neither of them knew me from a can of paint, I thought they were just talking out the sides of their necks." Once my juvenile idioms prompted pockets of laughter to break out amongst the congregation, I was able to relax. "I remember Jon saying: 'Don't worry because the results will speak for themselves.' Back then I didn't know what he meant. But I understand now. When I think about my former, dead-end life before coming to the Way..." Stopping here, I looked down and shook my head. "Folks, back then I wasn't a very good person."

"But that was then, this is now," yelled Brother Ralph. "Now you're saved!"

"Yeah," agreed Brother Rob. "That slate's been washed clean!" Then his wife, Rosa, co-signed her husband's declaration with an emphatic, "Amen!"

"So, what happened while you were on leave?" Jon asked.

Once he posed the question on everyone's mind, the room once again became silent.

"First of all, I want to say 'thank you' for praying for me." Then I spent the next several minutes recounting my phenomenal ten-days north of the Mason-Dixon line. Some of the women were moved to tears while I explained the miraculous turn-around in my family situation. Curt and Jon were laughing the entire time I explained the drama surrounding the Jetta; and Rosa, being a strong Latina, showed my sister-in-law respect by shouting: "That's right, can't keep a good woman down!" However, it was the final episode at Rutgers that sealed the deal. By the time I finished rehashing my EOP adventure—which included the mysterious phone-call that lead to meeting Dean Reed—the entire room was bug-eyed and speechless.

Finally, Rob broke the silence.

"Hey Tak, me and Rosa want tickets when you guys go to the Orange Bowl—and don't forget I asked you first."

Rob's request caused everyone to laugh.

"Gotcha Rob," I played along, "two tickets for you and Rosa."

Before the atmosphere grew too festive, I wanted to conclude by mentioning the students who had accepted Christ. "Hold up, believe it or not, you haven't heard the best part yet." Then I announced their names. "Andrew Lee, Miriam Carter, and Joliet Martin. Although you may not know them in the flesh, they're your new, spiritual siblings in Christ." Following a cursory look at the dumbfounded faces nearest to me, I explained in more detail. "These are the students at Rutgers who prayed with me to get saved—

hallelujah!"

"*HALLELUJAH!*" boomed the congregation much louder than I had expected. When Curt ran over to hug me this set off a chain reaction; and within seconds a line had formed. As people shook my hand or patted me on the back, those who remained seated showered our impromptu ceremony with applause, whistles, and grunt-barks. During the ruckus, I spotted Pastor Bart moving quickly toward the stage—he was almost running.

After stumbling up the steps the pastor grabbed the microphone. "Please sit down everyone," he almost yelled. "Unfortunately, we're running late this evening, so let's have a seat so we can get started."

As Rob released me from a bear-hug, I scanned the room and, like me, everyone was confused. This is because after church members finish giving their testimonies the congregation always provides feedback. "Pastor, just a moment please." So, when Rosa raised her hand and started speaking, I was glad I was not the only person who noticed this deviation from the normal procedure. "I have question about something Sam said in his testimony. It'll only take a minute—"

"I'm sorry Rosa," Pastor Bart said without compassion. "Ask me after church—"

"Actually, the question is to Sam, not you. I was wondering—"

"Everyone, please open to the Book of Jonah. Tonight, I want to discuss the parable of Jonah and the Whale." Having introduced his topic, the pastor started reading: "*Now the word of the LORD came to Jonah, the son of Amittai, saying: 'Arise go to Nineveh, that great city, and cry out*

against it for their wickedness has come up before Me'."
Glancing around the room, the pastor's eyes lingered on me
while he caught his breath. "But Jonah decided not to obey
God's command, for he had plans of his own. Instead of
going to Nineveh, the capital city of Assyria, he boarded a
ship bound for Tarshish, which was located in present day
Spain." Gazing at his audience with a puzzled expression, the
clergyman then asked a question. "Why would Jonah, a
devout prophet from Galilee, deliberately defy God's word?"

*I prayed the pastor was not going where I thought he
was going.*

"The Bible says Jonah was motivated by fear and
vengeance," the pastor emphasized. "In the past, the
Assyrians had committed atrocities against his people. Since
they were Israel's enemies, it's easy to understand why he
would be afraid to go there; and also, why he might want
them to be punished. However, these were not his reasons.
You see, Jonah understood God's nature; therefore, he knew
if he witnessed to the Assyrians as God had instructed, his
enemies would be shown mercy. So, he decided to go
elsewhere and waste his time. But folks, the Almighty has an
agenda to keep too."

Having emphasized the last sentence, the pastor
turned the page and took a sip of water.

"God caused a typhoon to attack the seafaring vessel
transporting Jonah!" Pastor Bart yelled with emotion. "The
Bible says it was so bad the sailors knew it had to be an
omen. After casting lots, they realized the blame lay with
Jonah for their grave misfortune so they confronted him.
Once Jonah confessed he was fleeing from the Lord, the crew
decided it was best to throw him overboard." Closing his
Bible, Pastor Bart looked at his congregation. "This evening

I'd like to pose the same question to you. If you find one amongst you who is being disobedient to God's plan, is it not better to throw him overboard? Or shall we allow his punishment to become our own? In law, this is called being an accessory to the crime. Don't be an accessory to prideful sin!"

Being seated in the front row, this limited the number of people in my peripheral vision but I could feel their staring eyes as if dozens of laser beams were being aimed at my occipital lobe.

Pastor Bart, carefully avoiding my glare, continued to push the accelerator down even farther. "*Pride!*" he yelled. "That's why Jonah disobeyed! Sure, he was scared, and of course he wanted the Assyrians to be punished. These human emotions played their part, no doubt. But ladies and gentlemen the bottom line was: Jonah had gotten a big head! He actually thought if he didn't go to Nineveh, this would prevent God's word from being spread there—as if God couldn't manifest his glory through others. Well folks, some of us here tonight are suffering from this same type of 'big-headed, false-pride.' Let us pray to exorcise these demons from our midst..."

That was enough! Yet as I contemplated walking out, I glanced down at my King James Bible. The gift Ken had given me years ago was sitting on my lap; it seemed to be calling me. Grabbing it, I flipped the pages until I came to the Book of Jonah.

Minutes later, I was engrossed in the words.

By the time the verbal lynching concluded, I felt numb. Once I stood up, I could not get out of there fast enough. The people around me—the same folks who shook my hand less than an hour ago—now fled from my presence. When I turned down the main aisle, I watched everyone 'make way for the bad-guy.'

Arriving at the exit as I reached for the door Curt snatched my wrist. "Tak, wait a minute!" he said in a reprimanding tone. "You're taking things too personally."

With my arm still in his grasp I used my other hand to point at the frail man who was observing the two of us from the pulpit. "So, you admit he's up there shinin' on me."

"Not just you. He's talking about all of us," Crawley declared.

"Really?" I scoffed. "Well I just saw Brother Sam walk out before me. Why didn't you stop him? I mean, since the pastor's talking about all of us, Sam might be upset too, right?"

Just then Jon, Reggie, Chill, and some others came up beside Curt.

I will never forget this mental snapshot. Looking at the people I had spent all my time with over the past two years, there was a whitish-gray aura surrounding them as if they were dead. In the blink-of-an-eye I understood this image represented a reflection from the past, not unlike the black-and-white photos in Dean Reed's albums.

"Curt I gotta go—peace!" Stating this in earnest, I twisted my forearm from of his grasp and walked out of the Doorway of Christian Unity…forever.

Tears streamed down my face as I stretched in the parking lot. In spite of this, instead of sorrow or regret, I felt a great sense of relief. Setting off from that store-front building in Fayetteville for the last time, I felt free as a bird let out of its cage. Released from the shackles of religious dogma, with no dead-weight to hold me back, the mixing of my sweat and tears once again unveiled the source of the universe. Symbolized by the sun or a black dot in many ancient cultures, this energy is the very same power which resides within Jon, Curt, Reggie, Chill and me. This realization led to understanding that becoming 'The Christ' has nothing to do with attending any particular church, being baptized, or even getting saved.

Having received this revelation, my mind's eye ricocheted back toward the dimension of time and space. Touching down in the shoppette parking lot—the first place I met Curt and Jon—I gasped for breath knowing the circle was complete.

"Come in."

Hearing a knock on the door the next evening, I knew it was Curt and Jon without asking. As they entered the room, I interrupted my Bible study to greet my *jegnas* with brotherly hugs. Despite having spoken to both of them just yesterday, laying eyes on the 'dynamic duo' caused a knot of nostalgia to tighten in my chest like I had not seen them in ages. Shaking off this weird premonition, I did my best to show nothing but respect by thanking them for everything they had done for me. Although my words expressed gratitude, they were insulted realizing I considered them old news.

"What's with all this 'thank you' jazz?" Curt wanted to know; his smile suddenly switching to a look of scorn.

"Chill out Curt," Jon said before turning in my direction. "We spoke to Pastor Bart about toning down his

194

message. He wants to talk to you, maybe even apologize for some things."

"Thanks, I guess. But I hope you didn't do that on my behalf because I won't be attending any more services at the Way."

"You say that now," resumed Curt in a smug tone. "You're still emotional, just give it some time."

With a wry grin on my face I gestured toward my bed. "Fellas, you're still not getting it," I said. "Please have a seat." After they sat down, I plopped down on a small throw-down rug and leaned back against my wall locker. "Let me try explaining another way. First of all, I'm not angry nor do I feel any regret or sorrow. This is one of those rare occasions when two parties just need to go their separate ways. Since no one is 'wrong' no apologies are required. In laymen's terms: it's just time for me to move on."

Seeing their puzzled expressions, I shook my head.

"Both of y'all heard the testimony I gave about what happened in Jersey—the Holy Spirit moved! If you can't see God's hand in that, I don't know what else to tell ya."

"So, what're you gonna do now, Tak?" asked Jon, "just backslide back into sin?"

Hearing his generic, brainwashed response made me exhale in disgust. "Just because a person doesn't attend *your* church that automatically means they're some kind of evil heretic? What about all the righteous people in California, Calcutta...or Timbuktu for that matter?" Squinting my eyes, I stared at them quizzically. "Brothers, we're nearing the end of the twentieth century. Is it just me, or does this orthodox logic sound a bit outdated? Perhaps even ridiculous? Honestly, I believe I've evolved beyond the church system."

"What's that supposed to mean?" inquired Crawley in

a tone of defiance.

"Curt, why was Jesus teaching his disciples? So, they could follow behind him forever? No! In that case, why would he bother to teach them at all? *You* taught me that!" Standing up, I summoned patience before resuming. "Even had Jesus been spared his crucifixion, the plan all along had been for the disciples to spread the word themselves. That's why they had to become 'the Christ' too. Well, yesterday, I got publicly crucified and now I feel I've graduated into Apostle-hood."

"Here you go again with your *Lone Wolf McQuade* type thinking—" Crawley began before I cut him off.

"More like *Kwai Chang Caine* leaving the Shaolin Temple, nah I mean?" Stating this with a grin, I then thumbed my nose to mimic Darrel's imitation of *Bruce Lee*.

"You think this is some kind of joke?" Crawley snapped, approaching me in an aggressive manner.

Jon immediately stepped between us. "Curt calm down!" he reprimanded.

Perhaps it was self-centered of me not to consider how my leaving would affect my brothers. For over two years, Curt, Jon, Chill, Reggie, along with a few others, comprised my family but Curt and Jon were the elders. So, accordingly, Curt was expressing his fraternal 'tough-love' the only way he knew how—he wanted to fight!

It took a few seconds for Jon to push Curt away from me. Once Jon was certain the situation was under control he looked at me but continued speaking to Curt. "Tak already knows Jesus for himself so he has to make this decision alone." Following a final glance at both of us, he released Curt's arm and walked to the door. "There's nothing else for us to do here—let's go."

As I watched the two reasons why I got saved walk out the door, I wondered about their futures. Would they ever figure out they were being pimped? A better question was: were they willing to become pimps themselves in order to head their own churches? I never saw either one of them again.

Dealing with the folks I had prayed with to get saved proved a bit more challenging. The first time I spoke to Chill and Reggie they maintained their poise but their disappointment was evident. Before we ended our conversation, they encouraged me to visit Eugene and Darrel. "Just for some closure," Chill emphasized and I agreed. So, on Friday evening I drove to *Quincy's* knowing everyone would be there following their witnessing session. My timing was impeccable. As I arrived Reggie's pick-up was just entering the parking lot, with Chill in the passenger seat and the two brothers riding in back.

"Wassup strangers?" I yelled through my open window.

It took them a second to locate where the voice was coming from.

"It's Tak!" yelled Darrel, pointing at where I was parking my car. With that, both boys leapt out of the truck while it was still moving and ran toward me.

"It's good to see you guys!" I said, stepping out of the car to give both youngsters a hug. After Chill and Reggie came over, we got in the Jetta. While I was rehashing the same message, I said to Jon and Curt, Eugene started crying.

"Pastor B gets the *gasface!*" he uttered between sobs.

"Me and Gene think Pastor Bart was wrong," said Darrel, co-signing his little brother's sentiments. "So, we decided we wanna go with you."

"Yeah!" agreed Eugene.

"Go with me?" I asked with an astonished grin. "Go with me where? To Rutgers?"

Realizing the absurdity of his statement Darrel cast his eyes downward, looking embarrassed.

Recalling Curt's confrontational behavior a few days ago, I did not underestimate the possibility this visit had to likewise become emotional; thus, before it had a chance to become a tear-jerker I wanted to get going.

"Brothers," I said looking around the car. "I love you back…I really do." Then I twisted around in my seat and extended my hand. It took Eugene a second to wipe his face with his shirt before he grasped it. Once his hand was in mine, I resumed. "The time comes when we have to stop being boys and stand up to be men. To do this, you'll have to choose your own path just as I'm following mine because no two men's paths are the same." Releasing Eugene's hand, I scanned the faces in the car again. "I learned so much during my time at the Way and I'm eternally grateful for this. But now it's time for me to leave. If any of you decide to leave that's your decision…but you need to do it because it's *your* time to leave and not because you're blindly following behind someone—even out of love."

Praying and fasting for three days and nights—just like Jonah did in the belly of that fish—I did not have any remorse or guilt come Sunday morning. Sleeping soundly until ten o'clock, I woke up feeling brisk and refreshed. After enjoying a lavish brunch, I had a constructive day in the weight room, at the pool, and finally on the track. Following a prolonged sauna session, I showered and went to the mess hall.

I remember that dinner being the most delicious meal I had ever eaten there. Considering it was the same food we always had, perhaps my level of appreciation reflected my mind-state: I was super-relaxed after a good work-out; plus, I did not have to worry about being late for the evening service. When the mess sergeant insisted I try some sweet-potato pie, I declined, wanting to get back to my room for a Bible study before taking my nightly run.

On my way to my building, I spotted Reggie, Chill, and a third guy walking toward the parking lot. As we made eye contact, I recognized the frail, white man with them: it was Pastor Bart. *Just my luck!* I smiled, realizing had I opted for a slice of pie I would have missed them altogether.

After greeting the pastor in accordance to his age and position, he proposed we gather in Reggie's room for a talk. Once everyone entered the room next to mine, Reggie and Pastor Bart sat on Reggie's bed while Chill and I squatted on the floor. Within minutes, I grew weary listening to the pastor's softened version of the witch-hunt sermon he gave on Wednesday. As my eyelids grew heavy, he asked me a question.

"Takuan, why do think God commanded the whale to eat Jonah?"

"I dunno." Although I had studied the parable over-and-over, I felt no inclination to debate.

Chill, knowing what the pastor wanted to hear, did his best to fill the void. "Was it because Jonah was being disobedient?"

"Exactly. And how do we know that's true?" Seeming agitated at my lack of participation, Pastor Bart again encouraged me to respond. "What do you think Takuan?"

"I dunno." Again, responding thus, I just wanted him to say his piece so I could get on with my life.

The pastor, realizing he was losing me, quickly answered his own question. "Because the whale spit Jonah out exactly where God had told him to go."

"*Wrong!*" I blurted out, completely forgetting my vow to remain silent. The truth was: I was sick-and-tired of him changing God's words to serve his needs and I couldn't take it anymore.

"What's wrong?" snapped the pastor.

"The Bible doesn't say that," I stated emphatically.

"Of course, it does, in the Book of Jonah—"

"No, it doesn't," I repeated. "I've read that chapter a thousand times since Wednesday. It says: *The LORD spoke to the fish, and it vomited Jonah onto dry land.*"

"Yes. And that dry land was the wicked city, Ninevah."

"If that's true Pastor," I countered just as quickly. "Why does God tell Jonah in the *next* chapter—and I quote: *'Arise, go to Nineveh and preach the message I tell you.'* He says go to 'Ninevah' all over again; so obviously he was somewhere else." Not satisfied my point was clear, I explained further. "For instance, if God were to say to you right now: 'Pastor Bart, arise and go to North Carolina,' wouldn't that be strange? Wouldn't you tell Him you're already here?"

"Takuan, I think you're missing the point—"

"No, I'm not; I'm onnit-dog-gonnit! The point is you have a habit of changing the Bible's parables to suit your needs." When he tried to interrupt for a third time, I silenced him with a wave of my hand the same way my sister-in-law muted Ken. "Just a minute Pastor, this is important. You taught us we had a personal relationship with Jesus—*personal!*"

Taken aback by my assertive stance, the clergyman swapped methods by agreeing. "Yes, I did."

"Well sir, you have a personal relationship with your wife, don't you?"

"Why yes, of course I do," Pastor Bart reluctantly responded, appearing uncomfortable.

"Pastor, if your wife has something to tell you—something important—would she ask someone else to give you the message? Or would she just tell you herself?" Without waiting for his response, I poured it on. "Sir, what happened to *my* ability to talk to the Creator? Don't you preach that? That through Jesus I can ask Him whatever is on my heart? The strange thing is when I put those teachings—or should I say *your* teachings—into practice unmistakable signs and wonders occurred. So much, in fact, the end result was I got exactly what I asked for. Not only have I been accepted into Rutgers without having my application reviewed, I'm also on the football team—without a tryout! Think about it: my new coach, right now, has *never* seen me catch a football or run a pass-pattern…but he allowed me on his team. While these decisions were being made, the Holy Spirit's presence was so tangible both counselors assisting me thanked God several times themselves. And peep this: one of them claims to be an Atheist!"

"Just a minute Takuan—"

"Pastor, please allow me to finish," I interrupted right back. Just as it is written in *Acts 2:43*: *'Everyone kept feeling a sense of awe; and many wonders and signs were taking place.'* But what happens when I return here and tell y'all—

GAIKOKUJIN - The Story

the Christians who supposedly believe in God's miraculous ways—about these heavenly signs and wonders?" Pausing here I made eye-contact with everyone in the room. "You give me some tired story about Jonah and the Whale!"

Pastor Bart stared in silence for a couple seconds before abdicating. "Takuan," he finally said, "I'll pray for you."

"And Pastor, I too will pray for you…good night!"

From Student to Master

Compulsive behavior is a personality trait. In my final year of the Army, I was breaking a mean sweat three-times-a-day exercising. If you add in my nightly runs, which occurred around five-times-a-week, a pattern of obsessive-compulsive behavior can be identified. Being devoted to honing my mind, body, and spirit, I considered my daily regimen to be healthy—and it was. But it was also addictive. For almost two years, this character flaw remained hidden behind my religious fervor; so, once I severed ties with the Way I started spending even more time at the gym than before.

Pairing up with Carney almost every night for the next six weeks, my strength seemed to double overnight. Each evening at eighteen-forty-five sharp, we exchanged a pound at the gym's entrance before going to the weight room together. During this walk the master would announce the evening's schedule, along with whatever improvements I needed to make.

"Tonight, we're working on our chest. Oh yeah before I forget, Tak, when you're on the bench don't fidget around so much," Jerome instructed. "Just lay down and get set.

Remember, the goal is to relax your entire body except the muscles you're working on…that's where you focus straight *fiya* into!"

"That's what I've been doing," I protested.

"*What?* That's bullshit!" Carney replied, shrinking his face into a frown. "Man, if you're not wiggling your toes, you're repositioning your legs three or four times—all this unnecessary movement wastes energy. Tonight, we're gonna work on efficiently channeling your *chi*."

In order to improve my technique on the bench-press I tried various tips that I picked up from the veteran weightlifters. According to Carney, the key adjustment which resulted in my becoming a worthy partner was closing my eyes and tucking my legs in the air. "You finally learned how to focus," he had told me. This subtle adjustment proved crucial to prepare for the hard hits my body was going to receive on the gridiron in a couple months. Now, back in student-mode, I observed my *sensei* closely; my goal always being to match his intensity. On the day I pressed three-hundred-seventy-five pounds—which was more than I had ever expected to lift in this lifetime—my confidence shot through the roof! The fact I had never heard Carney brag about topping the mighty four-hundred plateau made me suspect I was breathing down his neck.

"Alright y'all…" Having completed a set, Carney sat up on the bench wearing a grin. "As you can see, the stakes have risen to three-eighty so you rooks, got two choices: either push it up—or shut it down and get off my bench!"

Following his announcement, the five members in our workout dwindled to only three. Jerome, Buswell, and me.

"So," Jerome barked as he confronted us with his hands on both hips. "One of you grasshoppers think you're ready to snatch the pebble from my hand?"

"Oh no, of course not Teacher, for we could never hope to measure up to your supreme excellence!" As *Buzz* ceremoniously bowed with both palms joined in front of his chest, the rest of us shared a laugh at his Tibetan monk-like sarcasm.

Seconds later, I laid down on the bench, closed my eyes, and took a deep breath. "Let there be strength in peace and peace in my heart." Having recited the mantra which summoned my warrior-spirit, I was now ready. "One, two, three, lift!" After Carney helped with the initial thrust, I held the bar for a moment to confirm I could control the weight. Then we, together, slowly lowered it to my chest. "Okay you can let go."

Following a second to gather myself, I pushed from deep within; and in one mighty heave my elbows locked. Sitting up, I looked at Jerome and winked before rising to my feet and slapping Buzz on the back. "You gottit," I encouraged while stepping passed him on my way to the water fountain.

"Oh no doubt," Buzz replied, staring at the sagging bar.

Although I played it cool, in reality, I was absolutely ecstatic. From across the room I watched Buzz struggle for almost ten seconds before eventually getting the weight up— with minimal assistance from his spotter. As they returned the bar to its resting place, I approached Carney. "I think I'm ready for a shot at the title," I said with a grin. "When're you leaving for Ranger School?"

Upon hearing my question, Jerome busted-out laughing. "Pretty good! What're you clairvoyant?"

"Whaddya talking about?"

As Carney replied he wiped his face with a blue and white towel. "I'm not rolling out until next month but two hours ago Top told me I gotta pull detail on Pope Air Force Base, starting on Monday 'til my departure date. So, after this weekend the next time any of y'all see me, I'll be a Ranger—*hoo-ah!*"

"And you were gonna sneak away without saying anything, huh?" I joked.

"Hey, name one champion in any sport who begs challengers to square-off against him," he declared with a frown. "Sheeit, one of you sissies might wet your pants."

Once some bystanders heard what we were discussing, the crowd came to life.

"Wassup y'all?" yelled Buswell. "I'm taking all bets that Amaru is gonna take Carney out—who doesn't think so? Put your money where your mouth is!"

As the spectators dwelled on Buzz's proposition, he and another guy added a thin plate to each side of the barbell, which was already drooping on both sides.

"This is three-ninety," Thomas announced. "Who's up first?"

"Hold-up, y'all getting way ahead of yourselves!" Frantically waving his muscular arms, Carney interrupted the bookie and his agent. "This contest, bet and all, was engraved in stone almost a year ago. So, Buzz, you need to buzz your 'Johnny Come Lately' ass back over there and take a chill-pill."

Buswell, looking unfazed, countered in a loud voice. "Translation y'all: Carney's scared!"

Hearing this, the crowd busted-out laughing.

"Nah, nah, he's right," I interjected on Jerome's

behalf. "We're working-out now; so, we can't have the competition today." Looking over at Carney I then repeated my previous question. "So, when's your last day in here?"

Grinning in his usual way, Jerome shrugged his shoulders before giving pounds all around. "Let's do it this weekend, cool?" Without waiting for a response, he glanced at the clock on the wall. "Gotta go pick-up wifey right now, so I'll see y'all Saturday at nineteen-hundred hours—be there or be square. Oh, and by the way," he grabbed his towel and looked around the room. "This ain't just about beating Amaru—anyone here is welcome to lose."

Minutes after Jerome walked out, some guys were still chuckling at his candid remarks while others mumbled about whether or not they planned to be here this weekend. During the confusion, I approached the sagging barbell, believing everyone's attention was occupied. Even though three-eighty went up quite easily, I was having my doubts about three-ninety. Buswell, always one to be observant, caught me in my moment of uncertainty.

"Hold up y'all…" Hearing this, everyone turned to look at Buzz. "I thought Carney was shook," he continued, "but now Amaru's over there looking a little *chicken-shit-ish* himself!"

In spite of taking offense to the suggestion, I had to laugh at his choice of words before blasting back. "Buzz, you over there sounding like a guy who wants to put-in some work," I replied in a challenging tone. "Let's do it right now, me and you. You're up first!"

Once the street brawler from Gary, Indiana was challenged, he wasted no time before lying down. After he looked ready, I assumed the spotter's position at the head of the bench. "Step off!" Buzz lashed out, perhaps in an effort to gas himself up. "Don't touch nothing—I got this!"

"Alright Hercules," I said, taking a step back. "You're halfway there, you got the talking part done."

By the confident way Buzz snatched the bar from its resting place and controlled it down to his chest, I thought he was going to lift it. However, no sooner than it began rising did the bar stop—at about the midway point—and from there it took a rapid nose-dive. Even after the bar fell onto Buzz's chest, I remained standing two paces away with my arms folded.

"You better try harder because you don't need any help, remember?" I teased.

"*Stop...playin'...Amaru*!" Buzz muttered in a barely audible tone. It was painfully obvious he was suffering under the massive load.

"Okay, okay lemme see what I can do." Saying this with a chuckle, I stepped forward and grabbed the bar. "Are you ready? Lift!" After we failed to move the weight even an inch, two more guys ran over to help. With me in the middle and one person at each end, it still required an extreme effort to guide the barbell back to its resting place.

Once the bar was secure, for the next five minutes, we laughed and told jokes at Buzz's expense. I was still imitating his strained facial expressions when I approached the bench. "Hey *Kool Herc*," I teased once more, "I ain't as hard as you, gimme a spot."

When Buzz stepped forward, I lay down and got set. "Let there be strength in peace, and peace in my heart," I chanted before closing my eyes. "Ready, one, two, three—lift!"

For a couple seconds I held the bar in the air before

we slowly lowered it to my chest. "Okay, let go," I directed. With my eyes still shut, I felt enough pressure on my chest to crush my sternum. While I gathered myself for one mighty explosion the other activity in the room came to a standstill as onlookers moved closer to watch.

"Come on Amaru!" cheered one spectator.

"You gottit!" screamed another.

Once my mind was clear, I took a deep breath and focused 'straight fiya' into my chest—and in one fluid motion the weight moved. After locking my elbows, I opened my eyes just in time to see Buswell grab the barbell, and together, we guided it onto its resting place.

Sitting up, I was surprised to find so many looks of astonishment staring back at me. "Yo, did I lift that by myself?"

Showdown

On Friday afternoon, Carney climbed the stairs to my PLL office. "Three-ninety, I heard—congratulations!"

"Ssup Sergeant Carney." Although I greeted him casually and even gave him a pound, I made sure to address him by his rank. "It was unofficial," I said with a smirk. "Buswell might've helped me."

"Nah, Thomas said he watched. No one helped you," replied Carney in a confident tone.

"Well I'm not so sure. Anyway, that's what tomorrow's for, right?"

Although this was nothing but a friendly rivalry amongst a few weightlifting buddies, the atmosphere was at a championship pitch by Saturday afternoon. It seemed like everyone in my brigade knew about the contest. When a non-descript group of guys in the mess hall addressed me like I was a celebrity, I was more than a little surprised.

"Excuse us, Specialist Amaru," one of them said, stepping into my path. "You don't know us, but good-luck later against that show-off, Carney."

"Thanks fellas," I responded before shaking all five of their hands.

Arriving to the gym a few minutes before seven o'clock, I glimpsed Jerome in a brand new red-white-and-blue, spandex one-piece. Seeing him in this Captain America get-up—even though he looked absolutely ridiculous—the only thing I was thinking about is how much I owed him. Just as Curt had set the pace during our runs, my steady progress in the weight room had been thanks to Jerome's efforts as much as my own. Two days ago, after I lifted three-ninety, Buzz and Thomas told me this was also Carney's max. Upon getting this news I realized, for the first time, I felt uncomfortable about surpassing my teacher. After all, my goal had been to catch Carney—not pass him.

Standing at the entrance of the weight room, I considered my next move before anyone noticed my presence. Feeling a tap on my shoulder, I looked to my left and found Buzz standing there grinning.

"Amaru, you okay?" he asked, "why you standing over here?"

"I thought I forgot my towel so I was deciding if I should go check one out or not," I fibbed, "but I just noticed it's right here in my bag." Having said this, I pulled out a white towel and showed it to him.

As Buzz and I entered, Jerome saw our reflections in the mirror. "Yo Amaru, how you like my new outfit?" he yelled across the room. "I bought it three months ago specifically for the purpose of spanking your ass!" Having made this bold declaration—and while he still had everyone's attention—Carney pivoted sideways and placed his right hand on his left wrist before rotating his upper-body to the left. Making sure to keep his shoulders back and left leg slightly bent so his toes barely touched the ground, he completed what body-builders call the 'side-chest' pose. Taking a deep breath to inflate his chest, he then smiled. "Figure if I gotta embarrass my boy," he said looking at my reflection, "I might as well look fly while I'm doing it."

Seconds later, I approached Carney and a few others to greet them. As the room was teeming with comments and conjecture, I did my best to ignore the stares. While I stretched in silence, my fellow contestants, led by Carney, did a warm-up set one at a time. On my set, I was still lost in thought, contemplating what I should do.

"Alright," stated Jerome, let's kick this party off at three-seventy-five…cool?" Once everyone agreed, Carney, in his skin-tight costume, lay down and readied himself.

At this point, I knew there was no turning back.

During the first two rounds, all four participants lifted the weight with no problem. After pushing up three-eighty-five in convincing fashion on his third go-around, Jerome jumped-up talking trash.

"Okay, now we're gonna see exactly where you boys are at!" he stated in a cocky tone.

As in the case of most teacher-student relationships, Carney knew our limits quite well but we could only speculate on how high his ceiling extended. Accordingly, it came as no surprise that after his rant both Buzz and Sullivan failed to make the next cut.

"Two suckers down and one to go," Jerome jeered the departing contestants, even smacking Buzz on the butt, before turning his attention to me. With an emphatic wave of his hand, he gestured for me to lie down. "Aight Tak, show me what you got."

He did not stop talking until I readied myself to lift. *Three-eighty-five…three-ninety…three-ninety-five…*

Carney struggled for so long I honestly did not think he would be able to get it up. And for this reason, when he eventually locked his elbows I must say I was impressed. As he stood up, he was uncharacteristically silent. This got my attention. Absent of his usual grin he did not look like himself. Seeing his stony countenance brought to mind my glimpse of Curt's harried appearance while he and I were staggering down Ardennes toward the finish-line. With this in mind, I was looking forward to likewise seeing Jerome tread in deep, unknown waters.

After lying down on the bench, I smiled. "Is that a new max?" I asked.

"I don't know what you're grinning at," the master chastised, glaring down from his standing position. "You better save that energy!"

Little did he suspect the reason for my smile was because I had found the solution to my dilemma. After pushing-up three-ninety-five in one swift motion, I walked to the water fountain and gulped down mouthfuls of water. As Buzz and Sullivan added a plate to each side, I reflected on how far the three of us had come.

By the time I returned, Carney was preparing himself to lift.

Chiseled into his features was the single-minded

resoluteness a warrior exhibits who is about to engage his enemy. Since no one had ever seen Carney pushed to his limit, to say everyone was curious would be an understatement. And the master did not disappoint. After extending his arms three-quarters of the way, he only needed to lock his elbows. For several seconds, I watched Carney as he teetered along the border which separates victory from defeat before gravity finally had its way, defying his heroic effort.

Once Sullivan guided the bar to its resting place, Carney sprang to his feet completely un-vexed. Grinning from ear-to-ear, he turned toward me and pointed at the barbell. "Grasshopper, that's four-hundred-fucking-pounds!" Then, flipping the same hand over and extending his fingers, he revealed a small stone in his palm. "If you bad enough," he challenged, "snatch the pebble from my hand!"

As you might imagine, the whole room erupted in laughter.

This is why I respected Carney so much. With his title on the line he never switched-up his game; he was the same, confident, colorful personality we all knew and loved. The truth is many people talk a good game until it's time for the rubber to hit the road—then they're either nowhere to be found, or, if they do show up, they got a plethora of excuses to rationalize their lack of success. Considering this, I recalled something Jerome once told me when we first started training together: "Tak, the only thing I fear in life is growing old and looking back…" Pausing here, he drilled his eyes into mine. "And wondering what would've happened if I'd just had the balls to be a fuckin' man."

In spite of the disappointing groans from the

bystanders following my failed-attempt, I was pleased to end in a tie. Standing up, I exchanged pounds with Buzz and Sullivan before hugging Jerome. "Amaru," he uttered with a hint of skepticism once I had released him, "this ain't over. When I get back from Ranger School we'll do it again, okay?"

"Okay," I replied before adding: "do your *thang* at Fort Benning—and God bless you!"

Even though Jerome, just like Buzz and Sullivan, had extended his fist to give me a pound, for some reason, I was suddenly overcome by a feeling of sadness; so, I decided to hug him. At the time, I attributed my extreme emotion to nothing more than a side-effect of the tremendous adrenaline rush which accompanies any physical competition of this magnitude. That being said, is it possible this was my intuition telling me to embrace him?

At any rate, this turned out to be the last time I ever laid eyes on Sgt. Jerome Carney a.k.a. King of the Weight Room.

"Muthafucka, I told you about calling me nigga!" Yelling this in anger, Smith came toward me but before he could cover the ground separating us, Davis and Stock grabbed him.

"Let him go," I said, feigning a yawn.

As they struggled to hold onto Smith, I leaned back against a deuce-and-a-half and folded my arms. Watching the three of them tussle, I grinned at what I believed to be nothing more than Smith putting on a macho-simulated performance. In all honestly, I hoped he would somehow escape their grasp so I would be forced to defend myself. For the past several months, Smith had been slandering me behind my back and I was sick and tired of hearing about it. So, when

Sgt. Will got sent away for a few days this created the perfect opportunity for a confrontation.

"Let him go," I calmly reiterated. "He ain't gonna do nothing but run his mouth. Stock, let him go."

Stock and Davis looked surprised at my cavalier attitude.

"Yeah lemme go!" screamed Smith like a raving lunatic.

It was not until Sgt. Boswell, along with two other mechanics, ran over to restrain him when I took a good, second look at Smith. "Uh-oh," Billy nonchalantly sprinkled salt on his open wound, "you really wanna get busy, huh?" Asking this, I walked closer and stopped a few feet from where he was still wrestling with the mechanics. "Tell you what Smith, if you're really in need of an ass-whooping, rest-assured there's one waiting in the barracks one floor above you. You know where I live. Knock three times."

"Stock, get Amaru outta here!" screamed Sgt. Boswell.

*1989 was a pivotal year in Hip Hop. It marked the official reintroduction of the dirtiest, the filthiest…the most bigoted word of them all: **NIGGER!** The modern adaptation of the infamous N-word was pronounced 'nigga' and the spokesperson for this movement was the rap group appropriately named 'NWA,' or 'Niggaz with Attitude.' I think most would agree that Easy-E, Dr. Dre, Ice Cube, MC Ren,* *and DJ Yella embodied the name of their group.*

While many inner-city youth, claimed the updated version of the controversial expression was a term of endearment, others in the black community vehemently rejected this proposal. Personally, I never thought about any self-hatred implications; it was simply a case of using the lingo I had picked-up along Murchison Road. Both Smith and Davis used the word constantly amongst themselves; so, by implying I was not 'black enough' to use it they unknowingly tapped my Jap complex.

Again, it is amazing Smith and I never came to blows.

"Good morning Specialist, can I have a word with you?"

Prior to formation on his first day back from Ft. Jackson, my platoon sergeant stopped me on my way to the company headquarters.

"Welcome back Sergeant Will. Of course," I replied.

Watching how my supervisor abruptly concluded his conversation with the supply sergeant—that plus his tone when he greeted me—I deduced he already heard about the Smith incident.

"Okay Sergeant Medina, will do, talk to ya later." After shaking the NCO's hand, Sgt. Will turned toward me. "Specialist, let's go over there."

Looking in the direction he was pointing, I spotted a bench about twenty yards away.

While we were walking, he asked a question. "Did you take that 5k generator over to the airfield yesterday?"

Because I was certain he was going to grill me about Smith, his inquiry took me by surprise. "Umm...well Sergeant, you mean the one Sergeant Boz asked me to deliver?"

"Yes."

"Actually, I was planning to handle that first thing this morning—after formation," I replied, trying to avoid responding directly. The truth was the errand had slipped my mind; somehow, he seemed to know this.

"Amaru, are you still a Christian?"

"Yes Sergeant, you know that."

"Well, I also know that lying is a sin."

By the blank, poker face he displayed, I was thrown even more off balance.

"You forgot, again didn't you?" Sgt. Will added before I could gather myself.

"Pardon me, Sergeant?"

"Specialist, you heard me loud and clear. Answer the question!"

Considering Sgt. Will just returned from South Carolina, I was wondering how he even knew about this. "Ah, umm…Sergeant I apologize. Delivering that generator wasn't listed as a high priority, so when I called the airfield and PFC Arnold told me they had four serviceable 5k's, I thought delivering it this morning would be okay." Forced into making a statement on the fly this was the best I could come up with. And for this reason. I was astonished my platoon sergeant busted-out laughing.

"Amaru, I bet you play a mean game of chess," Sgt. Will said once he had regained his composure. "But this time I got you in check." Seeing his smile vanish, I now understood why he had chosen an area away from prying ears for our meeting: he wanted to speak in direct, down-to-earth terms. "Now if I keep questioning you I could eventually box you into checkmate but I don't have time for this childish crap—and neither do you!"

While not quite emitting anger, Sgt. Will's visage was deadly serious. Confused, I remained quiet.

"*Amaru!*" he yelled.

"Yes Sergeant," I responded in earnest.

"For the last month the only thing you've been thinking about is the results of your early-out application. Specialist, I understand you got a lot riding on this decision but until we get word that you're officially outta here, I gotta manage the motorpool with the cards I've been dealt. And that includes having a PLL clerk who follows—or should I say *remembers*—his orders."

"I understand Sergeant," I replied, trying to cut his lecture short.

"Shut up until I'm finished."

"Clear Sergeant."

"And you *don't* understand…at least not yet. Amaru, you used to be the most reliable guy I had around here. If Sergeant Boswell and I both needed to be away from the motorpool, I felt fine leaving you in charge." Shaking his head, he cast his eyes downward. "I could never do that now."

"Of course, you could, Sergeant," I declared with confidence.

"Are you kidding? So, you can pick fights with Smith and Davis?"

"Nah, that's not fair Sergeant. You haven't even heard my side of the story."

"*What?*" he snapped in outrage, "your side of the

story?"

Since Sgt. Will was normally calm and even-keeled, it was perplexing to feel his wrath. In fact, this was only the second time my platoon sergeant ever raised his voice at me. The other was when I had taken upon myself to skip a mandatory night-training exercise, never considering the rest of my platoon would mindlessly copy my actions. "You don't understand the influence you have on the guys around you," he had scolded. And like that time, I perceived the reason for his disappointment was deeper than just my involvement in a simple argument.

Taking a deep breath, Sgt. Will looked skyward and exhaled in an effort to calm himself. "Sit down," he then muttered in a low tone, "there's something we need to discuss; something important."

I took a seat on the bench while my platoon sergeant remained standing.

"Amaru, what do you think would've happened if you and Smith had fought?" As I opened my mouth to respond he added, "I'm not talking about who would've won the damn fight, you, stupid jack-ass! What do you think Colonel Packer would've said? Is beating Smith up worth jeopardizing your chance to play football this season?"

"Sergeant, I have a right to defend myself—"

"Shut up!" Sgt. Will commanded, looking perplexed. Removing his cap, he wiped his face with a towel before resuming. "You got a lot to learn about how the world operates. If you have a blotch—any kind of negative stain— on your record, you can forget about getting out of here early. And don't you have to report to camp in August?"

"Yes Sergeant. I also have to attend an academic

summer program in July."

"And you're willing to trade all that in just to win a meaningless pissing contest?"

His reference to a 'meaningless pissing contest' jolted my memory back to the example demonstrated by Sgt. Rogers in Air-Assault School.

"Amaru, you're an exception to the rule…you know, that right?" Asking this, Sgt. Will paused to stare at me. "I've been thinking of the best phrase to explain your situation, and the only thing I can come up with is: you're a 'one out-of-a-million' type story."

"Excuse me, Sergeant."

"In my sixteen years in the motor pool—*sixteen years!*" he exclaimed, flipping his fingers to simulate counting. "I've seem 'em come and I've seem 'em go. Everybody getting discharged has some sort of master plan of how they're going to 'make it' on the outside. A few months later, we always hear the same stories about those guys: they're either in jail, re-enlisting, or dead-broke and thinking about re-enlisting. But you…" Sgt. Will pointed in my face. "You're the first person I've seen who's getting out on his own terms. Meaning, you actually have a *sane* plan to succeed in the civilian world."

Nodding my head, I acknowledged his wisdom.

"Everybody knows this new president—with his old-ass looking wife—ain't trying to help black people either," my NCOIC resumed. "But that doesn't matter because not only do you possess the natural ability required, until recently, you conducted yourself in such a first-class manner there was no doubt you would be successful."

"Until recently, Sergeant?"

"Yeah, until recently—did I stutter?" Asking this in an

aggressive tone, Sgt. Will again pierced my pupils with another expressionless stare. "Nowadays, you got your head so far up in the clouds I can see the stretch marks on your neck from here!"

I appreciated Sgt. Will's forthright manner. So much in fact, I forced myself to keep a straight face and not smile at how corny his one-liner was.

"By the way," Sgt. Will returned to his usual voice, "you still wanna go out to the field with Stock and Buswell?"

"You mean for Operation Golden Seal?" I asked surprised.

"Yeah, I normally don't allow both of my E-4s out of the motor pool at the same time, but since you ain't worth a quarter these days anyway, I might as well let Rodriguez practice being the PLL clerk." Winking at me, he then cracked a smile. "If your request is approved, you'll be leaving at the end of the month, right?"

"Somewhere around then Sergeant," I responded.

"Yeah, I've put it off long enough," Sgt. Will replied, sitting down beside me. "Rod's gotta get his feet wet while you're still here for him to ask questions. Amaru, go out in the woods and relax, you hear me? Don't think about college or anything stressful for the next week—that's an order."

"Clear Sergeant...and thanks."

Chapter 8: Operation Golden Seal

"Gentlemen, the United States Special Forces carry out five types of missions: counterterrorism, foreign internal defense, special reconnaissance, direct action, and my favorite of the bunch—unconventional warfare. During the five nights we actively engage the enemy, we'll be concentrating on the last three." Stopping here, our operation team-leader scanned each soldier's face before resuming his briefing. "Normally an infiltration team consists of twelve soldiers: a captain, a warrant officer, and ten NCOs. Each sergeant is an expert in one or more of the five, combat categories. For those who did not review the information disseminated to your company about this operation, the five categories are: medics, commo, weapons, demolitions, and field ops."

Having been assigned to this FTX at the last moment, I did not have time to go over the material; so, I was grateful for the major's detailed introduction. Major Brackett was a slim Caucasian with freckles that were barely visible due to a sun-bronzed complexion. Slightly taller than me, his curly brown hair was tinted with grey, especially along the edges.

"In case you haven't noticed yet," he continued, standing next to the long, wooden table where we sat. "There are a few differences between the model I just described and our team." After pointing out the obvious, that our team was comprised of five lower-enlisted soldiers, one NCO, and the major himself, he went on to explain something interesting. He said this mishap had been orchestrated on purpose in order to manufacture a dire situation which often occurs in the heat of battle. "In actual combat, it's not always possible to proceed according to the template. Men, this is simply because…shit happens. And believe you me, when the feces hits, the fan for real, a PFC could suddenly find himself thrust into an NCO's role." The major paused to allow his words to resonate. "I missed Vietnam by a couple years but I got a chance to whet my fangs in Iran, Colombia, and most recently in Panama. By the way, you know we're about to stomp on that cockroach, *Noriega*, don't you?"

After a round of enthusiastic barks erupted from everyone except me, the major resumed his briefing.

"Golden Seal is a 'war games' operation designed for evaluation purposes. Not only am I evaluating you; my superiors are evaluating me. And together, all of us here will be evaluating our simulated-enemy for this mission." Stopping here, the SF officer took a sip from his canteen. "Tomorrow morning, three hundred National Guardsmen from Florida are scheduled to arrive."

"The National Guard?" Stock whined, sounding disappointed. "We're going up against a bunch of weekend warriors?"

"Did you *not* hear me Specialist?" the major replied sounding pissed, "I said three hundred soldiers versus seven! And don't forget, those 'weekend warriors' went through basic and AIT just like you did. Looking down your nose at them—especially given our overwhelming disadvantage in numbers—is a sure way to get pinned behind the eight-ball once the shit starts flying. You understand where I'm going

222

with this Stockton?"

"Yes, I do sir. And I apologize—"

"Not interested in apologies. Just keep your mouth shut unless you got something important to say. And that goes for all of you, gottit?"

"Clear sir," we answered in unison.

"Now, where was I?" It took another second for our team-leader to stop glaring at Stock and regain his train of thought. "Oh yeah, evaluations. Gentlemen, your names were not selected from a hat with a blindfold on. On these types of high-speed operations, we only accept soldiers who've been personally recommended by their commanders. For those who are able to employ the tactics presented in the following blocks of instructions, you may be asked if you're interested in being reassigned to a Special Forces unit."

Although I was no longer interested in being assigned anywhere in the military, I was committed to doing my best because I was the Son of the living God. Considering this, I grinned as Major Brackett yelled over our heads.

"Sergeant Lattimer, where ya at?" On this cue, four strapping NCOs emerged from the GP medium tent erected a few yards behind us. Like the major, one of them was wearing his green beret while the others held the headgear in their hand. Before we became too distracted by the new human stimuli, Major Brackett regained our attention. "These instructors will coach you on your objectives," he said, gesturing at the approaching foursome. "They will not participate as team members; however, they will observe and later assist with final evaluations." Then Major Brackett looked at a memo pad and yelled out, "PFC Buswell, where ya at?"

"Right here sir," replied Buzz in a professional tone.

"Go over there and find Sergeant DeJesus…he's the ugly, bald guy on the left," the major said pointing at the NCOs, who were now standing ten feet in front of us. "And allow me to add he's one helluva medic. Although his face might not be pleasant to look at, that grotesque grill has already saved dozens of soldiers' lives."

Everyone chuckled at the major's choice of words as Buzz jumped up and expeditiously moved toward the man who was raising his hand. After Sgt. Abrams, Spc. Persons, and Spc. Mullins were likewise introduced to their instructors, only me and Stock remained. Once the NCOs, along with their students, walked away Stock and I looked at each other, realizing we were going to be schooled by the major himself. No sooner had this thought crossed our minds when Major Brackett gave his confirmation.

"And you two holdovers belong to me," the major said, taking a seat on the other side of the table so he could face us. "Since neither of you have a combat MOS, you'll be serving as cavalry scouts. Either of you geniuses know what a scout does?"

Not having the faintest idea, I was glad Stock responded. "Yessir."

"Oh really?" Major Brackett said with a condescending grin. "Okay let's hear it Stockton, what does a scout do?"

"Sir, a cavalry scout is a reconnaissance specialist who works behind enemy lines to obtain vital information on the enemy in order to distribute it to his commander. The scout is the commander's eyes and ears on the battlefield—"

"Okay, okay, goddam…I see someone's been studying for the soldier-of-the-month contest."

"You asked, sir."

"Yes, I did," the major confessed in a serious tone. "And that was a mighty-fine answer, Specialist."

For the next two hours, Major Brackett explained our mission in detail. As forward scouts, we were responsible for gathering information on terrain features, enemy strength, disposition, and equipment—out there all alone by ourselves. "Ultimately, you two will be the key to either our success or failure. If the information you provide is sufficient and accurate, we'll waltz right in there and do whatever we please." Taking a sip from his canteen, the major scrutinized our faces. "Are there any questions so far?"

"No sir," we responded.

"Then let's get you two outfitted. Follow me." Standing up, the major walked toward the GP medium.

After Stock and I received our allotment of smoke bombs and simulated artillery, we returned to the table to study maps of the area our enemy would occupy the following morning. When the others returned from their private lectures, my stomach informed me it was time for lunch. Once the major released us, our team got into two jeeps. Aware this would be our last cooked meal for the next five days, we planned to enjoy this trip to the mess hall.

Following our lunch break, we took our first patrol of the area. As we advanced through the dense underbrush, I tried to imagine what three-hundred enemy troops in the foliage might look like. At intervals of about twenty yards, the major and the NCOs pointed out various landmarks to help us navigate. "Committing to memory the positioning of certain terrain features will greatly assist you—especially at night," one of the cadre instructed.

We returned to our site just as the afternoon brightness

was receding into the twilight of evening. Together, we broke down the GP medium before munching on a salty MRE for dinner. Thirty minutes later, we again separated into our groups for a final block of instruction. This was followed by a very thorough, group Q & A session. At 20:30 hours, we loaded the tent and other equipment onto a deuce. As we did so, everyone continued asking questions. By the time we waved good-bye to the four instructors, we felt confident about our mission.

Having already constructed our shelter-halves that afternoon in a secluded area selected by the major, we walked for about twenty minutes to our new headquarters before deciding to hit the sack early. After all, we had a big day ahead of us.

At sunrise when the convoy arrived, Stock and I were already hidden in the bush. Cammied-up in olive-drab war paint, we sat under a huge sycamore tree watching what seemed like an endless procession of jeeps and deuces as they converged on a clearing about fifty yards away. About an hour before, Major Brackett positioned us on opposite sides of the clearing; but minutes after he left I snuck over to Stock's side so we could get our first glimpse of the big, bad enemy together.

"Ooh, check-out that blonde!" exclaimed Stock in a hushed voice. "She has some nice tits!"

"Get your mind out the gutter…or at least keep your sinful thoughts to yourself." Once I finished reprimanding him, I looked to see if his claim was accurate or not. "I'm surprised they got so many female soldiers though."

"And good-looking ones too, woo-wee! Nothing like the *he-male*, dykes on active duty. Hey, where're you going?" Stock asked in response to seeing me stand up.

"Back over to my post."

"Why? I mean, at least wait until they get set-up. Remember, Major Brackett said it's standard procedure to perform a police-call before setting up a bivouac; so, it's too risky to go now."

I knew Stock was right. I also recalled the major emphasizing that ninety percent of our daytime objective was just to avoid detection. "Okay, but I'm gonna climb this tree to see if I can spot their movements."

"Then who am I gonna talk to? Come on Tak, stay down here," Stock begged like a whiny, little brother.

After slinging the M-16 across my back with the butt of the weapon facing upward, I grabbed the lowest boughs of the sycamore to stretch my arms while simultaneously testing their strength. "Until you elevate the level of your conversation, talk to yourself."

Before I finished the sentence, Stock was already fifteen feet below me.

"Damn Amaru, since you got saved you're no fun anymore."

By the time I pulled my torso up for a third time, the shrieks, wails, and whistles of countless creatures drowned out my motor pool mate's complaints. Although the gaps between branches where my body used to fit snugly no longer accommodated my man-sized frame, since tree-climbing was something I had done regularly as a boy, I felt at home in the sycamore—sort of like I was in my element.

For the next several minutes I spiraled upward, tier-after-tier, with the wind whipping in my ears. Concentrating on nothing but kissing the sky, I climbed until I was able to peer over the smaller trees surrounding the sycamore. By chance, I happened to find a trio of branches which were connected in such a way they formed a niche that could support my body. Leaning back and relaxing in this naturally crafted recliner made me appreciate the breathtaking scenery above.

I was soon mesmerized by the circular patterns of a hawk far off in the distance as it glided effortlessly through the cloudless sky before marveling at how the heavenly mist of the Blue Ridge Mountains seemed to melt into the horizon. Eventually, my attention was arrested by the red, orange, blue, and even purplish-black objects flittering in my periphery. Returning my gaze to the creamy brown limbs of the sycamore, I focused on the tiny birds darting to-and-fro amongst the leaves and smaller branches all around me; they seemed to be checking me out.

"Ssup y'all?" I greeted my feathered friends with a smile.

Identifying cardinals, blue-jays, sparrows, woodpeckers, and even orioles, a few of the birds were close enough to touch. As I examined their odd behavior I became nervous, never having been in such proximity to wild animals. Then something dawned on me. Instead of admiring the beauty of the wilderness or bird watching, I was supposed to be *people* watching.

With this awareness, I looked down and spotted some soldiers walking in our direction. "Stock!" I yelled before realizing how high I was.

Hurriedly climbing down several feet, I stopped

abruptly when I saw three National Guard soldiers beneath me. Two of them were sitting exactly where Stock and I had been minutes ago, with the third soldier standing alone on the other side of the tree. Feeling agitated for having allowed myself to become distracted, my first priority was to find out if they caught Stock. To achieve this, I started climbing down again. Slowly, stealthily—the entire time scanning the area from my bird's eye view—I descended until I was close enough to hear the trio's conversation but still remain camouflaged amongst my chlorophyll cousins.

"*Shhh!* Maybe we'll hear it again. I'm tellin' ya I heard a voice up in the tree," said the well-endowed woman that caught Stock's attention earlier. However, the solidly-built guy next to her was too busy ogling her boobs to take her comment seriously.

"Maybe this is a talking tree?" he replied sarcastically. "I wonder if it tells jokes?"

As the stocky GI teased her, she playfully slapped him on the chest.

Finding a thick branch, I grabbed it with both hands and lowered my chest until I was laying on it like a lounging panther. While I did so, the blonde cum-dummy peeked to ensure the third guy was not looking before reaching out to squeeze the sergeant's bulging bicep. When she moved her hand to his crotch, by the way she started licking her lips, I thought she was going to suck his dick right there.

The things people do when they believe no one is watching them.

"This is a sycamore tree, I believe," blurted out the third person. A chubby-cheeked Scandinavian with dark freckles on his oval-shaped face, he appeared to be the look-out while they shammed in the shade. "Sergeant Howell, what kind of tree was Moses talking to in the Bible?" As the pudgy soldier with brown bangs peeking from under his kevlar turned toward his squad leader, the couple quickly recovered their bearing.

"I don't know," the sergeant replied, sounding irritated. "Do I look like a reverend to you, PFC Connors?"

Just as I was getting comfortable, believing I had everyone in my field of vision, another voice burst forth spouting Biblical awareness. "Probably wasn't a sycamore, Connors. I only say this because it's called a burning 'bush,' not a tree. But there is a sycamore tree mentioned in the Bible though—it's in the Gospels." Startled, I turned my head almost one-hundred-eighty-degrees to where the female voice originated from. Not only did I find their second look-out but, to my dismay, I also discovered a hole in my leafy camouflage. Even with my glasses on I could not be sure; however, it appeared the melanin-rich sista was looking right at me.

Seeing this made me freeze like a cockroach on the kitchen counter.

"Johnson, you got another Bible story for us?" the blonde asked.

"If you want to hear another one, I do," replied Johnson.

"*Oh Christ!* Not another Bible story, how about we give the religious talk a break, huh? Johnson damn near gave us a sermon the whole trip out here," complained the E-5.

While Sgt. Howell expressed his distaste for spiritual conversations, both Johnson and Booth began walking toward Connors. As Johnson walked she kept staring at mc; but it seemed like she was not quite sure if I was real.

"You said the story's in the Gospels?" Connors broke back in, ignoring his squad leader. "That's the New Testament, right?"

"Yeah." Replying thus Johnson removed her kevlar, which revealed neatly-braided cornrows over her milk-chocolate features. Having arrived next to both Connors and Booth, she pointed at me and started to say something but when neither private looked up she ended up switching to the story they wanted to hear. "The Bible says the Messiah, *Yeshua*, visited a town named Jericho—"

"There you again with your weird pronunciations," snapped the burly sergeant as he stood up to walk to the other side of the tree. "His name's Jesus, with a J!"

"Okay Jesus," Johnson replied unfazed. Even with her brow knitted into a frown, the glimmer in her eyes made her attractive nonetheless. "In Jericho, there was a tax-collector named Zacchaeus who was despised by the townspeople. When Jesus arrived, Zacchaeus was so overcome by the Holy Spirit he wanted to see the Lord for himself; but he had a problem. Zack was a little guy, kinda like Sergeant Howell, so he couldn't see over the crowd—"

"Who you calling little? You big-ass Amazon warrior!" the E-5 shot back with a vengeance as he neared the threesome.

Sgt. Howell's sudden appearance startled Johnson, causing her to turn her head and shoot the NCO a cynical look. Recognizing my golden opportunity, in one swift motion, I maneuvered to another spot in the tree with the agility of a lesser primate. By the time Booth placed a hand over the sergeant's mouth, I was already comfortable in my new location. Now positioned behind several leafy branches, I felt confident even if they looked up I would remain hidden from their view.

"So, what happened?" Sounding impatient, Connors kept the Biblical discussion alive.

"Zack decided to climb a tree that was growing alongside the road," Johnson resumed. "It was a gigantic sycamore, just like this one." Saying this, she gestured toward the massive root base and trunk which resembled a gnarled, claw-like appendage sticking out of the ground.

"So, Johnson, you're telling me this respectable tax officer wasn't embarrassed to climb a tree in front of the same people he collected taxes from?" Connors asked.

"Exactly," Johnson emphasized. "Once Zacchaeus came face-to-face with God, his only concern was to make contact with the savior; so, he didn't have time to worry about what the townspeople might think."

"Oh, I get it!" exclaimed the airhead as if this was a new experience. "Zacchaeus' thoughts became pure, right on the spot."

"That's correct," Johnson confirmed with a grin. "The Word states: *Blessed are the pure of heart, for they shall see God.*"

For the next couple seconds everyone remained silent to reflect on the meaning of the parable.

Finally, Connors grounded everyone back to the present moment. "Why we're talking about this anyway?"

"Because," replied Sgt. Howell with a stupefied look, "Booth said the tree was talking, remember?"

"Unh-unh, that ain't what I said." As she playfully protested, she once again tapped her squad leader's arm in a seductive manner.

"She said she heard a voice up in the tree," corrected

232

Spc. Johnson before adding, "I heard it too." Then she pointed at the area I had just vacated. "And I could've sworn I saw someone up there a minute ago."

"Yeah right," the sergeant replied in a cynical tone as he scanned where Johnson was pointing. "And what did the spy up in the tree say, Johnson?"

Bringing her hand down, she said with a smirk, "Truthfully, I thought the voice yelled: 'Stop!'"

"Stop? Stop what? What's that supposed to mean?" Sgt. Howell asked.

"I dunno," Johnson shrugged. "But if I had to take a guess, maybe it was the Holy Spirit telling *you* to stop committing adultery by fraternizing with the lower-enlisted females in our company." While Sgt. Howell tried to erase his stunned look, she addressed Booth. "Girlfriend, you do know he's married, don't you?"

"With two kids to boot!" chimed in the chubby dude.

Seeing Connors then glance at Booth's breasts, I imagined he believed with the sergeant's personal life exposed he had a better shot at nailing her himself.

"At ease!" grunted Sgt. Howell as Connors and Johnson busted-out laughing.

When a soldier appeared in the distance, everyone got quiet. Seeing him wave over to them, I deduced the police-call was over. After Sgt. Howell signaled back to the messenger, he began barking loud orders to give the impression his squad had been doing something constructive.

"Make sure no ammunition magazines or other equipment is left lying around. Connors, you got everything?"

"Yes Sergeant," Connors boomed back, playing right along.

"Okay, let's fall back to the rear," commanded the

NCO.

"Clear Sergeant," the three lower-enlisted soldiers echoed as one.

As Johnson grabbed her weapon and stomped away with the others she kept looking back. This made me suspect their departure might be a ruse to trick me into coming down; so, I remained in place, not flinching a muscle while I continued scanning the terrain.

About ten minutes later, I heard Stock's voice.

"Amaru? You still up there?" he whispered.

Looking straight down, I found Stockton staring through another hole in my cover but when I did not respond he started walking away; this let me know he did not see me. *Maybe I can make myself invisible*, I joked to myself.

Swinging to a lower set of branches, I saw Stock cower down as I shook the tree on my rapid descent. Once I was close enough to jump, I unslung my M-16 and landed with it drawn. Rolling into a firing position, I was careful not to point the lethal instrument at my friend.

"You're lucky you're on my side," I said with a grin, "because I almost killed you."

"Oh yeah?" Stock responded, looking even more unimpressed than he sounded. "Well, why didn't you kill those four LEGs that were lounging underneath you for the past half-hour?"

"Only because the major ordered us to lay-low—plus I didn't want to slay your girlfriend."

"Yeah right, Amaru. You know you were up there checking out them jugs!"

◆ ◆ ◆

234

As soon as it was dark enough I went to meet Stock so that, together, we could trek to the rendezvous point which was about half-a-klik away. The meeting with our team, scheduled for 21:45 hours, was in an out-of-the-way, secluded cave that was concealed by fallen branches, hardened mud, and other such natural debris. Even though Major Brackett had shown me and Stock the cavern early that morning, prior to the arrival of the National Guard, it was so remotely hidden that, in the dark, we had to circle the area twice before I finally spotted Spc. Mullins pulling guard-duty just outside its entrance.

Realizing Mullins did not see us I silenced Stock and, instead of engaging him with the password our team-leader had furnished us with, we decided to sneak up on him.

"*Oh shit!*" Mullins blurted out in a hushed tone. "Where did you two come from? I thought I heard something so I looked over to my right. When I turned back, you guys were standing here," he said, still slightly trembling.

As the three of us entered the mouth of the cave, Major Brackett greeted me and Stock before telling the others, who were speaking in hushed tones behind him, to be quiet. After unrolling a map of the area occupied by the National Guard, he set it on the ground and told everyone to squat down around it. For the next ten minutes, Stock and I briefed the team on everything we had observed that day. While one of us was talking and pointing at the map, the other held a flashlight fitted with a red lens. Our briefing included the locations of the exit points, the length of the guards' shifts, and their patrol routes.

"Amaru, Stock, good work," stated the team-leader after hearing our reports. "Now lemme tell y'all about our change of plans." The major's new orders surprised us. "We need to scare 'em a little bit. I noticed on my rounds that they're way too relaxed…looks like a damn, college frat party. So, one of us needs to make an appearance to shake 'em up—you know, let 'em know that we're out here and we mean business." Major Brackett paused here to allow his words to sink in before emphasizing his last point. "The trick is, whoever it is can't get caught because we're not evaluating their POW procedures until the final two nights."

Considering the major had been staring at me the entire time he spoke, I imagined he wanted me to undertake the solo mission. In spite of this, Sgt. Abrams stood up to volunteer. "Sir, I'll do it. I wanna show these youngsters how it's done."

"Get back down here—*now!*" In an attempt to maintain military-silence, Major Brackett suppressed his scolding tone but it was clear he was angry. Once Sgt. Abrams returned to the squatting position with the rest of us, our team-leader finished reprimanding him. "Don't stand-up again until you're told to do so. Do you understand me, Sergeant?"

"Clear sir." Although the NCO submitted to being disciplined, it was obvious he did not comprehend what he had done.

The major, sensing this, exhaled in disgust before explaining the sergeant's gaffe. "The reason we're huddling together like this is so we can study the maps. If anyone stands up or makes any sudden moves, it allows the beams of the flashlight to escape." Having finished his explanation, the major grabbed the flashlight from Stockton and extinguished it. "If the enemy sees the light, he'll trap us in this cave and that'll make this a mighty, short operation—don't you agree,

Sergeant?"

"Yes sir, I do. It won't happen again."

"It's not supposed to happen once—maybe from one of the lower-enlisted guys," the major said before sticking his finger in Sgt. Abrams face. "But you're an NCO so let's step-it-up, Sergeant! And as to your request to be the lone insurgent, I'm afraid that's a negative because I need you here to disseminate my orders to the troops." Having vetoed the sergeant's request, our team-leader then looked at me; his features were barely visible in the sliver of moonlight seeping through the cave's entrance. "How about it Amaru?"

And make an appearance did I ever.

In spite of the razor-sharp coils of concertina wire looping around their compound, once it was dark, I found a way to enter and exit their perimeter—almost at will. The fact these National Guardsmen were not committed soldiers could not be emphasized enough. Lacking the discipline of full-time recruits, I learned whenever I approached their guards, if I waited patiently, they would unfailingly walk away to take a piss, go look at something, or one time they even compromised their night vision by striking a match to light a cigarette. As soon as I noticed any such discrepancy, I waltzed right by—sometimes within a few yards of them. In retrospect, it seems like someone should have detected my presence at least once. But they never did.

I was really starting to believe I could make myself invisible.

On my initial trip into enemy territory, following fifteen minutes of intermittent low-crawling, I found myself lying near the mess area. Confident I had entered undetected, with no one in sight, I dared to stand knowing it was well after lights-out. Tiptoeing around inside their perimeter, I was careful not to look directly at the glowing ashes of a bonfire. Passing by the dying embers, I quietly grabbed two, fold-up chairs; I stood one on top of a table, and the other I gently laid on a generator. I did this simply to provide harmless evidence of a nocturnal visitor. Then I heard some voices inside one of the GP mediums; this caused me to quickly get back down on all fours.

Crawling closer, I stopped when I was in earshot of the three men's conversation. Lying on my stomach, I listened to them small-talk about their first day in the woods. Judging by their tone, the size and location of their tent—not to mention they were talking kind of loud—I deduced this must be the commander's tent. Since my objective was to make an appearance, I figured what better way than to greet the commanding officer, himself?

While I considered my options, someone exited the tent.

The moonlight revealed the silhouette of an average-sized male. As I heard a voice inside the tent ask, "Where's Captain Daniels going?" I tried to subtly creep back into the shadows. Nevertheless, the figure continued to unerringly approach like a heat-seeking missile. By the carefree way he was strolling along, I was certain he did not see me so I was hoping he'd continue walking right by. But he didn't. Instead he stopped a few feet in front of my prostrated form and started fumbling with his belt buckle. I almost started laughing realizing he was about to take a piss—right on me. With no other recourse available, I jumped up screaming with my M-16 pointed at his face.

"*Ahh! Ahh! You're dead—dead!*" In addition to the echo of my booming utterances, the grim cries of several

238

night creatures could be heard responding in the darkness.

"*Uhhhh!*" blurted out the startled captain.

It took him a full second to regain his composure. Once he did, he took offense to the grin he glimpsed on my face. "Soldier, who the hell are you smiling at? Do you know who I am? And get that thing outta my face!" With his final declaration, he reached out to smack the muzzle of my weapon.

Tilting the tip of my weapon down slightly—just enough to dodge his hand—I then re-aimed it at his head, all the while wondering if he had urinated on himself or not. Before the captain could object any further I heard the sounds of approaching footsteps and, realizing the nearby sentries were on their way, understood I had to leave. "Captain Daniels, it's been a pleasure killing you this evening but I gotta go now. Oh, and sir, remember you're dead—so rest in peace!"

I started running just as a pair of soldiers sprinted onto the scene. To slow down their pursuit I had to cancel their ability to see in the dark; so, grabbing a simulated grenade from my pocket, I activated it and waited a few seconds before dropping it in their path. *Boom!* After it exploded, I changed direction and made a dash for the tree line.

"Oh shit! Where'd he go ?" yelled one sentry.

"I got him! He's right here," the other responded.

"*Get off!* That's me, you fuckin' idiot!"

"I see him," screamed a third voice from the blackness. "He's over there!"

Once they spotted me, it turned into an old-fashioned foot race. With three soldiers closing-in fast, I had to accelerate to avoid capture; this, despite knowing the coiled blades lay in my immediate future. Just as I sensed the prickly barrier someone touched my back. Suddenly, I was flipping through the air and something sharp grazed the top of my head. Then the wind was knocked out of me—and I almost lost consciousness—as my body crashed hard against the ground.

While I was still airborne something hit the barbed wire.

"Ahhh! Oh shit! Damn, damn, damn, I'm bleeding bad!"

"Me too! Medic! Someone call, a fuckin' medic!"

"Calm down!" scolded the third soldier who had arrived seconds after the collisions. "Both of you gotta relax."

Though it may seem strange, I had come to the conclusion my spirit was screaming out against my will so I instinctively covered my mouth with my hand. After lying there in silence, I eventually grasped it was my pursuers who were doing the yelling, not me. Sitting up, I felt a sharp stinging sensation on my right shin and only then did I realize I was on the other side of the barbed wire.

While listening to the soldiers, whimper about their injuries, I peered back through the veil of darkness and was barely able to distinguish the wounded pair along with the third soldier who was nursing their wounds. With no mention of me being made, I guess they figured I had already escaped. Following a brief, bodily function-check, I was pleased my legs had no trouble responding to my command to get up and run.

As I was fleeing the scene, dozens of soldiers were converging on the area.

Minutes later, I reached a spot in the woods where the moonlight was peeking through the saplings; so, I sat down on a log and rolled up my pants to examine my legs. Concerned about a sticky-liquidy sensation I felt leaking into my boot, I needed to know how badly I was bleeding. Fortunately, my inspection revealed nothing but some superficial cuts, most of which had already scabbed nicely. Feeling relieved, I re-bloused my pants inside my boots and tied my laces. When I stood up, the ground vibrated from a mind-jarring explosion; this was Major Brackett's signal. It was followed by staccato gunfire and grenades detonating all over their compound.

In our pre-assault briefing, the major had assigned each soldier a specific point to strike along the enemy's perimeter. Our team-leader had stressed how important it was that everyone attack at the same time. Everyone, that is, except me. My objective that evening was to make an appearance to distract their sentries. During the chaos which would undoubtedly occur the rest of the team was to move themselves into attack-position.

Having accomplished my mission in stellar fashion, I grinned knowing I had their company commander's head on a spike.

The next couple days were carbon copies of our initial success. Those bumbling civilians had no idea how to defend their base camp. On the second night, the major and Mullins detonated smoke bombs and artillery simulators on the northern side of their bivouac area. When the National Guard's defense team ran toward the commotion, the rest of us attacked their perimeter from the south and the south-west.

The following night, we nearly repeated the same plan except in reverse. Once Stock and I had circled around from the south, we announced our presence with our explosives. As we made our escape, we heard rapid-fire rounds and simulated bombs detonating along the northern flank.

By day four, we had gotten cocky.

Waking up to a huge ruckus, initially, I thought it was the same pat-on-the-back conversations over coffee we had enjoyed every morning so far. And it was. However, in addition to the normal laughter and recaps of the previous night's success, I noticed Buzz and Stock were writing on small pieces of paper. After sitting up, I put my glasses on and watched them jot-down short phrases, fold the bits of paper, and place them in a pile sitting between them.

"Mornin'," I greeted everyone with a yawn. What y'all doing?"

"Last two days, Amaru," said Sgt. Abrams while pointing at the pile of scribbled notations. "Check out the props for tonight's operation."

Once I stood up and stretched, I walked over and grabbed a couple of the folded bits of paper. They were writing one-liners like 'Pow! You're Dead!' Or, 'We're good ain't we?' After a brief examination, I refolded them before tossing the bits back in the pile.

"So," I said between yawns, "the plan is to leave these messages inside the perimeter, around the compound? Is that it?" Asking this, I hoped my repeated yawns demonstrated I was not impressed.

"Yeah Amaru!" Chuckling like a mad man, Mullins then started beating his chest like a crazed gorilla. "We're really gonna embarrass those part-timers tonight!"

"These are Major Brackett's orders?" I continued my inquiry.

"No, mine," declared Sgt. Abrams.

Hearing this, I grabbed my toothbrush and wash rag. "Oh," I mumbled on my way to the latrine.

"Hurry up Amaru! You gotta help too. We need as many of these as possible," Sgt. Abrams spoke in the direction of my receding form.

When I returned, I got dressed and prepared my gear for the day but I never wrote any memos. Beyond thinking his idea was corny, Sgt. Abrams was starting to get on my nerves. The NCO had been riding me about every little detail for the past two days—ever since Stock had unintentionally revealed I snuck over to his side on the first morning. While Stockton was giving details about our observations, Sgt. Abrams noticed he kept saying 'we' instead of 'I'. "Wait a minute Specialist," the NCO had interrupted, "Major Brackett assigned you to the east-side of the perimeter and Amaru was on the west-side, right? So how did you two end-up together?"

Had I been the one being questioned, instead of Stockton, it would have been easy for me to pretend I had just made a grammatical error. But after all, having a past laced with street-hustling and witnessing, I had acquired the gift of gab. Whereas Stock, being a Californian surfer who was born and bred on the beaches of San Diego, he did not have a dishonest bone in his body; so, it was easy for Sgt. Abrams to get the truth. And of course, all this took place in the presence of Major Brackett and the entire team.

Later, when Stock and I were alone, he meekly approached me with his head down. "Tak, I'm sorry for tellin' on you...I didn't try to, it happened by mistake."

"I know," I replied to my friend's apology. "Don't sweat it, what's done is done."

In retaliation to Sgt. Abrams' intensified scrutiny, I started calling him 'Johnnie Rulebook.' Or if I really wanted to piss him off: the 'LEG sergeant.'

When *Johnnie* noticed me resting with my head propped on top of my rucksack instead of sitting next to the other guys who were writing memos, he approached bearing the air of an authoritarian. "So Amaru, what is it?" he asked. "You think you're too good to write messages?"

"Of course, I do, Sergeant," Billy accepted his challenge with open-arms. "That's a job for a secretary, someone like you. Besides since you're the only one here who doesn't do anything—well, except boss us around and bother everyone—you're the only one who has any time." Saying this, I glanced over at Stock and asked in an irritated tone. "Why're you writing those? Let them do that." Then I explained my rationale. "Who do you, think's gonna be out there placing those things on their equipment? Us, that's who—me and you. And guess what the LEG sergeant here," I said hooking my thumb at the NCO, "and these three will be doing while we're out there taking this unnecessary risk? They'll be back here jerking-off and swapping war stories. Come on, the sun's up we gotta go."

Although I had the included the others in my critique, Buzz, Mullins, and Persons knew they were not my intended targets. Since it was rare to see a lower-enlisted guy chew-out an NCO, everyone remained silent.

"Wait a minute Stockton," Sgt. Abrams said in a defiant tone before pointing at me. "What're you trying to say, Amaru? Hell, I'll take your spot right now and show both of you how it's done!" With his greasy, slicked-back hairstyle and fake Benson Hurst accent, it was obvious the Jewish E-5 was trying to pass for Italian.

"Calm down, calm down," interceded Major Brackett. Appearing from nowhere holding a map, he seemed unconcerned the sergeant was in an uproar. "Gentlemen, we gotta tighten this shit up. With three-hundred-plus enemy soldiers a little more than a stone's throw away, the last thing we need is some snot-nosed in-fighting." Having made this statement, the team-leader turned toward his E-5. "Sergeant Abrams."

"Yessir."

"Get these three to their stations—come on, let's look alive around here!" Then he pointed at Stock and me. "And why the hell are you two still here? How can you be my 'eyes and ears on the battlefield' if you're standing right next to me? Get outta here!"

Stock and I jumped up and grabbed our weapons. But before we could get far Major Brackett called our names as if he just remembered something.

"Stock, Amaru come here for a second."

Knowing the team-leader was agitated, we quickly jogged over to him.

"For the record," he said, looking back-and-forth between Stockton and me, "which one of you is getting caught today?"

"Haven't decided yet sir," Stock honestly replied.

"*Haven't decided yet?*" the major repeated, sounding frustrated all over again. "Well, what're ya waiting for?" Then he closed his eyes to gather himself before speaking in a calm tone. "Look, whoever surrenders, don't forget to initiate the POW evaluation immediately upon being apprehended."

"Got it sir."

"Yessir."

Shortly after leaving our base-camp, Stock and I decided by playing 'rock-paper-scissors.' Even though I lost, he volunteered to be taken prisoner in my stead. "Maybe the blonde will guard me tonight."

"Dream on," I replied.

Then we split up.

From my favorite vantage point high up in the sycamore, I surveyed the dedicated men and women of the National Guard's 261st Aviation Brigade. Following three days away from civilization, they appeared altogether different from the happy-go-lucky group me and Stock initially observed. Gone were the goofy grins from overworked, office workers happy to have an excuse to leave their cubicles and experience nature. As the number of females gawking at exotic plants dwindled, likewise, the men were no longer startled by their encounters with wild creatures.

In spite of their new toughened appearance, I was barely paying any attention to them. This was because I was more concerned with the platoon that had just arrived a couple hours ago. Minutes after leaving Stock, I observed an unidentified group of soldiers advancing through the forest. My first impression was they were only passing through the area. Nevertheless, just in case, I went to warn Stock which turned out to be a good decision. Together, we followed them until they started setting up their base-camp about five hundred-yards north of the National Guard's perimeter. Seeing this, we decided Stock should continue keeping an eye on them while I returned to spying on the larger group. What we forgot to discuss was whether or not Stock would still get caught. And if so, by which group?

As I sat in the tree contemplating the motives of these newcomers, scores of birds suddenly took off into the air. Most of them flew away but some took refuge in the leafy branches of the sycamore. Since becoming a scout I learned whenever birds jettisoned all-at-once in this manner it meant intruders were approaching.

"Mankind...*shiznick!*" After whispering one of the kosher substitutes I used to avoid swearing, I looked straight down fearing a worst-case scenario had presented itself. And it had. "The shammers are here earlier than usual," I moaned.

Once again having gotten caught-up admiring the pristine wilderness, I had failed to abandon my observation post before patrols began roaming the area. Peering down through the leaves at my adversaries, I racked my brain on what to do next knowing how much they loved lounging in the shade. Just thinking about being forced to remain in the tree made me nervous because I really had to take a piss!

Climbing down to my previous lookout position, it felt like déjà-vu seeing Sgt. Howell and Booth sneaking a kiss while Spc. Johnson and PFC Connors, along with a few others, sat on the other side of the sycamore discussing the latest gossip.

"I'll be glad to get back to civilian life. Don't get me wrong, this nature shit was cool in the beginning but I need to wash my ass!"

The character who emerged that morning with the most memorable comments was a funny private-first-class, named Lester. Not only were his antics entertaining but he also looked comical. Having small beady eyes in a big, block-shaped head, his beige complexion somehow combined with a shrill, high-pitched southern drawl to make his superbly-timed jokes hilarious.

"Me too," replied Connors. "But before we go, we gotta catch those thieving sons-of-bitches that dumped everything out of my duffel bag last night."

"I wanna get 'em too but let's not exaggerate," Lester replied with a grin. "If they were stealing shit, they definitely would've taken that *Hustler* magazine I saw laying outside your tent this morning. Now I know why you're a perverted ass always hits the sack so early. You in there beatin' your meat, huh?"

As Connors' face lit up bright-red, everyone except Johnson busted-out laughing

"Calm down, they got all of us," she coolly replied. "And guys do me a favor. Can you ease up on the profanity?" Saying this, Johnson sighed like she was tired of repeating this request.

Once there was a lapse in the conversation the rotund E-3, still smiling sheepishly, returned to the topic. "You know what? I heard Captain Daniels say only one of 'em is a green beret."

Hearing him talk about us, I strained my ears to listen.

"Well, if that's true, the rest of them are imitating that guy real, good 'cause I have yet to see any of 'em up close. Every time we spot 'em, they detonate their explosives in our faces and disappear," countered Lester.

"I saw three of them last night—" Johnson started to

248

explain before Sgt. Howell cut her off from the other side of the tree.

"Shut up Johnson, you didn't see squat! Remember everybody, she's the one who said there was a guy in the tree talking."

"Unh-unh I said that, remember?" Booth corrected the sergeant.

"Oh yeah you're right. But then she followed-up your phenomenal claim with…hmm, let's see, how should I put it? A *Predator* sighting?" Saying this, Sgt. Howell stood up and helped Booth to her feet before the two of them started walking over to join the rest of their squad.

Lester, whom I deduced had a crush on Johnson, tried to defend her while simultaneously quell the debate with more of his witty satire. "I dunno Sergeant," he said, smiling at the couple as they stepped over the twisted, contorted roots protruding from the ground. "It's tropical as hell out here…this is exactly the kind of environment Predators are attracted to, you know."

"And," Connors added with a grin, "we are a military component with heavy weaponry; so… the great 'Extraterrestrial Hunter' might consider us a formidable challenge."

"Yeah right," Lester turned on his buddy. "The second he checked-out that spare tire you're packing around your waist, he'd know we were nothing but a bunch of civilians playing Cowboys and Indians out in the woods.

As laughter erupted, Sgt. Howell ended the sci-fi banter.

"Johnson, what you saw last night was probably some of the soldiers Cox and I spotted this morning. Those dudes are active-duty from somewhere in Georgia. And I heard it's their job to capture the midnight marauders by tomorrow."

"Sergeant, I don't think so because they just got here a couple hours ago," Johnson replied looking doubtful.

"Yeah but who knows? A few of them were probably snooping around last night to get the 'lay of the land' so to speak. Can't remember the name of their unit but they're supposed to be the real deal," stated Sgt. Howell.

Lester, reluctant to change subjects, returned to the fantasy conversation.

"Ay Connors, remember the Predator had that cool device on his arm to make himself invisible?"

"Not really invisible," corrected Connors. "More like it somehow blended his body into the background scenery. Yeah, I remember…was it called 'inviso'? Did anybody else see the movie?"

It had taken a couple days of practice but eventually my climbing skills improved—or should I say returned to my childhood level. Having spied on 'the enemy' from my aerial post several times, I had gotten to know them pretty well. In spite of this encouraging development, I felt very uncomfortable at the moment because I urgently needed to relieve myself. *Man did I have to go!*

Just as I was deciding on what to do next, two helicopters flew into view from the west.

"Speaking of high-speed gadgets, check out those Black Hawks!" exclaimed Connors when no one replied to his question about the movie. "Did you know they're equipped with Global Positioning Systems? That means they're plugged into a satellite that pinpoints their location anywhere on the planet."

Taking advantage of this deafening distraction, I

climbed lower with the dexterity of a squirrel. When I was just above their heads—clearly in view had they stopped gawking at the choppers—I jumped. Dropping to the ground, I rolled into the prone position exactly where Sgt. Howell and Booth had been kissing minutes ago. Thanks to the thunderous whirring sounds roaring overhead, my descent went undetected. Nevertheless, with eight pairs of eyes on the other side of the sycamore, intuition hinted it would be mockery to attempt sneaking away in broad daylight. For this reason, plus the fact I had not heard anything about Stockton being captured, I decided to surrender. *But not before having a little fun!*

The National Guard soldiers continued watching the Black Hawks until they landed on the airfield, which was located on the other side of the perimeter. Before any of them had a chance to notice me I moved closer to the trunk of the sycamore and sat down. Now seated Indian-style just a few yards behind Connors, I began speaking in as calm a voice as I could muster. "I don't think it had a specific name…if I remember correctly, it was just some kind of time-bending, cloaking device." As everyone whipped their heads around I raised both knees, wrapped my arms around them, and grabbed my wrist. Startled beyond belief by my presence, they just stared in silence; so, I kept talking to fill-in the awkward moment. "I'm talking about the Predator's thingamajig, not the Black Hawks."

Connors was the first to regain his ability to speak. "Who the hell are you?"

"And where'd you come from?" added Johnson.

Then everyone hurried over to scrutinize their uninvited guest.

"Whoa, whoa," I declared, revealing my empty hands

in a gesture of peace. "We're all on the same team. My name's Amaru, I'm with the unit that's been assigned to capture the OPFOR renegades who've been harassing your brigade. If you don't mind, I have a few questions." Due to an outbreak of acne, I had neglected to cammie-up that morning. Therefore, I was hoping I did not look like an 'enemy scout.' Fighting off the urge to smile, I resumed the charade by lacing my fingers together, placing my hands behind my head, and leaning back against the tree while everyone else remained standing in a semi-circle around me. "Has anyone made visual contact with the enemy? Captain Daniels reported there are about twelve of them. Can any of you confirm this information?"

"*Bullshit!*"

When Specialist Johnson yelled everyone—including me—was astonished she had used profanity. Quickly realizing I was not supposed to be aware of her prudishness, I coughed to disguise my momentary lapse.

"So," the specialist eyed me with suspicion lacing her tone, "you're one of the grunts from Georgia, huh?" In response to my nodding head she then slayed me with her next question. "If you're not from Fort Bragg why is there an Airborne tab on your shoulder? You know what?" she resumed without allowing me time to respond, "I think you're one of the guys we're looking for. Connors, Maxwell, arrest him!"

"At ease Specialist! And you two, stand-fast where you are," the E-5 addressed the three lower-enlisted soldiers before turning to confront me. "I'll handle this." Despite the fact Sgt. Howell was the least professional amongst them, considering he was the only NCO present, this meant, by default, he was in charge. "Specialist Amaru, what unit are you in?"

Once questioned by the NCO, I stood up and assumed a relaxed, at-ease posture. "Charlie Company, five-oh-seventh Parachute Infantry Regiment, Sergeant."

"What post is that?"

"Fort Benning, Sergeant."

Since they were LEGs, I assumed they wouldn't know this was the Airborne School.

"Specialist Johnson," Sgt. Howell began, rolling his eyes at her. "Last time I checked Benning was in Georgia. And if he's in a parachute infantry regiment that would also explain the Airborne tab."

"Maybe," she tried to argue, "but it doesn't explain—"

"At ease Specialist, I have this under control, okay?" Without waiting for Johnson to comply, he turned back toward me but I spoke first.

"Sergeant...Howell," I pretended to read his BDU shirt. "I need to speak to someone in charge, preferably an officer." Hoping to make as big a splash as possible, I wanted to drop the news that I was an OPFOR freedom-fighter right in their commander's face.

'Freedom Fighter' I liked the sound of that.

"We caught one of 'em!"

Hearing a voice yelling our way, everyone turned toward the three approaching soldiers.

"Oh Sergeant Strauss," replied Sgt. Howell, sounding surprised to see his supervisor. Before walking over to greet them, the burly E-5 addressed me one more time. "Amaru, you might be in luck. Don't move, I'll be right back."

"Clear Sergeant," I replied, "but I'm gonna take a

leak, if you don't mind." Feeling some uneasiness concerning these new arrivals, my bladder reminded me it had not yet been relieved.

"Okay but don't go far," he said good-naturedly before calling out to Connors. "PFC, keep an eye on him." Then he started walking toward the advancing figures. "Sergeant Strauss, what was that? I couldn't hear you before."

I hesitated long enough to get a good look at the oncoming trio. A lanky, white man was flanked by an olive-complexioned guy who walked like a duck and a dark-skinned soldier with a stocky build. It looked like the guy bringing up the rear had a stubby beard on his face so I imagined he had a shaving profile. While everyone trailed alongside Sgt. Howell to meet them, only Connors accompanied me as I walked in the opposite direction.

"I said, we caught one of 'em," the E-6 repeated once he was closer. "Well, actually he turned himself in but—" Suddenly Sgt. Strauss stopped in mid-sentence. "Who's that over there with Connors?"

Having my back turned, I couldn't see Sgt. Strauss but with only twenty yards separating us I could hear him clearly and imagined he was pointing at me. However, since the NCO had not addressed me directly, I continued walking. Connors, looking back and forth between me and the members of his squad, began to sense something was amiss.

"Alright, that's far enough," barked Connors.

"At ease PFC," I snapped, hoping to make him tentative. "Not only am I *not* your prisoner, I also outrank you—remember that the next time you address me." After a few more steps I was able to find what I was looking for: a medium-size shrub that would effectively put an obstacle between me and Connors without cutting off visual contact. Briskly double-timing behind the bush, I unzipped...*what a relief!*

Seeing Connors watching me closely, I hoped to create a little more space. "Hey, do you mind giving a guy a little privacy?"

"Oh sorry." Embarrassed, Connors turned around to face the others. Due to what Sgt. Strauss said next, this turned out to be crucial.

"Is that guy wearing an Airborne tab?"

"Yeah why?" responded Sgt. Howell.

"Because the grunts from Fort Stewart don't have Airborne tabs but the captive we got in custody does."

"*Fort Stewart?* I knew it!" Spc. Johnson exclaimed, turning her head to search the area. "Ay, where'd he, go?"

By the time Connors spun around to do something heroic, I already had my M-16 leveled at his dome. "Bang-bang, you're dead," I taunted in a mocking tone. "Now lie down like a good sport and count to fifty." While Connors pondered what he should do, I pulled a grenade simulator from my cargo pocket and showed it to everyone. "You're all dead!" I yelled with a grin. "Just let me go, okay? I didn't know my buddy already gave himself up." With that, I flung the explosive at them. "Y'all be cool—peace!"

Boom!

Utilizing my world-class credentials, within seconds, I was so far ahead of them, I was surprised they even bothered giving chase. Nevertheless, since I enjoyed stretching my legs against the terrain, I was glad they did. After a few twists and turns, I ran straight through the densest part of the forest. By the time reinforcements arrived, I had already switched on my 'inviso' and blended into the scenery. I did, however, stick around long enough to confirm the new voices belonged to the combat team from Ft. Stewart.

Amazed at how easily I was able to lose my pursuers, I realized the forest had become my home over the past couple days. Every nook and cranny—from the flowing brooks to the blossoming flora—was now my ally; and I could read its pathways and passages as easily as a civilized man understood a road map or a street sign.

"What're you doing back here?" inquired Sgt. Abrams. "You know you deserted your post, right? Hey, I'm talking to you!"

After walking passed the annoying E-5, I approached Major Brackett and reported the arrival of the unidentified troops. I was stunned by his cold reply.

"Interesting," he said, "and why did you come back here?"

"Um, well sir…" I was baffled to come up with a good answer. "I figured you needed to know about the new troops right away."

"Specialist, you thought we failed to notice a whole platoon marching through the woods in the bright morning sunshine?"

"Not only that, sir. But *who* they are, I just thought—"

"You know what Amaru?" Major Brackett interrupted, "technically, the sergeant's correct. What I mean is, what if the enemy was heading this way right now? With Stock taken out, we'd have no way of knowing they were coming."

"Clear sir, I apologize for my oversight and I'll return

to my post at once." From my perspective, the major was siding with the sergeant against me. Why? I didn't understand but at this point I just wanted to leave.

"Like I said, totally unprofessional…I knew you couldn't hack it, Amaru!" Sgt. Abrams did not miss his golden opportunity to belittle me. "You've let the entire team down with your lack of discipline!" Walking up to me, he stuck his finger in my face. "Repeat after me Specialist: 'I will guard everything within the limits of my post and quit my post only when properly relieved.' It's the first General Order we learned in boot camp, dammit!"

Sgt. Abrams was the only member of our team who did not have any set-responsibilities. As the only non-commissioned officer, his principle duty was to train the lower-enlisted guys as he supervised us. In other words, in addition to disseminating the major's orders, he was supposed to be teaching us soldiering skills so, in the near-future, we could advance to the NCO level. Nevertheless, instead of showing us anything useful or conducting any training, while everyone else was working, he just sat around the base-camp repeating the major's orders. Other than that, he chilled-out until nighttime. For this reason, the last thing I was concerned with was hearing any evaluation he might have on my conduct; especially because it was obvious he just wanted to grandstand for the major. In my mind, to pay any attention to this clown's critique would have been the same as a first-team player—who is currently in the game—worrying over what a bench-warmer might be whining about on the sideline.

"Sergeant, with all due respect, in my opinion one of the reasons for our success to this point has been because of the information me and Stock have provided about the enemy."

"Oh no doubt about it," the major calmly concurred as if he wanted to add fuel to the altercation.

"But," I continued, "I'm not trying to take all the credit because, as you mentioned, it's been a *team* effort. The major and Mullins have been planning our attacks with precision while Buzz and Persons have been supporting them by handling whatever needs to be done around here. The three of them also rotate the night-guard duty, right?" Now it was my turn to point at him. "But you don't. So, Sergeant, my question is: besides holding a few of the major's maps, running your mouth from the passenger seat of a jeep, and having some memos written—you didn't even do that yourself—exactly what have, *you* done for the team?"

Sgt. Abrams stood there in silence.

"Exactly," I said in disgust, "I rest my case." Then I grabbed my weapon and started walking away.

"Hey, I'm still talking to you, where do you think you're going?" Then Sgt. Abrams ran into my path to stop me. "You've already failed Specialist, so I'm replacing you as a scout."

Then he pivoted toward our team-leader to make his request official.

Before Major Brackett could respond, I protested. "No way sir, that's my post! I know my way around out there because I've invested the time and effort." Then I pointed at Sgt. Abrams again. "This soft, city-slicker won't last five minutes out there—he smells like *Brut* for goodness sake!"

Following a brief snicker at my last comment, the major gave Sgt. Abrams permission to replace me. "And Buswell," he called out, glancing over to his left. "You're leaving with the sergeant too—you're Stockton's

258

replacement. Both of you," the team-leader stated looking back and forth at Buzz and Sgt. Abrams, "get your gear ready and report back for a pre-deployment briefing."

"Clear sir," Buzz and Johnny chorused.

Hearing this, I walked away pissed off.

There was no doubt I was stung by the major's decision but it did not take long for me to recognize the up-side to remaining in the rear. While the new scouts were receiving their briefing, I lay down in the shade to get some shut-eye. Minutes later, when I heard footsteps, I opened one eye and spied Sgt. Abrams walking by with Buzz trailing behind him. "Amaru," he said glaring at me, "now I'm gonna show you how it's done." After uttering his favorite slogan, he and Buzz disappeared into the brush. Once they were out of sight, I closed my eyes again and rolled over onto my side. Just as I was getting comfortable, Major Brackett canceled any thoughts I had about getting some sleep.

"Sit up Amaru," the major scolded. "In spite of what you might think, we're not back here taking naps." Then he gestured toward some stones big enough to sit on; we used them to eat our MREs. "I wanna hear more about this combat team from Fort Stewart. Mullins, Persons, come over here."

Although the major had acted aloof and disinterested when I initially reported the troops, now with Sgt. Abrams gone, he grilled me with detailed questions. As I relayed everything I'd heard from my perch in the sycamore, his eyes grew wide in astonishment.

"Wait a minute," the team-leader shook his head in disbelief. "You're saying you've been *listening* to their conversations?"

"That's correct, sir…this is what I was trying to tell you before."

When I finished my report, the major folded his arms and smiled. "I like your style, Amaru," he said before addressing the three of us. "Tonight, we're gonna abort our normal offensive in favor of a reconnaissance mission. We need to learn more about this 'real deal' combat team." Then he pointed a finger skyward. "Men always remember: '*If you know your enemies and know yourself, you will not be imperiled in a hundred battles.*[3]' Following a brief scan of everyone's face, the major resumed. "Let's check-out our guests—see if they're any good."

That night, we rendezvoused with the scouts later than usual. In spite of Sgt. Abrams insisting he had a sure-fire plan of attack, the major announced our change of tactics. Instead of mounting an incursion, we were each designated a sector of the forest to watch. "Don't engage anyone," ordered Major Brackett. "Just record any details about this new enemy that'll help us outmaneuver them. At the very least, we need to know how many soldiers they got patrolling the forest." Before ending he eyed each of us. "Gentlemen, tomorrow is the final day of Operation Golden Seal so we wanna go out with a bang. But for tonight, just hide and watch, gottit?"

"Clear sir," we all chorused before heading off in separate directions.

Since the sycamore was inside my assigned zone, I went to it straightaway and started climbing. I had barely made it to the panther perch when three silhouettes, moving in a triangular formation, approached with the finesse of a trio of hunting lioness. Because they advanced one at a time, and only after a lengthy pause between each movement, at first, I thought there were only two, not three, soldiers. Even before

---

[3] From the *Art of War* [孫子兵法], by Sun Tzu

Sgt. Abrams' scream echoed through the blackness, just by what little I had observed, I knew these were no ordinary soldiers.

For over an hour I laid deathly-still in the darkness. About every eight minutes or so, I heard twigs snapping and leaves being crunched so I substantiated their teams were rotating in patrols, and not just randomly searching through the forest. However, for the past forty minutes, the moon, which usually aided me, had been hidden behind a patch of clouds so I was not sure how many men comprised each group. Looking skyward, there was no way to determine how long the moon would take to escape its cloud-cover so I started contemplating on a way to get close enough to count them.

Since the major liked the *Art of War* so much, I was reminded of the copy I used to browse at Jeff's house. I remembered one of the tenets which intrigued me instructed the warrior to appear wherever he's not expected. I figured the only way to get a good look at these Ft. Stewart soldiers would be to position myself in the last place they would ever think of looking. With this in mind, formulating a plan became easy. "They'd never think of searching *inside* the National Guard's perimeter," I mumbled under my breath.

It only took thirty seconds before I heard leaves being crunched below me. Knowing that after this patrol went by I only had eight minutes before the next one would arrive, I climbed down without delay. Once I ascertained they were far enough away, I dropped onto the ground and scurried toward the nearest sentry post. Although I moved quickly, I did not hurry. Having witnessed the deliberate, calculated maneuvers of the soldiers from Ft. Stewart, I was careful to, hesitate every couple seconds, scan the darkness and listen for footsteps—not unlike how a mouse, rabbit, deer, or any prey-animal advances through the forest while staying alert for predators.

Arriving at the wood line nearest the entry point, I was out of breath and my heart was racing. As luck would have it, my arrival coincided with the departure of about fifteen National Guardsmen; they were exiting the perimeter as I got into the prone position. I barely had time to count the soldiers and observe their leader having a hushed-discussion with one of the guards when footsteps from behind caused me to roll my body up against the trunk of a tree. I realized whoever was coming could not see me in the dark but, if someone happened to stumble, chances are they would know what they tripped over was a human body, and not a root, a rock, or other such natural feature of the forest.

Fortunately, no one touched me and I watched a squad of five walk by. As soon as the last soldier went past I sat up. Seeing others arriving from other directions until the number of returning Guardsmen totaled about the same amount of personnel exiting the perimeter, I understood the graveyard shift was relieving the evening patrol. So, in addition to the combat team from Ft. Stewart searching for us, the National Guard had a few squads out there too. This explained why some of the patrols I had encountered were very quiet and a few seemed a bit amateurish and sloppy.

While all this commotion was taking place, I knew it was a good time to gamble. My objective was to get as close to the entrance as possible. Having achieved this, I had no idea what to do next, nor did I care to think about it. Why? Because 'What to do next?' was the Beast's responsibility. My job was to be in position when the Beast did what it did best: create chaos or some sort of confusion. As far-fetched as this might sound, up to this point, this is what had been working. So, as they say, if it ain't broke why try to fix it?

Stepping out of the wood line far behind the last grunt who passed me, I followed him and the four individuals ahead of him toward my goal: the perimeter's entrance. With all of my attention focused on the two guards manning the gate, by the time I realized the guys I was following were merging with the other arriving soldiers it was too late to turn around. Now, with the moon having escaped the clouds, it was only a matter of seconds before my cover would be blown. Just as I was about to abandon my risky gamble and make a dash for the trees, the opportunity I had been waiting for presented itself.

"As always bitch-ass Bravo Company couldn't get the job done—not surprised!"

When I heard this slick comment and witnessed the violent shove that came right afterward, my instinct warned that a fight was about to break-out. Evidently, there was a competitive rivalry among the two companies. So, when three soldiers exiting the perimeter disrespectfully walked between the ranks of the arriving group, it only took one of them to utter something rude before a pushing-shoving match ensued. Once again, being in the right place at the right time, when I saw both guards engaged in breaking up the altercation, I just sauntered through the entrance—totally unnoticed.

Having slipped by the guards, I scampered about seventy yards. Staying close to the concertina—and away from the tents—I took refuge next to the same patch of barbed wire I had flipped over four nights ago. Within minutes, I heard footsteps approaching. It took a vast amount of discipline to remain still as twigs and leaves were stepped

on a few yards away—on the other side of the steel blades.
When the footsteps walked out of earshot, I sighed in relief.
Remaining quiet as a mouse, I spied through the darkness and
listened as numerous patrols made their rounds. Even with the
moon again partially hidden I was close enough to count, in
most cases, either three or five soldiers in each group. Having
just witnessed the National Guard's five-man patrols, I knew
the combat team from Ft. Stewart comprised the three-man
groups.

After a while I got so comfortable it was difficult to
stay awake; so, I dozed off and on for the rest of the night.
Whenever I woke up, I stayed awake long enough to hear one
of the groups passing by—then I fell asleep again.

Hours later, realizing the footsteps had finally ceased,
I sat up and stretched my numbed limbs like a drowsy jungle
cat. Feeling refreshed, I wondered about the time but I did not
dare illuminate my *Casio*. Judging the night sky, I calculated
dawn was less than an hour away. This led me to
understanding the urgency of my situation: I had to be outside
the perimeter before the sun split the horizon. In spite of this,
before making my departure, I decided to distribute the notes
Stock and Buzz had stashed in my pocket.

Smiling, I stood up and grabbed a few of the corny
one-liners. Making no more sound than a wolf prowling
outside a hen-house, I glided amongst the tents, liberally
scouring a section of the compound. When I got down to my
last memo, I actually crawled inside a tent and placed it next
to a soldier's head. This guy was snoring so loudly, it was not
nearly as daring an escapade as it might seem. Besides, by
this point, the Beast was guiding my every action.

Having accomplished Sgt. Abrams' order, I grabbed a

handful of rocks and approached the sentry post. After getting down on one knee, I cocked my arm back and threw the rocks over the guard's heads, out into the forest. Once trees not too far away started getting pelted by stones both sentries, never considering the source of the projectiles was behind them, took a few steps into the woods to peer into the brush. With their backs turned, I walked out just as the sun peeked over the lowest peak of the Blue Ridge Mountains.

Call of the Beast

When I woke up, the first thing I saw was Buzz and Mullins staring at me; they were sitting on either side of my sleeping bag. "What's wrong with y'all?" I asked, seeing the perplexed look on both of their faces.

"Blmx—" they both tried to answer simultaneously.

"Relax, one at a time," I demanded. "Buzz, what's up?"

"Sergeant Abrams got caught last night, and him and Stock still ain't back yet," he reported.

"Word?" Saying this groggily, I still did not understand why they were so worried. Judging by their countenance, if I didn't know any better, I'd have thought this was a real war. Sitting up, I rubbed my eyes. "Where's the major? Don't tell me he got caught too?"

"No. He left a half-hour ago to see if he could find out what was going on with Stock and Sergeant Abrams," Mullins answered still staring at me wide-eyed.

Earlier that morning, when I returned to the base-camp, it was drizzling. Dead tired and wet, I assumed everyone was asleep; so, after changing into some dry BDUs,

I collapsed underneath my shelter-half.

Seeing my lack of concern, Mullins managed to calm down a bit. "What happened to you last night?" he asked.

After I revealed my success, Buzz relaxed too.

"*What?*" Buswell exclaimed in a low tone. "You went *inside* their perimeter? You're crazy Amaru!"

Mullins seemed to agree. "Those renegades had the woods so locked-down last night that me, Buzz, Persons, and the major were forced to retreat beyond the boundaries of the training area just to escape being captured. When you didn't show up all night, the major figured you got caught too because they were everywhere."

"No, not everywhere," I emphasized. "They weren't inside the perimeter. Plus, you gotta remember one thing."

"What's that?" they both asked.

"I can make myself invisible, remember?" I said with a grin.

"Oh yeah, how could we forget?" While Buzz sarcastically replied, Mullins scoffed and brushed me off by waving his hand in the air.

"Gentlemen," came a robust voice from the tree-line. "Let's look alive this morning." After the major startled us with his sudden appearance, Persons also came sprinting into the base-camp, but from the opposite direction.

"They let Sergeant Abrams and Stockton go—here they come now!" Persons announced like the town crier.

Looking over the major's shoulder, we saw two weary silhouettes listlessly ambling toward us. It took an extra-second for me to recognize the dusty images were Sgt. Abrams and Stockton.

"*For Christ sake!*" admonished the major after he

turned around. "I hope you know you just led them right to us!"

"Good morning to you too, sir," replied a disgruntled Sgt. Abrams. "And they already know where we are. Check your sleeping bag."

"Sir, they said they left you a love-letter," Stock added.

Major Brackett immediately ran over to search through his equipment, and sure enough he found a white envelope. Following a quick look in our direction, he opened it and pulled out a piece of paper. As he unfolded it, one of the memos written by Buzz and Stock fell to the ground: 'Boom! You're dead!' After silently scanning the letter, Major Brackett then read the contents aloud. *"To know your Enemy, you must become your Enemy."*

"I guess they got a copy of the *Art of War* too." When I blurted this out in a nonchalant tone, the major stared at me, appearing impressed that a black kid from the street was familiar with the teachings of the master strategist, *Sun Tzu*.

"Major, he said he could've ambushed us already but it wouldn't have been fair," Sgt. Abrams continued his report. "Since you weren't aware his team had been invited to spoil your fun at Golden Seal this year."

"He who?" inquired Major Brackett.

"I dunno sir, he didn't exactly give us a self-introduction," stated the E-5 with a hint of contempt still in his attitude. "His BDUs were blank but he definitely had juice as a high-ranking officer."

"He had a British accent sir," broke-in Stock, "and he said we had an hour to move." Having completed his statement, Stock then turned toward his former cellmate to get something off his chest. "So, Sergeant Abrams, about your performance last night, is that how it's done?"

The lower-enlisted guys were still sharing a laugh at the NCO's expense when the team-leader refocused our attention back to the mission. "Stock, you said the officer had a British accent, right?"

Once the major asked this question all laughter ceased.

"That's right sir," Stock replied.

"Okay everyone, listen up: we gotta break the camp down and be outta here in ten minutes—let's move."

Eight-and-a-half minutes later, with rucksacks on our backs and rifles in our hands, we were walking through the forest at a brisk pace. This trek continued in complete silence for several hours, until well into the afternoon. When we finally stopped alongside a winding stream, everyone except the major looked sweaty and fatigued. As the rest of us sat down, Major Brackett, not appearing tired in the least, paced back-and-forth like an anxious child on Christmas Eve.

After a few minutes, he chanced breaking military silence.

"Lieutenant Colonel Thames," whispered the major. He appeared to be speaking more to himself than to us.

"Excuse me sir," replied Sgt. Abrams.

Seeming to ignore the NCO, the major recalled details straight from his memory. "Ronald Thames was originally commissioned by the British Royal Special Forces but was later reassigned to our military by the queen herself."

"A British guy? Assigned to us? For what?"

Hearing Sgt. Abrams' defiant response, Major Brackett chuckled. "For the purpose, and I quote her highness: 'To assist in the upgrade of the American ground-forces.' And just like her," the major continued, "Thames is an arrogant son-of-a-bitch. However, to his credit, allow me to add he has earned a reputation for being a very thorough chap." Removing his headgear, the major scratched his head. "I've never met Thames personally but from what I've heard if he's in charge my guess is he's toying with us. He probably wants his men to practice tracking us through the woods."

"What're we gonna do, sir?" inquired Stock.

Contorting his face like Stockton had asked a dumb question, the major smugly replied. "What any sensible person does when confronted by a superior force—cheat." While the lower-enlisted guys grinned at one another, the major tapped his breast-pockets as if he was searching for something. "Where's my commo, man?" he asked, pulling a piece of paper out of his right pocket.

"Right here sir," responded Mullins smartly.

It took a few seconds for the major to read whatever was written on the paper; then he looked up at Mullins, almost as if to ensure he was not talking to the wrong guy. "Bring me the radio and the AA-144 map." It seemed Major Brackett had hit upon something and was eager to implement his idea so, although Mullins already appeared on his high-horse, the major wanted him to move even faster. "Come on son, I ain't got all day!"

"Here you are sir," Mullins said as he ran over and handed the requested items to the major.

The battle tactician grabbed the map, unrolled it, and laid it over some rocks. "Get HQ on the line," he said before adding, "and see if you can patch me through to Colonel Jeter."

"Will do sir." No doubt racking his brain about what Major Brackett was up to, the specialist rushed to follow his instructions with a big grin etched on his face. As Mullins cranked up the radio, our team-leader addressed the rest of us.

"It looks like we're gonna be here for a few minutes, so Amaru," he said looking at me.

"Yes sir," I replied.

"I want you and Stock to backtrack a hundred yards to see if we have any company."

"Sir, what about me and Buzz?" asked Sgt. Abrams, sounding upset.

Never even glancing at the NCO, the major responded without skipping a beat. "The rest of you, sit down and break for lunch." After hearing his orders, the E-5 turned away from Major Brackett and gave me a dirty look. It took all of my Christian discipline to restrain Billy from issuing his trademark wink.

As Stock and I walked away, we glimpsed an animated Major Brackett spitting map coordinates into a field-phone. "Sounds like he's calling for an air-strike," Stock said. "But how the hell can that be simulated?"

Once we walked about the length of a football field, we decided to take cover in a well-camouflaged thicket. While we sat there scanning the terrain, I started opening an MRE.

"What're you doing?" Stock asked, sounding alarmed when he heard the plastic packaging being ripped apart.

Knowing there would be no time to eat when we reassembled with the others, I had decided to get my grub on now. "They been chowing-down since we left," I replied in an irritated tone. "By the time we get back, the major's gonna be ready to roll-out." Citing the tendency Major Brackett had revealed several times, I was already tearing into the salty

270

concoction.

"Yeah, you're right," Stock concurred. "When he came to check on me two days ago I was starving 'til he left." With this emphatic declaration, he pulled an MRE out of his cargo-pocket.

About six minutes into our meal, I spotted something moving in the brush. Since the movement came from the direction of where our team was assembled, even prior to recognizing what it was, I already suspected it might be Sgt. Abrams tiptoeing through the tulips—this guy was so predictable. Saying nothing, I wiped my mouth with the tissue provided in the MRE before softly kicking Stock's boot to get his attention.

When Stock saw what I was pointing at, he started laughing under his breath. "What a goofball," he whispered before taking a swig from his canteen. "Do you think he's trying to sneak up on us?"

"What else could he possibly be doing?" I replied in a hushed tone, taking my final bites. "Let's clean up before 'Johnny Rulebook' reports us for eating on duty."

Inserted between a grassy knoll, some boulders, and a clump of bushes, we were hidden no doubt about it. Nevertheless, from twenty-five yards away, had the sergeant stopped to collect himself, he would've noticed us just as easily as we could see him. As I considered if being hidden in plain sight qualified as invisible, Stock revealed he had a plan. After pressing an index finger to his lips, he gestured for me to sneak around to the right. When I started moving, he began walking in the opposite direction.

Keeping a wary eye on Sgt. Abrams, I watched him clumsily crunch dead leaves and dislodge stones with his heavy, uneven gait. Seeing this, I wondered if Stock and I were even half that conspicuous. Scanning the forest, I searched for my partner and, even though I knew where he was, it still took me several seconds to pick him out from his surroundings. Once I found him, I noticed he was almost in position so I put a little more pep into my step. By doing so, I discovered what the difference was between the sergeant and us.

Harmony.

With numerous twigs and leaves scattered on the ground, even wild animals cannot trek through the forest in silence. Yet, if one were to acquire the knack of synchronizing his movements with the rhythms of the organic orchestra, meaning nature herself, it was possible to blend-in with frequently occurring sounds. After several days of being secluded in the wilderness, Stock and I had learned to cover our furtive movements with the mating calls of cicadas, croaking frogs, or even changes in the wind patterns.

As I considered this, the breeze stirred up the stronger branches so I took advantage and moved even faster. Once in place, I signaled to Stockton with a raised fist. Seconds later when I saw his signal to ambush our quarry, I snuck up behind Sgt. Abrams, grabbed his arm, and whispered in his ear.

"Boo!"

"*Ahhhh!*" Completely startled, Sgt. Abrams snatched his arm out of my grasp, pivoted in the opposite direction, and ran straight into Stockton.

Stock, with his hips sunk low and head up, led with his shoulder and exploded right through the NCO's mid-section, lifting him off his feet. Seeing such superb tackling technique, I thought to myself it was a shame he never played football. As soon as the panic-stricken NCO's back touched the ground, he threw a fit.

"*Get off me!*" he shrieked.

"*Shhh* Sergeant, it's us!" To silence him, Stock announced who we were as quickly as possible. Then he stood up and gave me a hi-five before both of us pointed down at Sgt. Abrams, who was still lying flat on his back, and busted-out laughing.

This made the NCO angry; and he threatened to report us.

"Report us?" I snapped in a hushed tone. "For what?"

"For assaulting a non-commissioned officer, that's what!" he replied, glaring back at me from his now-sitting position.

"Sergeant cut-it-out," Stock declared sounding disappointed. "The only reason you're angry is because me and Amaru are laughing—we were just havin' some fun." Then he reached down and grabbed the sergeant by the hand while I snatched his other arm. "But for the record," Stock continued as we helped the NCO to his feet, "if I'm questioned, I'm just gonna say I thought you were one of the National Guard soldiers."

"Me too," I concurred. "And anyway, you shouldn'tve been tryin' to sneak up on us."

"I wasn't!" Sgt. Abrams whined.

Before the debate could escalate any further Major Brackett, once again, manifested out of thin air. This time the team-leader had an amused smirk on his face. "Sergeant, what the hell was all that noise? Don't tell me that was you screaming again?" Just as the E-5 opened his mouth to respond, the major waved his hand for silence. "You know what? I don't even wanna know." Then he looked at me.

"Specialist, is there anything back there worth reporting?"

"No sir, it's all clear," I stated in a military tone despite my grin.

"Okay let's go," the major commanded.

With that, we started walking back to where the others were.

Mullins was the first to spot our approach. After whispering something to the others, he began folding the map he was referencing. Upon our arrival, Stock and I were surprised to find four shelter-halves erected near the stream. With the entire team assembled, the major issued our next orders while emphasizing the need to go deeper into the woods. "We gotta circle around our enemy," he insisted. "So, I want everyone to put a clean set of BDUs, a towel, some drawers, socks, and a t-shirt in a wet-weather bag—move."

While everyone was packing their rucksacks, he gave us another command.

"Ground the rest of your equipment next to the shelter-halves—and be careful not to trip any of the wires." Only then did Stock and I notice the entire area had been booby-trapped with simulated, claymore mines. "Anybody who tampers with this...*ka-pow!*" the major said with a sinister grin. Then, seeming to read my thoughts, he commented further. "Don't worry, we're not sleeping here tonight, this is a decoy. Besides, after that womanly yelp by the sergeant, we'd be fools to remain here. Let them find this camp and die. We'll come back tomorrow and police this up after the FTX is over." Saying this, he looked at his watch. "We gotta hurry if we're gonna make our appointment. Our destination's a couple klicks north of here...come on, I'll explain on the way." Having completed his instructions, he walked past the phony home-base, over to the stream. "I hear that Thames fella is a real bloodhound, so to erase our trail we're gonna walk in the water," he said pointing at the current. "Men, take off your boots and socks."

After rolling up our pant legs, we placed our socks inside our boots and tied the laces together before hanging them around our necks. Stepping into the tepid current, I was surprised because the water was deeper than it looked; it reached about half-way up our calves. Sloshing upstream through these swamps, I imagined we were dodging slave patrols along the Underground Railroad.

About an hour later, the major stopped to consult a map before telling us to walk out of the stream onto the bank. Once everyone dried their legs and donned their boots, we hiked for another two hours. When we came across a yellow SUV parked in the middle of the forest, everyone except Major Brackett took cover. At first, I thought the unknown POV was stuck in the dense undergrowth. However, I soon realized it was actually resting on what used to be a dirt road but in recent years had been overtaken by vines and other greenery.

As we stealthily approached the vehicle, a cheerful voice boomed out from within.

"Who's the best right-fielder of all-time?"

Completely disregarding the need for silence, the major replied in a loud voice. "Oh, that's easy, Roberto Clemente – Pittsburgh Pirates."

Hearing this odd, challenge-password combination, I realized this guy and the major were friends. Despite this I remained hidden along with the rest of the team, excluding the major, when a towering Caucasian emerged from the driver's side door; he was wearing a t-shirt, some raggedy blue-jeans, and sunglasses under a baseball cap.

"It's okay," the major announced casually, "he's on our side." When Major Brackett walked over and shook hands with the imposing giant, we all stood up. "Men, come over here," our team-leader commanded.

Once we were standing around the major and the bearded man, the huge lumberjack-like stranger, wearing a sly grin, introduced himself with a country accent.

"Name's Babcott, Joe Babcott. Pleased to meet y'all…I'm your cheatin-transport service."

After loading up the gear, we piled into the van. When Joe started driving, he announced we would be in transit for about ninety minutes. Hearing this, everyone settled in to catch some z's.

But not before hearing a bit of this master plan.

"According to the major, Thames believes he's got you guys on-the-run," Joe spoke as he checked the rearview mirror. "His team's probably scourging the mountains we're driving through right now, thinking they're gonna overtake you in an hour or so." Saying this, he shared a chuckle so raspy and hoarse it sounded like he was dying from emphysema. "By the evening, you guys'll be back near the National Guard's perimeter and Thames'll never expect y'all to be there." Stopping here, Babcott looked at Major Brackett. "Can I tell 'em why not?"

"Sure, go ahead," the major replied with an attitude of indifference.

"Boys, this ain't the first time this Thames fella's been snuck into Golden Seal to show-off his combat team doin' them British SAS field-maneuvers. What I'm tryin' to say is: he knows the rules—including what resources are available to y'all. And, believe me, those resources don't include having access to no vehicles." Again, checking the rearview, he took a drink from a bottle of water. "But I'll be damned if I'm gonna just sit back while that arrogant limey is allowed to come in—unannounced as always—and embarrass our boys. Let's see how good he is when the playing field's more level. Bear in mind, it still ain't equal 'cause he got all kinds of shit at his disposal, but at least y'all'll have a fighting chance." Having completed his statement, he went into another wheezing fit of laughter.

In spite of his casual apparel and sporting a beard, Joe did not seem like a civilian. While listening to him and the major planning our strategy, I started to wonder if he was a member of the often-talked-about-but-rarely-sighted Delta Force Team. This was my last conscious thought before I was overcome by sleep.

Glancing at the moon, I muttered my appreciation for another rainless night. Scanning the forest, it took me a few seconds to spot the point-man waving me forward. After likewise waving back to Stock, the third man in our sneak-patrol formation, I grabbed my rifle and sprinted to the location Spc. Persons had just vacated. Just as I dropped into the prone position, I heard a stifled yelp. *Something had happened to Persons!*

Raising my fist, I froze Stock in place.

Straining my eyes in the moonlight, I patiently waited for some sign of life ahead of me. After what seemed like forever, but actually amounted to a minute and some change,

Persons finally waved me forward again; however, he did not
advance to his next position. Seeing this, I approached
cautiously and, even before arriving to his side, I smelled the
stench of blood. This time the concertina wire had taken a
bite out of one of our guys. Briefly scanning the hillside, I
noticed several coils had been added since yesterday.

Sequestered behind thick shrubs, Persons and I
inspected his injury with a red flashlight lens. Although it did
not appear serious, considering he had not tried to stand, I
refrained from commenting. When the rest of the team caught
up, the major shook his head in disgust. "The bloody Brit will
stop at nothing to win—even in a training-simulation." Then
he tapped Mullins on the shoulder. "Switch the lens to blue,"
he muttered in a grave tone. Once Mullins changed the lens
and flashed the light, the injuries appeared altogether
different. Along with the ripped holes I saw on Person's
uniform seconds ago, there were now previously unseen
blood stains covering both legs. Eerily, the crimson liquid
was glowing white in the sapphirine beams. "Son, you're
gonna be alright. It looks a lot worse than it really is," the
major lied. "Can you walk?" Seeing Persons look of
uncertainty, Major Brackett called his E-5. "Sergeant
Abrams."

"Yessir."

"Do you know how to perform the Fireman's Carry?"

"Yessir but—"

"Good. I want you to transport Persons back to the
rear. Don't leave his side until a doctor is working on him.
Understand?"

"Yessir but—"

"But what Sergeant?" the major sounded irritated.

"Couldn't someone else do that, sir?"

"*Sergeant!*" Although the major's voice was muffled, his no-nonsense glare projected his anger. "We're in the middle of a mission here so I don't have time for your ego-maniacal bullshit. You have your orders—move." Without wasting another second, Major Brackett sat down and began wiring a booby trap.

While Sgt. Abrams carefully slung Persons onto his back and disappeared in the direction we just came from, our team-leader addressed the rest of us.

"Gentlemen this is it. As you can see, Thames and his black-op renegades are playing for keeps. By now, he's probably figured-out we slipped by his search patrols. From here, me and Mullins are gonna separate from you three. Have all of your senses alert out there—expect the unexpected." After we nodded, he dispatched us on our way. "Buzz, you got everything set-up?"

"Yes sir," Buzz responded affirmatively.

"Amaru, Stockton," the major continued, "you know what to do, right?"

"Yes sir," we chorused.

"And don't forget, once Buzz gets captured, check to see if they call for a medic before you fall back. Then just sit tight and wait for the signal to attack," our team-leader said referring to the simulated bomb he was carrying in a harness over his shoulder. "In forty-five minutes, I'm gonna set this baby off. At the same time, Mullins will detonate flares over the compound. Remember, our targets are the commander's tent and their supplies."

"Yessir," we whispered back.

"Good luck soldiers!" Muttering these final words of encouragement, Major Brackett individually shook our hands before parting company with Mullins.

Following the major's orders, the three of us trekked to the east-side of the National Guard's base-camp. Once there, we began low-crawling across the meadow which separated the perimeter from the forest. Buzz was on the far-left, Stock in the middle, and me on the right, with ten-yard lanes between us. I could barely see Stockton next to me with the moonlight again having been reduced by clouds to a faint luminescent glow. The two of us had become intimate with the forest over the past few days; and for this reason, I knew something was different that night. Feeling the need to make heads or tails of my fleeting intuition, I crawled toward one of the few trees dotting the glade. Having arrived next to it, I stood up to get a better look.

Almost immediately, the sounds of running footsteps caused me to duck back down.

"There he is, right there!"

"I got him. Oh shit, he's not moving!"

"Flash a light on him," commanded a third soldier.

"*Damn!* He's bleeding, call for a medic."

Once I heard this, I smiled knowing Buzz had successfully pierced the 'ketchup packs' before they reached him. This part of our mission complete, I stood up again and searched for Stock, hoping he was already pulling back. Unable to see him in the darkness, I turned to leave when another voice shouted.

"There's another one over there!"

Unsure of which of us he was referring to, I remained behind the tree. It took only a few seconds before several black silhouettes unerringly ran over and surrounded Stock.

"*NVGs!*" I whispered, realizing they were using night-vision goggles.

Considering I had not been able to find Stock just seconds before they spotted him from twice the distance, figuring out their latest gimmick was a no-brainer. 'Expect the unexpected!' Hearing the major's voice in my head, I reached into my cargo-pocket for two artillery simulators. For this situation it was important to use artillery simulators, not grenades, because grenades just explode; they do not whistle before detonating. Following a brief examination in the moonlight to ensure I had the proper weaponry, I ran ahead a couple feet to heave them high above Stock and his captors. It was my hope the sparks and whistles, followed by two deafening explosions, would cause enough panic and chaos for Stock to escape. Outnumbered the way we were, that was the best I could do for my buddy.

"There's another guy over there," the same soldier yelled. "Wait! He's throwing something at us—*look out!*" As his warning rang out, sparks began shooting over their heads along with loud whistling sounds.

Boom! Boom!

Before the airborne bombs detonated, I had already dashed back to the tree-line. After galloping a couple hundred yards, I secluded myself under the outstretched branches of a pine tree. I was surprised no one had given chase. Lying there on my stomach, I intently scanned the area for troops. Even though I detected no movement, I could not shake the feeling I was being watched. For this reason, I looked skyward. Considering helicopters had been arriving and departing at all times of the day and night, it never occurred to me the *Huey* flying overhead was tracking me. Nevertheless, when it stopped above the pine tree I was hiding under, my instincts warned this was hardly an accident; then I remembered

Babcott's comment about Thames having all kinds of resources at his disposal.

That must be Thames' bird—and if it is, they got NVGs too!

Before I had consciously registered this, my feet were already in motion. Dashing an additional forty yards, I fell to the ground when I heard voices. From the prone position, I watched three groups of soldiers—arriving from three separate directions—surround the pine tree I had just vacated. Altogether, the guerrillas numbered about thirteen or fourteen.

"*Dammit!*" cursed the squad-leader. "He's gotta be around here somewhere—spread out!" Then, the same angry guy snapped at someone through his walkie-talkie. "Behind us? Where? Give me a military direction, lieutenant!"

Seconds later, the black shadow in the sky flew over me and hovered again. This confirmed my suspicion the ground troops were communicating with the pilot. Jumping up, I ran to the next, temporary location in the middle of nowhere. Although I was expecting company any second, it was still astonishing how fast they arrived.

Boom! Boom! Boom! Boom!

A series of explosions several yards to my rear startled me. The intermittent flashes, in flickering sparkles of light, revealed one soldier with a pair of NVGs strapped to his kevlar as well as the stunned expressions of several more. In addition to exposing my stalkers, the strobe-light effect created by the repeated explosions illumined the area enough for me to recognize the patch of concertina behind them was the same patch of wire which had wounded Persons. Somehow, I had circled back to the exact spot where our team split up; which in turn, had caused the guerrillas chasing me to run into the major's booby trap. Even in the heat of the moment I knew that I had had nothing to do with the execution this ingenious strategy; while at the same time understanding this could not have occurred simply by chance—it was more than just a stroke of good luck.

"Yeah!" I yelled to make sure my adversaries saw me pointing at them. "We got you…you're all dead!"

This only made them more determined to catch me.

"*Get that muthafucka!*" one of them yelled.

Just the thought of being chased through the woods at night is enough to arouse a feeling of stark terror in anyone. Nonetheless, for people whose skin is of a darker hue, this imagery evokes something deeper because, for us, lynching's have become the very symbol of our holocaust—especially in the Americas. So, the fact my pursuers were mostly whiteboys, not to mention the forest I was running through happened to be in the deep-south, all of these factors I suppose, was enough to trick my subconscious into believing my life was actually in danger. To be honest I'm not really sure what triggered it. The only thing I can say for certain is, from this point, the normally 'little voice' in my head which sometimes gives advice really stepped-it-up and began transmitting loud and clear. Time and time again, whenever all hope seemed lost and I found myself surrounded by three, six, or even nine silhouettes, something inside me would say: '*Turn left!*' or '*Duck down!*' And once I followed these instructions I disappeared from my enemies' sight.

"Fuck!" someone screamed. "He was right here…where'd he go?" After a couple seconds, another voice yelled out. "There he is, to your right—he's crawling. Look down!"

Right then, the moon popped out from behind the clouds and the chase resumed.

Minutes later, I gave them the slip long enough to take refuge in a rocky hillside where a series of flat, smooth stones was stacked to form what looked like a staircase leading into the side of a cliff. A couple days prior, when I first came across these rocky steps, I wanted to inspect them to see if they were man-made or not; but with no trees to provide cover it was too risky.

Within seconds three soldiers came into view. Too tired to flee I crouched down, having decided to rest until they spotted me. But they never did. "Ah-ha, I get it," I whispered to myself. "Most of them don't have NVGs—only the squad-leaders do."

KA BOOM!

When the major's timed explosion shook the ground, I was in the process of tiptoeing behind my pursuer's backs. As the flares illuminated the sky like a sports arena, in a near panic, I dove to the ground and rolled my body into an unseen gully at the base of the stair-like structure. Naturally concealed by a few small shrubs, I had failed to notice this drainage ditch in the middle of the afternoon; so, I knew a person lying in it at night would be almost impossible to see. Prior to closing my eyes to preserve my night-vision, I saw several more soldiers approaching from the opposite direction. A few were holding their NVGs in their hands while they took advantage of the lit-up sky to scan the forest with their naked eyes. I prayed none of them turned around to spit—*some of the guys were right next to me!*

One of the newcomers stopped to question the first three who had arrived.

284

"We followed him here. Are you sure he didn't get passed you guys?"

"No way he got by us, Sergeant," replied a man with a deep voice.

None of these soldiers seemed surprised by the major's mega blast or the pyrotechnic demonstration which followed. This suggested that Thames' boys—not Major Brackett—had detonated them. *Had the major and Mullins been captured?* I wondered to myself. *Or, perhaps they had been forced to leave their gear behind while making a hasty retreat.* Reviewing the facts, I recalled the major saying he would set 'this baby' off, referring to the simulated bomb, in forty-five minutes; but even without checking my *Casio* I was sure that no more than thirty minutes had passed since our team separated. With this in mind, I imagined the combat team, after procuring the incendiary devices, had decided to detonate them in an effort to trick the members of our team into exposing themselves. Having convinced myself thus, I considered what to do next.

Boxed-in by a sheer cliff face, my only avenue of escape was to go past them. Or, I thought to myself, perhaps I should remain where I was until they dispersed. This seemed like my best option until I considered those incessant helicopters which, even now, were buzzing in the vicinity. Playing the scenario out in my head, I imagined that once the flares were extinguished the occupants of one of the Huey's, with their birds-eye view, would spot me before these troops had time to leave the area.

Having vetoed the contingency plan to remain hidden, I decided to gamble and take my chances. "Twenty, nineteen, eighteen…" I started counting backward under my breath, recalling the major saying a flare could remain burning for as long as forty-five seconds. Having guessed around twenty seconds had elapsed, I could barely hear my conscious-mind screaming about how irrational it was to risk everything on an improvised clock in my head. "Five, four…" Whispering thus, I prepared to stand praying no one had turned around to inspect the cliff behind them. "Two, one…"

Right on cue the flares went out.

Opening my eyes, I came to my feet and stepped out of my hiding place in one efficient motion. After hopping over a small shrub, realizing I had to move quickly, I glided past my pursuers using three long strides before their pupils had time adjust to the darkness. They reeked of sweat and dirt.

No one saw me.

At this point, Operation Golden Seal descended into nothing more than a manhunt through the forest. Again, and again, whenever the guerrillas spotted me, they gave chase like a pack of rabid hounds; this forced me to pull-off a series of Houdini-type escapes one right after the other. Due to these back-to-back-to-back close calls, I was dead tired and ready to drop. Realizing I could not maintain this pace much longer, I felt the urgency to do something unexpected.

On all fours, I wriggled my way to the edge of the woods; knowing that just beyond the tree-line was a dirt road. When I spotted a humvee slowly approaching, I stood up behind the massive trunk of a magnolia. Not only did the tree block their view, it also prevented any traces of my body heat from being detected by their thermal-imaging technology. Feeling safe for the moment, I peered between the leaves and spotted four other vehicles barely visible in the distance. Once I realized the roadway was under constant surveillance I knew it was only a matter of time before the search teams combing the forest, with their dominant numbers, had me cornered—unless I could sneak across the road. Since the guerrillas were convinced they had me trapped on this side, I imagined if I could cross undetected, I might fall-off their radar altogether. *I've got to find a way to cross*, I thought to myself. *But how?* No sooner had I asked this question when the corners of my lips curled up into a grin—for I had discovered the golden thread to unravel Col. Thames' strategy.

This portion of the forest was divided into sections by dirt roads created by the Army engineers. Once enough trees were cut down to clear an area wide enough for a road, the engineers used the felled timber for its foundation. After chopping off the branches, the logs were placed lengthwise next to each other along the desired pathway. The final step was to bulldoze mounds of dirt, mud, and Carolina clay over the logs; the sun and the rain did the rest. Since the roads were raised a few feet above the ground, a narrow trench was created on both sides. Normally serving to channel the excess flow of rainwater during a storm, my hope tonight was this narrow alley would be my safe-haven.

The magnolia tree I was hiding behind stood about twenty yards from the road—which is a long way to low-crawl out in the open. Nevertheless, there was no time to relocate to a better position because I could hear footsteps approaching. Judging by the search patrol's slow deliberate pace, I knew I had not been spotted; so, this enabled me to hesitate just long enough to allow a pair of humvees, moving along the road in opposite directions, to crisscross. As soon as the military vehicles passed each other, I began to low-crawl at a moderate pace, wagering the occupants of both jeeps had just finished searching the area where I was crawling.

For almost two minutes, I was exposed to the open-air with nothing to hide behind. In short bursts, I crawled for a few seconds before stopping to listen for any approaching footsteps. Then I continued. By the time I reached the trench I was exhausted all over again; but with no time to waste, I quickly dropped the two handfuls of dirt and rocks that I'd collected along the way into its black gulfs. Following a brief pause to ensure my visit was not intruding on any resident rattlesnakes, I entered.

Before I could catch my breath, a deuce slowly approached. Having no tarp covering its cargo area, I stared at the handful of soldiers riding in the back. With my glasses on, I could barely make out the NVGs mounted to their kevlars; and just as I had anticipated, all of them were intently staring *over* my head into the forest. Remaining in the ditch, I proceeded to trail along in back of the deuce. Having deduced the pilots were not inclined to search near one of the ground patrols, I stayed in place a couple paces behind the huge utility vehicle even when helicopters flew overhead. After a half hour passed with no bounty-hunters showing up, I knew my plan was a good one. Marching back-and-forth through that canal, I stayed behind the deuce and watched the occupants of the truck as they searched the darkness in vain.

Three hours later, a squad of grunts emerged from the tree line; this was the only time I abandoned the trench. However, since the squad-leader had removed his NVGs to confer with the officers in the deuce, and the other soldiers were taking a break, no one saw me scamper back into the forest. On their return into the wood line the troops ambled within several feet of my hiding place. As the squad-leader strapped the NVG to his kevlar, I heard him rebuke a corporal who insisted that all of the rebels had been apprehended.

"That's a negative, Corporal. Captain Daniels expressly reported that the soldier we're looking for is black—"

"One of the six captives back there is black," argued the corporal.

"I know, if you'd just let me finish," responded the sergeant in a calm tone. Even though the NCO kept his cool, it was clear he did not appreciate being second-guessed by his subordinate. "I pointed that out, but the captain said the prisoner we got is definitely not him. He said on their first night, the guy was standing right in front of him with his weapon drawn; so, he's one-hundred-percent sure of what the soldier looks like. Captain Daniels claimed he'd recognize that guy's smart-alec grin anywhere. Sounds kinda personal to me…I s'pose this guy's been causing a ruckus."

As the sergeant led his troops back into the foliage, I was reeling at the news that the entire team had been caught—*even the major!* Relieved I had a plan for success, I returned to my cozy cubby hole and caught up with the deuce.

Hours later, I was still dragging my body through the slender passageway when the helicopters started landing one by one. Fatigued and famished, I sensed the sun's radiance was about an hour beyond the horizon and I knew the nighttime festivities were finally coming to an end. About ten minutes later, someone on the truck with a British accent gave the order to 'Shut it down!' Hearing this, I smiled through my anguish.

"Guess you ain't as thorough as they say," I whispered to myself.

Crouching low, I allowed the deuce to leave me

behind. After it sped off in a cloud of dust, I grinned through the dirt and grime caked-on my face. Yet, before I could pat myself on the back, a search party exited the woods. With their eyes cast downward, they appeared demoralized and exhausted. Holding my breath once more, I prayed no one saw me as they stepped through the ditch, all around me.

Having made that narrow escape, I realized the need to be patient because I was unaware of how many squads were still roaming the bush. This led me to my week-long sanctuary, the sycamore tree. Climbing up, I perched myself on my panther platform one last time. Twenty minutes later, my intuition informed me it was safe. On the climb down, I noticed my body had stiffened up—*man was I sore!*

Once on the ground, I crept toward the enemy camp. Finding no sentries did not surprise me. Their field-exercise just hours from being over, these National Guardsmen probably thought the combat team from Ft. Stewart had caught all of us. With no guards, present, I boldly strode toward the tent where I had executed their commander four nights ago. No longer feeling tired or sore, there was an invigorating pulse beating within that demanded its release. Unable to deny the Beast this moment, I pulled out the rest of my artillery and loaded a fresh magazine.

After setting my weapon to automatic, I tossed the rest of my simulators, both artillery and grenades, at the areas our team-leader had instructed us to attack. Just as the whirring, whistling sounds broke the silence, the grenades started detonating one-at-a-time: *Boom...Boom... Boom!* These were followed by the even louder artillery explosions. Aiming my M-16 at the sky, I pulled the trigger to allow the staccato fire from my black rifle join the melee of blasts occurring all over their compound. Half way through this explosive display a savage, hideous shriek burst-forth from my body.

"Rahhhhhhh!" the call of the Beast roared through the forest.

By the time the first heads popped out of any tents, I was already vanishing into the wilderness. With the receding moon smiling on my back, the faint howling of a wolf was heard replying in the distance. This, despite the fact Red Wolves had been extinct in North Carolina for nearly a decade.

Beaming at the red ball of fire penetrating the skyline, with Operation Golden Seal officially in the books, I double-timed along a dirt road. It felt good to stretch my cramped hamstrings and even better to break a sweat. I was traveling southbound hoping I was not lost. Now I wished I had paid more attention when Major Brackett was showing everyone where to muster after our mission. At the time, I figured because Stock and I worked as a team I would just follow him.

"Our new base-camp is Joe's farm," the major had said with a chuckle.

Recalling an image of the map, I was almost certain the major had been pointing at an area about two miles outside the woods I just left. Since Mr. Babcott utilized several acres for his cows, pigs, and chickens, when I caught the overwhelming stench of manure, I grinned knowing I was moving in the right direction. Following the nauseating odor until it became unbearable, I came upon a large white estate surrounded by several smaller dwellings. Eyeing the property through the gate, I was reminded of the plantation imagery provided by *Roots*.

After approaching the gate's entrance, I was astonished my instinct to remain covert prevented me from walking into the yard like a normal human being. On the other hand, I also felt naked, now realizing the gut-feeling sense telling me what to do was no longer transmitting. Since I had depended on a continuous flow of these extrasensory hunches over the past several hours, I was at a loss on how to proceed. Consequently, I remained hidden behind some bushes for the next five minutes in a state of confusion. Before I could make sense of my situation a blurry shape exited the house; so, I put my glasses on. Seeing a bearded Caucasian grab his morning newspaper from the mailbox, I felt relieved, at once recognizing the man's rugged sharecropper build.

"Good morning Joe!" I shouted over the twelve yards separating us.

"Ohh," Joe sounded mildly surprised. "Good morning Amaru…and welcome to my humble abode," he clamored while scanning the area. "Where ya at?"

Seconds after his good-natured reply, I stood up and saw my OPFOR comrades—looking cleaned-up, showered and shaved—exiting the house one-at-a-time. To my surprise, Sgt. Abrams was the first soldier to greet me as I entered the yard.

"Specialist Amaru, great work out there!" the NCO stated with his hand extended. "You did one helluva job!"

Following his handshake everyone likewise approached to offer their congratulations. With all the guys

292

surrounding me, our team-leader then summed-up his evaluation of my performance. "You know what Amaru, I've been thinking about this and, in my opinion, maroon doesn't really suit you," commented the Special Forces officer with his arms folded. "I bet a *green* beret would match your capabilities much better."

Once everyone realized there was an offer embedded between the lines they stopped talking.

"Sir," I replied in a sincere tone. "I'm flattered, I really am. But actually, I'm hoping my next assignment will be given to me by a professor at Rutgers University." Then I explained my collegiate aspirations in more detail. In spite of Joe insisting it was great news—especially the part about playing football—my former team-leader shook his head in disappointment.

"It'll never work," Major Brackett spoke the words like a prophet. "You'll be back."

"Really sir? You think so?" I uttered in astonishment.

"Oh definitely," the major replied without malice. "Amaru, don't get me wrong, I think you're intelligent enough to go to college. But what about after college? Let's face it, there ain't no place in the pansy-ass, civilian world for the warrior-spirit you got." With an elbow propped on the fist, of his other arm, the major stroked his chin with a thumb and index finger. "Yeah," he nodded as he spoke, "you'll be back."

"Okay sir." Baffled at his conclusion, I just smiled. "When I do return, you'll be the first soldier I look up…I'll even buy you a drink." This made Stock and Buzz laugh because they knew I quit drinking alcohol over a year ago.

Amidst the chuckles and pats on the back, Joe said the best thing someone in my condition could hope to hear.

"Amaru, your ruck sack's already in the house. Hurry upstairs and jump in the shower. My old lady put together a southern-style breakfast with all the trimmings."

"And everyone's waiting on you!" joked Sgt. Abrams.

Shaved, showered, and with a full belly, the images of the past five days seemed like nothing more than a passing dream. That is, until we remembered we still had to police-up the gear remaining in the forest. So, you can imagine our surprise when we returned to the training area and found all of our equipment neatly stacked on the airfield—and next to it, standing at attention, were hundreds of soldiers.

Upon exiting our vehicle, the throng saluted us. Not quite understanding what was happening, we glanced at the National Guardsmen before locating a separate, much smaller contingent, next to them. It seemed the thirty or so soldiers comprising this platoon had made an extra-effort to stand away from the part-timers. Possessing an altogether different demeanor, they glared defiantly while the commanders of both groups approached us.

"Good morning sir," Major Brackett stated as he saluted smartly.

"Good morning Major," replied a man speaking with a British accent and wearing the oak leaf of a lieutenant-colonel. "Can we have a word in private?"

While the officers shook hands and conferred, we locked eyes with the combat team for a few seconds before turning toward each other and starting our own conversations. After all, we were not standing in formation like they were; the only reason we stopped after exiting our vehicle is because they saluted us.

A minute later, Major Brackett returned.

"I've been ordered to introduce the members of my team," stated the major in a serious tone. Without another word, he mustered us into a formation. "Team, attention!" Once we snapped to attention, our team-leader turned around to face the eight-man entourage. Ten yards behind them three hundred and thirty soldiers remained as still as statues. "Colonel, it's my pleasure to introduce the soldiers comprising this year's OPFOR component." Following his opening salutation, the major pivoted and pointed at the ground to illustrate where he wanted us to line up. "Sergeant Gerald Abrams." Even though I was next in rank the major introduced me last. "Specialist Andrew Stockton…"

Starting with an O-3, whom I recognized as Captain Daniels, the officers one by one began shaking hands and exchanging comments with each member of our team. Eventually the procession made its way to me.

"So," remarked a dark-haired soldier wearing the olive-drab flight-suit of an Army pilot, "I finally get to meet the assassin who strikes his victims when they're taking a piss!"

Following a good laugh with Captain Daniels about our encounter on the first night, I hobnobbed with the lieutenants and warrant officers who had manned the search-vehicles and helicopters. I was astonished when, to a man, all these guys spoke like they knew me on an intimate level. Moreover, it was done with such deference they made me feel like a famous celebrity who was at the airport greeting his fans; the only difference was I did not sign any autographs. When one lieutenant asked if I had found any secret tunnels, I busted-out laughing so hard that I had to support my upper-body by putting my hands on my knees. While I was still crouched-over catching my breath, I spied a pair of spit-shined jump-boots as they stepped before me and stopped. Standing up, I locked eyes with Colonel Thames.

For a brief moment, the skinny officer paused to give me a silent once-over; which conversely gave me the opportunity to check him out too. At six-foot-three the 'Bloody Brit' was taller than I had imagined. Very pale-skinned with brown hair containing tufts of gray, his long, oblong face drew attention to a pointy nose and a severely jutting chin. These sharp angular features made him look like a pirate, especially whenever he squinted his blue eyes, which he did often. His quirk, it seemed, was not due to poor vision but rather just out of habit. Once he finished scrutinizing me, he stepped forward and extended his hand with the air of a European dictator.

"As a child I used to wonder," LTC Thames opened as we grasped each other's palm, "if it was possible to touch an invisible man. And if so, would his hand feel solid like yours? Or, would it evaporate into nothingness like a ghost's?"

At the mention of my self-coined nickname, I felt Buzz's elbow tap my ribcage. Not knowing how to respond, I just stood there, confident the lite-colonel was not finished talking.

"Two hours ago," Thames resumed, "we scoured the woods looking for an answer to how you were able to evade our night-vision technology. We found scores of your footprints alongside the road." Stopping here, he pointed at me. "You were following one of our vehicles back-and-forth through that canal, weren't you?" By asking this, Thames was humbly acknowledging his own defeat. Shaking his head, the Englishman never allowed me to respond. "Quite clever I'd say. Here we were looking under every nook-and-cranny way out in the thicket…and the entire time you were right there under our very noses. It seems you took the maxim: 'Keep your friends close and your enemies closer' quite literally. Specialist Amaru, plain and simple, you out-foxed us last night…keep up the good work!"

Since Col. Thames resembled an old crony pirate, at first, I thought he was criticizing me but soon realized that, far from being bitter, he was actually commending my effort. "Thank you, sir," I replied without ever confirming his theory.

He did not seem to need it.

After loading the stacked equipment onto a deuce, everyone jumped into the cargo hold to be transported to their respective units. When Major Brackett offered to give me and Stock a lift in his personal jeep, we looked at each other knowing there was no way to refuse—even though we had been looking forward to spending that last ride together with our team. Following a round of farewell hugs with our former comrades-in-arms, Stock and I grabbed our gear and climbed out the back. As we walked toward the major's humvee, we waved our final good-byes to the rest of the guys still on-board the deuce.

Having arrived at the jeep, the major's driver was shaking his head in disbelief as he opened the door for us. "You *must* be the man!" the young black PFC said, raising his hand to give me a pound.

"Wassup?," I said, bumping the driver's fist with mine. As Stock and I got in the jeep, I was wondering why the dark-skinned brother was so excited.

Seeming to notice my dubious disposition, PFC Reynolds connected the dots. "Until now," he said, adjusting his rearview mirror so he could see us. "I've only driven officers; so, this is the first time any enlisted butts have touched the backseat of this limo—and y'all ain't even NCOs!" Before he finished speaking the major appeared so Reynolds, knowing he had to stop talking, quickly asked the question he wanted to know. "So, what happened? What did y'all do to deserve a chauffeur-driven ride?"

Until that moment, I had not considered it strange that Stock and I were going with the major. Since he was the one who trained us, with the exception of Mullins, we had spent the most time with the team-leader; so, I just thought it was a last token of his camaraderie. However, when the major instructed Reynolds to drive to the Special Operations Command (SOCOM) Dining Hall instead of our company headquarters, it was obvious an honor reserved for a select few was being bestowed upon us.

At the mess hall, Major Brackett took Stock and me into a room reserved for officers and introduced us to high-ranking officials in the Special Forces, describing us as 'exemplary soldiers.' Following the meal, the major told me and Stock to go ahead to his jeep while he had a few words with his colleagues. Upon our arrival, the major's driver was shaking his head again. "And," he said, resuming his previous conversation, "y'all get to eat in the VIP suite with the big-brass? Come-on fellas, stop holdin' out," he pleaded, this time shaking Stock's hand while staring bug-eyed. "What the hell did y'all do out in the field?"

When PFC Reynolds stopped the jeep in the parking lot next to our company headquarters, the afternoon formation was already underway. While Stock and I grabbed our ruck sacks and other gear, the major exited the vehicle. "Good day Captain, First-Sergeant," he greeted the CO and Top in the no-nonsense manner of the US Army. "Excuse me for interrupting, but I wanted to return these two outstanding soldiers in-person, so I could tell you how much of a pleasure it was to have both Specialist Amaru and Specialist Stockton serve on my team. They did an excellent job!"

"Thank you, sir," Top and the CO replied in unison. By this time, Stock and I had put our equipment on the ground and were standing a few paces behind the major.

"Good afternoon sir."

"Sir, good afternoon," both of us greeted and saluted our company commander.

Once the captain returned our salutes, the first-sergeant approached us and shook our hands. "We knew you two would do a good job," Top praised as the CO beamed his appreciation with a benign facial expression. As Major Brackett returned to his jeep, following another salute, Stock and I grabbed our stuff and double-timed over to the motor pool platoon. I barely had time to ground my gear when Top called my name.

"Specialist Amaru, front and center!"

As I jogged back to where Top and the CO were standing, I noticed the BMO and Sgt. Will were also walking toward the front of the formation. Looking around, I wondered what was going on and for a split second, in spite of my hero's entrance, I feared I might be in some sort of trouble.

"Specialist," Captain Pearson stated wearing a solemn expression I had never seen before. "While you were in the field you received orders from Washington."

Having been distracted the last couple days, I had all but forgotten about the impending decision hanging over my head; so just hearing the phrase 'orders from Washington' instantly restored weeks of tension. Before I could ask the next obvious question, Sgt. Will started shaking his head. "Like I said *Mister* Amaru," my platoon sergeant said with a grin. "You're that one-in-a-million story." Following the comment by my NCOIC everyone became silent again; it seemed they wanted me to sweat for a few more seconds.

It did not take long for my patience to wear thin. "Sir," I spoke in earnest. "Did it get approved?"

After another poker-faced hesitation, Captain Pearson finally spoke. "Like Sergeant Will said *Mister* Amaru …" then he smiled. "Congratulations and good luck at Rutgers!"

As everyone chuckled at the candid way I was being addressed as 'Mister' they stepped forward, one at a time, to shake my hand. "Wait a minute," I interrupted the celebration after calculating it was somewhere around the twenty-first. "My ETS date isn't until the twenty-fifth so I still have a few days left as *Specialist* Amaru."

Seeing everyone's blank stare made me understand I needed more information.

"What's today's date anyway?" I asked

"The twentieth," shot back the BMO.

"Yeah, so I have five more days—"

"That's a negative," interrupted Sgt. Will. "According to these orders from the Department of Defense," he said, waving a piece of paper in his hand, "your ETS date is today." Realizing I did not believe him, my platoon sergeant simply handed me the documents. "See for yourself."

Taking the parchment from my platoon sergeant, I scanned down past the seal of a bald eagle grasping a bundle of arrows and an olive branch…*I could not believe what I was reading!* When I looked back up, Captain Pearson summed up our meeting.

"Amaru, you've already stood in your last formation," the CO stated with a grin. "You gotta start clearing immediately and I'll explain to S-4 why you're running so late. Also, make sure you call the Soldier Support Center to schedule an Out-Processing Briefing."

"Clear sir," I replied with a gigantic smile.

After saluting my former company commander, I executed my final about-face. As I was running toward the barracks, I suddenly felt the urge to stop. Just once, I wanted to watch Top call Sgt. Will, Stock, Chill, Reggie, and the rest of HHC 3/759th Aviation Regiment to attention—without me. Now, looking back at that moment over twenty-five years later, I wish I would have stood in that formation just to experience it one last time...*sike!*

Chapter 9: No Good-byes...only Good Memories

At my out-processing briefing, I was given a laundry list of requirements to fulfill. ACAP, Transportation, Finance, Education, and the Transition Services Branch were some of the stations I had to clear to receive an authorized stamp. For the next couple days, while I sat in multiple waiting areas, the previous two-years-and-nine-months swirled in a mist of memorable moments. The entire week would have been absolutely perfect had it not been for a flat tire on the Jetta and one department called CIF. The Central Issue Facility was the turn-in point for our equipment.

The Army operates according to its own priorities; which unbeknownst to some is not simply dictated by a soldier's rank. Due to the unusual circumstances surrounding my discharge, I did not contact the Soldier Support Center until the date of separation on my orders. This is a far cry from a normal situation where out-processing begins two weeks prior. So, in spite of the presence of mostly officers and NCOs at the briefing, my case took precedence. This was nice until I realized that, as a result, my appointment at CIF had been set for the next day. I should have rescheduled in order to have time to clean my TA-50 but, having no idea that CIF had a reputation for being the most difficult station to clear, I figured I'd simply wipe-down my gear instead of giving it a thorough cleaning. If, by chance, I failed to get it clean enough I'd just end up with a new appointment anyway; so, it's the same as rescheduling, right? Not exactly. What my line of thinking failed to take into account was just how strict and demanding these already finicky clerks can become if they don't like you—not to mention the embarrassment that accompanies these types of situations.

The next morning, I was seated in a bland gray waiting area with ten other soldiers. Of the ten only one had ETS orders; the others were being transferred overseas, mostly to South Korea. While we greeted each other, all of them took a glance at my equipment and agreed I'd never clear CIF today.

"Specialist, this is the first time you've had an appointment at CIF, isn't it?"

"Yes Sergeant, how'd you know?" I naïvely responded.

"Because when it comes to accepting TA-50, CIF is famous for being...*hmm*, let's say very meticulous."

Another NCO, seeing the confused look on my face, translated 'meticulous' into easier to understand jargon. "He means they're a bunch of nit-picking assholes."

His translation caused everyone to laugh.

At 09:30 hours, we were greeted by a stubby Caucasian male with droopy jowls and a round, compact nose who introduced himself as 'Specialist Macy.' Once the brown- haired clerk escorted the eleven of us inside a warehouse, he pointed at eight, long tables lined-up at the front of the gigantic room. "Spread out," he said. "And once you've found yourself a space, go ahead and start placing your gear on the table. I'll be by to inspect it shortly."

The tables were long enough to provide everyone with

a separate work area. After going to the fourth row, I turned right and walked to the end of the aisle, far away from where Macy was standing. Prior to opening my duffel bag, I looked around the warehouse to take in my surroundings. Behind these tables was a gated-counter which separated us from a large storage area. Somewhere in the back rows of that supply area, a female's voice could be heard shouting out number / letter sequences which I deduced were bin locations. Although she was not visible, the two male privates following her directives could be seen racing amongst the rows of equipment placing items onto shelves. Once I confirmed Spc. Macy was the sole inspector, I glanced over at the pudgy E-4 on the other side of the room to make sure his back was turned; only then did I start setting my stuff on the table. For this reason, I had to chuckle along with everyone else when Spc. Macy—without even glancing in my direction—flunked me from fifty feet away.

"*You!*" he yelled as he jotted notes on a clipboard, "the dirtbag in the fourth row. I can smell that Carolina clay from here. Pack that nasty shit up and gettit out of my warehouse!" Like most military bureaucrats, Spc. Macy took his job very seriously. "And don't bring it back until you've washed it thoroughly—*capeesh*, Specialist?" To confirm his message was being received, he turned to glare at me. "I don't know what the hell you think this is, Amaru!"

When it came to inspecting TA-50, Spc. Macy was a strait-laced stickler. He ended up sending me to the laundromat four times before finally accepting every piece of equipment. In fact, CIF was the only station I had not cleared by Friday afternoon, thereby causing me to stay an additional weekend at Ft. Bragg. Nonetheless, even with this small inconvenience, my last week in the Army was akin to being awake in a blissful dream.

Three days later, when I arrived at the motor pool to clean out my office, I was glad only a few of the guys were present. After exchanging greetings, plus a few jokes with a new dispatcher, I went upstairs. Ten minutes later, the same private-first-class entered my office without knocking. "Hey Amaru, what's the status of that light-switch for vehicle H-9?"

When PFC Raga caught me in a tearful moment I was embarrassed.

"Oh, my fault, I should've knocked," admitted the russet-red complected Cuban. With his crew-cut and toothbrush moustache, he looked like Charlie Chaplain with a tan.

"Nah, it's cool," I said, wiping my face with a tissue. After walking over to a metal cabinet, I grabbed a small package from a shelf and handed it to him. As I did so, it dawned on me this menial task would serve as my final action in the motor pool.

"Thanks Specialist." Before Raga exited, he stopped to say one more thing. "Hey Amaru, everybody knows how much blood, sweat, and tears you put into this place so I'm glad I got a chance to meet you before you left. And again, I want to apologize for interrupting."

Hearing his kind words in such a sentimental moment forced me to fight off a second surge of emotion. "It's cool man," I replied with a grin as I grabbed another tissue. "Hey do me a favor, don't tell the guys downstairs I was crying, okay?"

"Okay," he uttered with a smile.

"Thanks Raga. And remember cuz," I said pointing at

him, "it's never too late to accept Christ into your heart."

"I know, thanks. Hey listen, I want to ask you something before you leave...nothing important." His smile having faded, he was now wearing a somber expression. "It can wait until after you're finished in here."

"Yeah alright," I replied blowing my nose. "See ya downstairs."

Once Raga left, I stuffed the rest of my belongings in a bag and sat at my desk. Since I had established that PLL office from scratch, my mark was on every inch of the room; so, no matter where I looked there were so many memories, both good and bad. Following a short prayer to express my gratitude, I stood up and grabbed the bag. As I walked toward the exit, I composed myself before extinguishing the lights and locking the door for the last time. While I was descending the stairs, it occurred to me that Raga might want to get saved; this upset me because I realized I had been so wrapped up in my own situation I had failed to think about his. When I got on the floor and did not see him or anyone else, I walked toward the dispatcher's office. After likewise not finding anyone there either, I jogged across the bay to Alpha Company never suspecting when I opened the door to the office I would get the surprise of my life.

"Congratulations Amaru!"

Standing in the doorway, I was blown back by the voices of nineteen people. If I had not seen it with my own eyes, I never would have believed the members of both motor pools could fit into the tiny space around the dispatcher's desk. Once everyone filed into the bay and shook my hand, Sgt. Will assumed the spokesperson duties for the entire group.

"Specialist Amaru," the E-6 said, stepping forward, "we want to congratulate you on what you've accomplished." Although my platoon sergeant saluted me with words of support, he wore a sober facial expression. His next remarks explained his cold look of indifference. "I never told you this before so I wanted to make sure I did today. When I became the motor sergeant a year-and-a-half ago, there were some shady rumors floating around the company about you."

Hearing this, a couple mechanics stifled back a chuckle.

"As your direct supervisor," Sgt. Will continued, ignoring the gibes, "it was my job to investigate every one of them. Having said that, I can say with certainty, I never found even one shred of evidence to support any of the allegations. Like the BMO said," with this he pointed over my shoulder at Sgt. Polkowlsky, who was standing behind me. "You've been nothing less than an outstanding soldier." Then, making a fist, he stuck out a thumb and jammed it into his own chest. "I personally witnessed how you raised this battalion's standard of excellence—and not only in the motor pools and supply rooms. Thanks to your example, the PT standards along with the general attitudes of the younger guys have improved dramatically. And trust me," he insisted, "your efforts will continue shining around here long after you've scored your first touchdown. Specialist, thank you for a job well done! And never forget what you told me."

"What was that, Sergeant?"

"There's no such thing as good-byes—only good memories."

"I told you that?" I asked, thinking he might be confusing me with someone else.

"Yeah, you don't remember? Sgt. Will responded

sounding disappointed. "You said it right after you told me our bird went down in Honduras."

About a year ago, a Chinook crashed during an exercise in Central America resulting in five deaths. Among the mortally wounded was Staff Sergeant Tubbs, who was good friends with Sgt. Will. On that fateful evening I happened to be the CQ-runner; so, I was the person who had delivered this morbid news to the various section-chiefs—which included the motor sergeant.

"Oh, that's right," I replied, now recalling I had repeated the proverbial phrase many times that night. "No good-byes," I stated with a grin. "And Sergeant, thanks for all the memories." Then I gestured behind him. "That goes for all you guys…thank you!"

With that, Sgt. Will and I embraced in an emotional hug which prompted another round of applause. As he released me, the BMO stepped forward to shake my hand. "*Dammit Amaru!*" Sgt. Polkowlsky said, choosing a disposition more in accordance with the macho image of the Army. "It sure has been a pleasure having you around here!" Following the BMO's exclamation, I was bombarded with numerous shout-outs, pats on the back, and words of support. As good as it was to be acknowledged by my supervisors and peers, the climax of my farewell came when Smith and Davis approached. Both wearing huge grins, they took turns shaking my hand.

"Amaru," said Smith once Davis released my palm. "Yesterday, the battalion commander's driver, Specialist Marley, told us something interesting about you. He said the colonel black-mailed you into coming to our basketball practice that time." Before I could respond he snapped his fingers to emphasize his own lack of awareness. "I should've known something was strange when the colonel showed up with those two majors and a captain we never seen before."

"Yo Amaru," Davis broke-in, "is it true that Colonel Packer said if you didn't join our team, he wouldn't sign your early-out request?"

When Davis asked this, the bay became dead silent.

"Check-it-out," I said, thinking of the best way to avoid creating any controversy. "Y'all still gotta live, breathe, and eat around here so don't even sweat the details about that." Then I pointed at Smith. "What's important is that intelligent, good-looking brothers like us found a way to rise above the *Willie Lynch* syndrome. Lord Smith," I said while presenting arms with my right-hand. "I salute you in peace!"

"And I you, Lord Amaru," replied Smith returning my salute. Following our theatrics, we hugged and shook hands. After likewise hugging Davis, in order to make everyone feel at ease, I took a free-shot at Smith's sidekick.

"But Travis," I said, hooking my thumb at Davis, "I dunno about your boy over here."

"What?" Davis blurted out defensively. "What's that supposed to mean?"

Before I could add the obvious punch line, Sgt. Will beat me to it.

"It means you dumb and ugly, boy!"

After everyone busted-out laughing, Stock and Ware walked out of the tool room carrying the main course for my Sayonara party. "Amaru," clamored Stock, "sorry we couldn't bake, you a cake but one of the cooks at the chow-hall was cool enough to donate these."

"He also told us to tell you, 'Congratz and good luck'," said Ware.

Looking at the same cherry, apple, and lemon *Hostess* pies I used to smuggle into the barracks during basic training, once again, I was brought full circle. "Specialist Arnold?" I asked, wanting to know where to direct my gratitude. "He's the one who hooked this up, right?"

"Umm…" With a mocking wink, Ware made it known these treats had similarly arrived via the black market. "You know what? I can't even remember dude's name."

Sgt. Will caught the vibe and immediately cleared his position on the matter. "Not only do I *not* want any of that junk food," he joked, "for the record, I don't hear any of this conversation."

After the BMO co-signed on Sgt. Will's sentiments, Davis used my camera to document our Kodak Moment. As we munched on our treats, Smith asked if I had taken a recent photo in my Class As.

"Speaking of taking photos, I know you already took an official joint for your grand mom, right?"

"I wanted to but I didn't have any time," I replied taking another bite.

"Hold up, hold up," interrupted Sgt. Will. "I thought I told you to get them taken when you first got back from Golden Seal?"

"Yeah, you did," I admitted. "And I was going to, until I found out how much time and effort went into out-processing. But at least I got my photos from basic training, those'll have to do."

Before the words finished coming out of my mouth, EVERYONE blasted my decision.

"*What!?*"

"Oh, hell no!"

Before the mob became too rowdy Sgt. Will held up his hand for silence. "Amaru," he said with a grave look of concern. "I can't order you to get new photos taken—but if I could I would. Trust me, in twenty years, when you look back you'll be happy you made the extra effort."

"And your grandma'll be happy too," chimed in Smith.

"Tak, whaddya talkin' about?" Stock then added for good measure. "This is a moment in time that requires official documentation!"

Needless to say, when I saw how everyone was in unanimous agreement, I decided to go through with it. Since it was for the record, I decided to wear a uniform sporting the Division's unit patch rather than the logo of an uncelebrated Aviation brigade. That evening, I called my homie, Atkins, from the oh-five. Since the Jetta was in the shop, he agreed to bring his Class-A jacket in his car to my barracks the next day, at lunch time.

On the following afternoon, after receiving the jacket, I commenced the meticulous ritual of preparing the uniform and polishing my jump-boots. Having already showered and shaved, I then got dressed before checking my appearance in the mirror. Once satisfied, I grabbed my wallet and walked outside.

The heat was so stifling that I immediately had to seek shelter in the shade. Even though I was hidden from the sun it was so hot that, within seconds, I began to perspire. As the liquid pouring down my face matured into rivulets of sweat, I wiped my brow and cringed realizing how drenched I would be by the time I walked the eight hundred yards to the taxi-stand. "I should've taken Atkins up on his offer to give me a lift," I sighed, closing my eyes for an answer to this dilemma.

Knowing Atkins wanted to spend time with his girlfriend before he hit the field next week, I declined his offer, thinking it would be just as easy to take a taxi into Fayetteville. Plus, I did not want to sit around waiting for him to be released for the day. After leaving the photography studio, I planned to walk five blocks to the garage where the Jetta was being repaired. By that time, I reasoned it should be a lot cooler and, even if it's not, the photo shoot would already be over so a little sweat won't kill me. As I puzzled over the issue, a horn started blaring in the parking lot. Never thinking the driver was trying to get my attention, I ignored the racket until a familiar voice called my name.

"Amaru! Yo Amaru, is that you? Open your eyes—it's me, Yates!" the voice yelled. "Where's Chill?"

When I looked down, I saw a stubby brown guy in BDUs waving his arms; and next to him was a car with its hazard lights flashing. "Ssup Yates," I replied, greeting him with a raised fist.

"Check out my new ride," Yates declared, proudly gesturing toward the light-blue *Nissan Sentra*. "I just bought her yesterday, whaddya think?"

"What do I think?" I repeated with the look and sound of satisfaction. "I think you oughta hook a brother up with a ride off-post!"

"You serious?"

"As a heart attack," I replied. "Oh, and Chill's not here."

"What? Are you sure? He told me he had to pull CQ duty last night, so he would have the day off today," Yates stated in a tone which suggested I might be mistaken.

"Yeah he's off today," I agreed, "but his girl picked

him up a couple hours ago."

"Oh, okay let's go."

Descending the staircase, I thanked my guardian-spirit; nevertheless, I was not all that surprised. Twenty-five minutes later, I gave the Atlanta native a pound before making the usual, farewell comments. "Thanks for the ride, Yates. And by the way, you got a nice car," I said admiring the spoked rims as I shut the door.

"Amaru, if I don't see you again before you leave, I just wanna say good luck…and God bless!"

"Brother, God bless you too—peace!"

As soon as Yates drove off, I looked at the plaza-directory billboard near the main entrance and failed to locate a photo studio listed amongst the various shops. Feeling agitated, once I started to sweat again, I ducked inside a drugstore to soak up the AC while I bought myself some time to think. Upon entering the building, I could not believe how good the air-conditioning felt. *It was great being back in civilization!* Just inside the double-doors, I spotted a janitor mopping so I approached him to ask about the studio. Once the sanitation worker revealed it was inside the pharmacy, I was relieved I did not have to go back outside.

"Thank you," I said expressing both my gratitude and relief.

Following the janitor's directions, I walked to the back of the store and had no difficulty finding the small studio. When I tried to enter, however, I nearly smashed my face against the transparent door before realizing it was locked. Following a closer inspection, I noticed a hand-scrawled message taped to the inside of the glass: 'Be back in 15 minutes.'

Once my wait had exceeded twenty minutes, instead

of roaming the aisles for the umpteenth time, I decided to remain near the photo studio and watch four employees as they rearranged light bulbs arranged to spell 'Drugstore' on an electrical sign with the word 'Pharmacy.' Seeing this, I imagined the word 'drug' had gotten such a bad rap in the 1980s that, instead of anything medicinal, it now conjured up images of skinny crackheads stealing VCRs or, even worse, strung-out pregnant women trying to prostitute themselves. This is when something occurred to me: why is it acceptable in society to be addicted to the pharmacy's dope, but doing street drugs somehow makes you a bad person, even a criminal? I mean, what's the difference? Do my brain, heart, and liver prefer Demerol over heroin? Or amphetamines over cocaine? Wondering this to myself, I promptly concluded: *not if it's Wiley's yayo!* Covering my mouth, I coughed to stifle a chuckle before something caught my eye which caused me to spin around.

"I see you!" I said pointing at the Peeping Tom who was clumsily peering from the next aisle. "What do you want?" After a pair of skulking eyes disappeared from between two boxes, the cardboard containers shifted themselves back into position next to one other.

A split second later, a woman's voice wailed from the next aisle. "You caught me!" the woman screamed in melodramatic fashion. "Oh, my goodness, I'm so embarrassed!"

Hearing this weak attempt at humility, I walked toward the end of the row wondering what type of lunacy awaited around the corner. Upon making the turn there was a young woman standing there waiting. Peering into the girl's face I knew, right off the bat, she was a 'GI Hoe.'

Ester the Molester

'GI Hoe' is a slang-term to describe desperate women who will do anything to marry a man in the military. In short, it means being a soldier-groupie. Large military installations like Ft. Bragg make a significant contribution to the economy of the nearest city. We used to joke if Ft. Bragg ever moved to another state how Fayetteville would fold-up like an abandoned tent. This type of dependency results in some of the local girls dreaming of being rescued by a 'Knight in a Shining Class-A uniform.' On our witnessing missions in Fayetteville, Curt, Reggie, Chill, and I had encountered more than our share of these aggressive hens. For this reason, even before she introduced herself, I already knew her story *almost* as good as she knew mine.

"Hi Specialist Amaru," the woman said, offering her hand with a bashful grin. "My name's Ester." If Ester had not later revealed during our conversation that she was twenty-two, judging by her dress and demeanor, I would have mistaken her for someone much younger. Nearly as tall as me and maybe a shade darker, the girl looked like she just rolled out of bed still wearing the same clothes she fell asleep in last night. Not only was her apparel wrinkled but her hair was not done. Short with a perm, there was a blue comb stuck inside to keep it in place.

"What's up sis?" I replied, grabbing her hand as casually as I could to demonstrate there was no attraction. Although I behaved in the detached manner of a polite stranger, Ester made it clear from the onset—when she refused to let go of my hand—that she was definitely interested.

"Oh my, your hand is so soft and soothing…can I hold on to it?"

"Umm, ha ha," I laughed to disguise my discomfort as I snatched my hand from her grasp and put it inside my trouser pocket. "Ester," I said, figuring this was a good opportunity to witness, "how's your relationship with Jesus Christ?"

"Couldn't be better," she replied without hesitation. "I've been a member of Mount Sinai Baptist Church my whole life. My cousin just became the pastor six months ago and I'm training to be a Sunday School teacher."

"Oh, that's nice," I replied, not knowing what else to say.

"Excuse me for thinking out-loud," Ester said, changing the subject, "but you're so young…" Saying this, she stared at my face. "You can't be more than nineteen or twenty, right? And you're already an E-4, that's impressive! If you keep it up, you got a shot to retire as an E-9. But," she raised her index finger, "even as an E-4 you got-it-going-on, honey! Did you know the president raised wages throughout the entire military last year? Now, your base salary's over nine-hundred-bucks! And that ain't even including housing and separate rats—"

"I live in the barracks so I don't get either of them," I interrupted.

"Of course, you do now silly, because you're still single." As she spoke, she playfully rolled her eyes. "But after we get married, we're gonna live off-post. And wait a minute, oh my, since you're a paratrooper, you also get jump-pay!" Firmly entrenched in her own world, Ester then started calculating numbers and rattling-off data that illustrated how a married couple could 'live-it-up' on an E-4's salary.

As insane as Ester appeared, I was impressed at how well she could work-out arithmetic problems in her head. Just as I was about to suggest that she pursue a career in accounting or financial consulting, her conversation plummeted from innocent and naïve, to down-right ridiculous.

"As I'm sure you know," she said in an earnest tone. "Both Reagan and Bush are big supporters of our Armed Forces family. That's why I became a republican last year."

"Oh, you're in the military too?" I asked, making sure to steer clear of politics.

But she ignored my question.

"You look *sooo* good in your uniform! *Hmm-hmm*, I can't wait 'til mama gets a look at you!"

I was actually thankful to hear this nonsensical reply so I could feel justified in ending this foolish conversation. "Well, well, look at the time," I commented sarcastically while making the effort to look at my bare wrist.

"No," Ester promptly replied, making it clear she was not ready for our conversation to end. "I'm not in the military but I'm a military-brat. My father was killed in Vietnam when I was still a baby."

"Oh, sorry to hear that. So, are you planning to join the service?"

"No…I'm not."

In an attempt to look shy, I noticed Ester was standing with her hands clasped behind her back, gazing down at the ground. As I observed her B-movie acting skills, I found it difficult to believe she actually thought anyone would take her seriously. "Help me out sis, I'm a bit confused," I continued my line of questioning. "A second ago, you mentioned 'our' Armed Forces family, what did you mean by that?"

Hearing the question Ester looked up and grinned; this revealed a large gap between her teeth which I had not noticed until now. Transfixed by her macabre smile, everything seemed to slow down; so, when Ester responded by suddenly pointing and saying: 'I'm gonna marry you!' I flinched.

"We're gonna have five children and live overseas!" Ester continued.

Standing there, I considered the possibility the woman might be clinically insane. This made me feel sorry for her; that is, until she tried to hold my hand for a second time. At this point, having no other choice, I once again snatched my hand back before raising both arms like a referee signaling a touchdown. "Slow down!" I said, giving Ester. the same advice, the *Brand Nubians* later recommended to *skeezers* worldwide. Lowering my arms, I folded them against my chest to discourage any further hand-holding attempts. "Sista, don't you think you're a little ahead of yourself?"

"*No!*" she snapped, putting a hand on her hip. "My mama taught me when I see something I want, I have to take the initiative."

Hearing Ester's firm reply, I understood she was determined to make this difficult. Then something occurred to me. Since her dream was to marry a soldier maybe all I have to do is tell shorty my plans.

"Ester—"

"Baby, you can all me 'Essy'," she interjected, batting her eyes to appear seductive.

'*Baby!?*'

Hearing Ester call me 'baby' was reminiscent of the time Tina referred to me as 'her man.' Nevertheless, since she was propositioning herself so boldly, I felt obligated to scan her from head-to-toe for any 'girlfriend' potential. This notwithstanding, with no make-up, perfume, nor any appreciation for fashion or elegance whatsoever, I almost became insulted this shabbily dressed girl in her faded t-shirt and beat-up dungarees actually believed she could pick me up.

"Ester," I tried again.

"Yes baby?"

"Today's my last day in the Army."

"Really?" she replied before my words had a chance to sink in. "Well—wait a minute, what're you talking about? Your last day?" The boyish grin having vanished, Ester then initiated an interrogation that I was only too happy to participate in.

The fact she was not impressed by my collegiate plans did not surprise me; what did however, was how she actually turned her nose up at the notion of pursuing a higher education. "So, you're just gonna walk away from all this?" she asked in a tone of disbelief mixed with disappointment and anger.

Not quite understanding her question—especially if she was including herself in the 'this' package—I remained quiet.

"You're just gonna ruin your life!"

"Is that supposed to be a joke?" I replied, completely at a loss for a more appropriate response.

"No, it's not!" Ester behaved as if I had crushed her only goal in life. Appearing somewhat neurotic by this point, she then launched into a two-minute rant listing the reasons why I need to quit talking what she termed 'nonsense.' "Hurry up!" she whined, "and re-enlist so we can get married!"

"Ester, Ester please calm down." Without waiting for a response, I pointed over her shoulder. "See that man behind you?" When Ester turned around, she saw a fat, white man standing in front of the photography studio. He was looking at us. The man, after propping the studio's door open, stood in the entrance and continued to stare with an amused look on his face. From fifty feet away, in addition to the boyish grin, a large coffee stain was visible on his breast pocket. "I have an appointment with him, so I gotta go."

Without further ado, I walked right past her.

"Wait—you can't just leave!" Ester shrieked, trying to grab my arm. But my first-step was so quick she ended up grasping wildly at the air.

I was praying she would not chase after me.

"I'll be waiting here when you're finished, okay? After you meet mama, you'll change your mind—you'll see." Ester spoke, in a confident tone.

As I walked into the studio, the photographer was still nibbling on the remnants of a doughnut. Watching him try to suppress a grin from forming on his triple-chinned visage reminded me of one of Belkis' famous sayings. In fact, she liked to voice this rallying cry almost as much as her acclaimed Golden Rule. "Never argue with a fool," she had warned, "because a bystander can't tell which, is which."

When I left the studio with my portraits that evening I was relieved the aisles were clear of any lurking GI Hoes. Two months later, while I was attending summer football camp at Rutgers, a red-shirt freshman named Josh said

320

something which reminded me of ol' Ester.

Following our second practice of the day and a refreshing shower, everyone piled into a convoy of vans for a ride to dinner. I rode with the same group of first-year players to every meal. Like myself, these newbies were being introduced to the life of a campus jock—which included being the target of female groupies. As our team van arrived at the cafeteria, we looked at the crowd of mostly girls, who were staring back at us through the windows.

"Tak," Josh said, pointing out the window. "See that chicken-head near the door? The girl in the red tank-top?"

"Which one?" I asked, "there's two girls over there wearing red tank-tops."

"The one talking to that tall dude," he continued. "She's smiling…see her? She has a big gap between her teeth."

"Yeah I see her."

"So, check it out, yesterday homegirl pushed-up *strong!* And guess what she said when I told her I already had a girlfriend."

"What?"

"She accused me of 'playing hard to get.' Can you believe that?" Josh stated with contempt.

"So, what'd you say?" I asked with a grin, knowing his come-back would be something funny.

For a split second, the six-foot-two, two hundred twenty pound, outside-linebacker just looked at me like I was stupid. Then his brows suddenly clenched together and the tips of his mouth turned downward into a frown. "I told that trifling hoe the truth!" he said, glaring out the window in disgust. "I ain't *playing* hard to get…I *am* hard to get—ain't nobody playing!"

Hearing Josh's reply, everyone in the van—including the driver—cracked-up laughing. Although it took a couple minutes for the van to be parked, most of the guys were still enjoying a chuckle as we stepped outside to greet our admirers. So, as you can imagine, the humor only escalated when the girl in the red tank-top, upon seeing Josh exiting the van, quickly ended the conversation she was having with the tall guy and started walking toward us. "Hi Josh!" she yelled out, sporting her gap-toothed grin.

"Good luck with that, homie," I muttered under my breath, walking away from Josh's side. As I did so, I wondered how my girl, Ester, was doing.

Chapter 10: A Final Quick Conversation

At 09:00 hours, on Monday, June twenty-seventh, I felt brisk and refreshed when I walked into the dining facility on Smoke Bomb Hill. Having exchanged farewells with Chill, Reggie, and the rest of my neighbors in the barracks, I was amped knowing that following a cheese omelet and a cup of coffee—plus one final stop at CIF—and it was all she wrote. I recall the food tasting really good that day; it was almost as delicious as the dinner I had in the very same building on my initial Sunday after leaving the Way. Having already placed my duffel bags and suitcases in the trunk earlier that morning, following my meal, I returned to the barracks just to brush my teeth.

With everyone at work the barracks were so peaceful that I decided to take a minute to relax in the foyer on my way out. Taking a seat on a wooden chair, I thought about all the guys here, both past and present. Then I took a moment to envision the future—at least what I conceived of the future. It consisted of scenes of people coming and going, GI parties, and guys just chilling outside their rooms with a beer talking. Throughout my life, I've always felt a great deal of anxiety when it's time to leave a place I've called 'home' for the last time. Perhaps it's a moment to conceive just how temporary and insignificant my physical existence is.

Standing up, I made my final salutations before stepping out of the foyer. Jogging down the steps, I recalled seeing Curt do a somersault off the balcony of a nearby building with the same design. This prompted me to say something I never thought I would admit. "Yeah, I'm gonna miss Fort Bragg!" With no one around, I dared to speak out loud and even laughed to myself as I crossed a road and entered the parking lot.

Seeing the Jetta waiting for me, I smiled, thanking God for my blessings. As I opened the driver's door, I heard my name being called so I looked in the direction of the voice and spotted a tall, lanky guy with a familiar stride running toward me. It was Specialist Robertson.

"Yo Amaru, hold up a minute!" he yelled, jogging across the parking lot.

Shutting the door, I leaned back against it until he reached me.

"Thanks for waiting," Robertson said, giving me a pound. "Listen, I just wanted to say 'peace' and 'good luck'."

"Thanks."

"And…" Robertson paused to make eye contact, "to apologize for giving you a hard time about getting saved. You didn't know this back then because I kept it a secret."

"What's that?"

"I had broken up with my girlfriend a few days before you started going to church…so I guess when you switched up your game I felt like you were deserting me too." Admitting this, Robertson looked at the ground and shook his head.

"So, you ain't seeing Alicia anymore?"

"Nah, everything's cool between us now; we got back

324

together a couple months later. Oh, that reminds me, she wanted me to tell you, "Good luck!"

Touched by his humility, I stepped forward and gave my former teammate and drinking buddy a hug. "Give your lady my thanks," I said before releasing him. "And tell her I said she has been blessed with a good man. Yo, did your roommate tell you I dropped by last night?"

"Yeah, that's how I knew you were ETSing today. By the way, congratulations on going to Rutgers! You gonna play wide-out or d-back?"

"Wide receiver, I hope. Yo check-it-out—" But before I could start talking, Robertson handed me a CD.

"Here," he said. "It's a little going away gift."

"What is it?" I asked, expressing my surprise.

"It's a new single for a joint by *Spike Lee*. Every time I hear it, it reminds me of you."

Scanning the CD cover, I saw the famous movie producer staring up at me with a box of pizza in his hand. Also, in the picture was a well-known, Italian actor whose name I could not remember. "*Fight the Power…Do the Right Thing,*" I said before reading the last line: "*Public Enemy.*"

"It just came out. You up on *PE?*" Robertson asked, wanting to know if I liked the group. "They're the dopest crew out right now, and they're bringin' that real Hip Hop!" When he went on to explain this single was coming off their yet-to-be released album entitled '*Fear of a Black Planet,*' I knew I was going to like it.

"Thanks man, I'll check it out," I gave him a pound to show my appreciation.

"Promise?"

"Whaddya mean, 'promise?' I need to make a promise?" I asked laughing.

"Nah I'm just playin'," Robertson said with a grin. "Look I gotta go. I'm supposed to be running an errand for Sergeant Gaines, and I should've been back by now." Following another hug and a pound, I watched Robertson jog away before climbing into the driver's seat.

My final tour of Ft. Bragg was splendid indeed. Taking the scenic route, I even cruised past the 18th Airborne Corps Headquarters to say farewell to my old Air-Assault buddy, Iron Mike. By the time I drove into the parking lot at the Out-Processing branch, I couldn't have stopped smiling even had I tried. Having received the last required stamp of authorization from a very polite and friendly Spc. Macy a half-hour ago, the only thing separating me from civilian life was simply handing-in the file containing my military records, which was sitting on the passenger seat next to me. Opening the door, I almost floated out of the car. "When I get back here, we're bound for 95 North boyeee!" I exclaimed, locking the door.

Entering building 4-2843, I climbed the stairs and went to the D-wing as I had been instructed. After finding room 261, I walked down the center aisle of a room that was bisected into two equal-sized seating areas. There were about twenty soldiers on the right-side of the room but very few sitting on the left. Both groups waited in silence. Standing in line, I resisted the urge to scream at the top of my lungs: *'I'll never wait in a military line ever again!'* Instead, I settled for a tranquil grin while the guy in front of me handled his business at the window.

"Next," barked a rude, Caucasian female with short black hair.

"Good morning, Specialist," I greeted the cranky

woman, placing my folder through the slot in the window.

"Mornin'," she mechanically responded, barely looking at me. Following a glance at my records, she slid them back through. "Have a seat on the left side and wait for your name to be called," she spoke and gestured at the same time. "Next."

As I entered the waiting area, I wondered why I had not been instructed to sit on the right side, where most of the people were. Once seated, however, I started feeling sleepy right away so it was nice to have all that empty space to stretch-out and relax.

I do not recall how long I had been asleep; the only thing I remember is a familiar voice disturbing my power-nap. "Hold up a minute Lewinsky, I know that ain't who I think it is!" As the voice grew louder in my ears I decided it was not part of my dream, so I opened my eyes. And there, squatting before me grinning like a hyena, was my former platoon sergeant, Sgt. Quick. Because I had never seen him look this happy before I was not sure if I was awake or still dreaming. My feeling of uncertainty was only exacerbated by his strange behavior.

"*Oh my God!*" Sgt. Quick shouted while staring at my face. "It's the Army's lucky day!" Yelling this in an exaggerated fashion, he stood up and threw his arms in the air like a lady who is possessed by the Holy Ghost. Then he pivoted to address the other side of the room. "Well, I'll be damned! Talking about a low-budget, two-for-one sale," he paused to chuckle and slap his own thigh. "Today, I get to witness two, that's right folks," he emphasized with two fingers extended, "*two* sorry slime-balls get tossed-out for the price of one."

"Hey, what's up Sergeant Quick?" I said with a yawn,

scratching my head. As I sat up and stretched my limbs, I wondered who he was talking to because the unknown guy standing behind him did not appear to be listening.

"Lewinsky sit down," Sgt. Quick snapped before adding a touch of sarcasm. "This here's someone you gotta meet!"

Once the blonde-haired, Caucasian private was seated in the row behind me, I tried to greet my former platoon sergeant again. "Sergeant, it's good to see you. I—"

"Good to see you my ass!" Sgt. Q taunted, sitting down in the chair next to me. "They finally caught up with you, huh Amaru? Guess you ain't as slick as you thought!" After my former supervisor finished cracking-up at his own comment, he turned in his seat and looked back-and-forth between me and his prisoner. "You two fuck-ups know each other?" When both of us shook our heads, Sgt. Q looked genuinely surprised. "No? Well, y'all just missed being sorry at the same time in my motor pool." Not waiting for a reply from either of us, the motor sergeant was beside himself with laughter.

After a few seconds, he took a deep breath to collect himself.

"Amaru," he said pretending to be serious. "I never thought I'd say this but it's damn good to see you too…" he hesitated before adding the punch line, "sitting in the Chapters Section of the Out-Processing Center!" Then he busted-out laughing again. "Man, I can't wait to tell Chief!" *Then he got his first hint it might not be such a lucky day after all.* "By the way, where's your NCO escort?" Saying this, Sgt. Q stood up and glanced around the room. "I need someone else to laugh with."

Until Sgt. Quick mentioned the 'Chapters Section' and something about me needing an escort, I had no idea what he had been babbling about. When Lewinsky and I made eye-contact halfway through his crude monologue, Lewinsky revealed his cluelessness too. Only then did I notice, for the first time, a sign dangling from the ceiling above Sgt. Quick's head which read: 'Chapters Here.' Seeing this prompted me to look across the room, and sure enough just as I suspected, there was another sign fluttering in the breeze provided by a fan. Because it was flapping like a flag on a windy day, it took me a second to make out its message: 'ETS Soldiers Here.'

Expiration Termination of Service (ETS) is only one of the Army Regulation's many chapters explaining the various types of discharges: honorable, general, and dishonorable. That being said, everyone knew the phrase 'chaptered out' referred to a less-than-honorable dismissal. Given the Army's dual nature any action which differs from the majority population—even if the result is something good—is automatically separated and filtered into the 'evil' category.

A-ha, I gettit. So that's why I'm sitting on the left side.

"Oh," Sgt. Quick resumed being an asshole. "Where are my manners? I forgot to introduce you low-lifes. Private Lewinsky," he stated before pointing at me, "this is Private Amaru."

"Come on Sergeant…" Standing up, I pointed at the insignia on my collars. "Are you getting senile in your old age, or what?" Then I pivoted and shook hands with Lewinsky. "I'm Specialist Amaru, pleased to meet you." Having released Lewinsky's hand, I looked at Sgt. Quick. "And technically, I'm an E-4 promotable."

"*What?*" the E-6 was instantly pissed off. "How the hell can you be an E-4?" Then he spun around and raised his voice. "Amaru, where's the NCO escorting your delinquent ass?" he asked for a second time.

"Sergeant, I'll explain everything if you'd just allow me to," I said with an innocent grin. "You got it all wrong, I'm not getting kicked-out; I've been given permission to ETS three months early because I got accepted to Rutgers University. Oh, and guess what? I'm on the football team too…so I'm gonna be runnin' back kick-offs just like I told you I would!" When I said this, I honestly thought my former platoon sergeant—who after all was a black man—would be proud of me. Proud of how much I had matured and achieved since leaving the Division.

Well I was wrong.

"You got permission to do what?" Sgt. Q bellowed in a pompous tone. "ETS three months early? *Stop lying!*" he jested with contempt. "I've never heard of that before. In what chapter, of what Army Regulation, is that covered in?"

Seeing this naked display of arrogance was appalling but I still did not give up. "Actually Sergeant," I replied, choosing my words carefully, "it's a directive from the Department of Defense in Washington DC."

"Oh, is that right?" Sgt. Quick responded between chuckles. "The Department of Defense, huh? And I imagine you have some paperwork to substantiate these wild claims."

"Of course I do, Sergeant," I said nonchalantly while extending the folder in my hand. "The orders from the Department of Defense are on the last page."

Seeing no hesitation on my part caused the NCO to stop laughing. Before taking the folder, he took a moment to inspect my uniform. In addition to my two promotions since leaving the Division, he sighed loudly when he noticed the Air-Assault badge sewn under my Airborne wings—*the very same Airborne wings he and Chief had painstakingly made the effort to slice-off with a razor blade.*

"What the fuck is going on down there in Leg Land?" he vented his dissatisfaction by rudely snatching the documents out of my hand. "You voluntarily terminated! That means, by Army Regulation, you aren't allowed to wear those wings anymore," he seethed, pointing at my chest.

"But Sergeant, just like the regulation covering discharges," I calmly stated, "there's a directive that overrules it. In my case, since my new unit—well it's my old unit now—has jump slots, my CO asked me if I wouldn't mind having my jump status reinstated."

"*What?* Your CO asked if you wouldn't mind—forget it, shut up!" he said clearly upset. "Let's have a look at these alleged orders." Looking down, he started flipping through my file so I watched in silence. By the time he came to the letter of acceptance and Coach Anderson's authorization—both of which had been typed on bright red and white, Rutgers letterhead—his jaw started to tighten. After reading them carefully, he turned the page and saw the orders from Washington DC granting my three-month hiatus. At this point, he was far beyond the boiling point. "This is a bunch of horseshit!" he yelled, flinging the folder at me.

As I stooped down to collect the papers which had fallen on the floor, a clerk called Lewinsky's name. "Come on, let's go," Sgt. Quick said without acknowledging my presence one way or the other. Hoping to make a final appeal, I reached out and grabbed his forearm.

"Sergeant, you gotta believe me," I pleaded, "I've

changed! A couple months after I terminated, I got saved. Since then, I've dedicated my life to serving Christ."

After yanking his arm out of my grasp, Sgt. Q took a step back to glare with disdain. "*Oh really?*" he replied in a sneering tone. "So, you got saved by the blood of Jesus, huh?"

Despite hearing the condescension in his voice, I nodded. "And I praise God He gave me the opportunity to thank you in-person before I left Fort Bragg. Sergeant, I appreciate everything you did for me when I was lost in sin." Peering into his eyes, it seemed he believed me for a split second. That is, until I failed to respond satisfactorily to his final question.

"Amaru, what's the name of your church?"

"The Door…umm, well the truth is, I had to quit attending church because—"

"*Bullshit!* You're a lying, con-artist Amaru! You always have been and you always will be!"

Before I could plead my case any further, he walked away with his prisoner in-tow. Watching him talk to the lady behind the glass window, I was beating myself over the head thinking of a way to convince him I had truly changed. As Sgt. Quick placed Lewinsky in the custody of the MPs on-duty, the solution I was searching for came to me. *Fuck him! I mean why was I so invested in what he thought anyway?*

Sitting there in silence, I watched Sgt. Quick walk past me on his way to the exit. Of course, he ignored me. Seeing him defiantly strut by holding his maroon beret, I tried to imagine what he would look like in a black beret with shades and a black leather jacket. This made me smile. "Sergeant Quick," I called out. "Wait a minute!"

Upon hearing his name being called the NCO stopped and exhaled in disgust before turning around with both hands on his hips. "What do you want Amaru?"

Seeing Sgt. Q's high-handed, swaggering posture set Billy off; so I had to get him! Rising to my feet, I stepped into the aisle for the confrontation. "*All the Way!*" I yelled as loud as I could.

Once again everyone's attention was riveted on us.

"*What?*" Sgt. Q snapped, sounding both surprised and embarrassed. "What's that supposed to mean?"

"Whaddya mean, 'what's that supposed to mean?'" I shot back in a challenging tone. "That's the Division's motto, right?"

"Right."

Then I pointed at him. "You're in the oh-five, right?"

"Right."

"And that's part of the Division, right?"

"Right."

At this point, some chuckles could be heard in the background so I couldn't stop myself from cracking a smile. Now speaking in a calm tone, I folded my arms. "So I'm saying it to you. All the Way."

Infuriated, Sgt. Quick tried to respond but realized he could not be heard over the growing laughter; so, after pushing a guy out of his way, my former platoon sergeant backtracked four steps and stopped. "Half-way!" he yelled pointing at me. "Amaru, with your sorry ass, only half-way!"

As I chuckled along with the entire room, a frustrated little man—who also happened to be a good soldier—stomped out the exit. With his 'Half-way' declaration still ringing in my ears, I realized this was the first time I had ever been associated with the term 'half' and thought it was funny.

I had truly come full circle.

Minutes later, I was still snickering about Sgt. Quick's witty come-back when my name was called.

"Specialist Amaru."

"Welcome to Fort Bragg—Home of the Airborne."

Two years ago, I promised myself not only would I make it to this moment but, when I did, I would pull off the road right here in order to admire the billboard that, back then, I used to hate. Although much had changed in my heart since I made that vow, just looking at this sign, which featured the various unit patches worn on the shoulders of soldiers at Ft. Bragg, even now, I could feel tinges of the desire to go AWOL; this feeling was especially strong whenever I returned from a weekend pass. Reclining the seat back, I interlaced my fingers behind my head just as *Lionel Richie* started singing the first verse of '*Jesus is Love.*' After a minute or so of gazing at the sign I popped out the tape and put the CD Robertson gave me into the stereo.

As I shifted into gear, the beat hit.

"A-ight, a-ight!" I said, nodding my head.

"It's nineteen eighty-nine! The number, another summer (Get down!) Sound of the funky drummer! Music hittin' ya hard 'cause I know you got soul...(Bruthaz and Sistaz!)"

"Fight the Power!" I yelled out the window with *Chuck D* and *Flava-Flav*. In between rocking to the beat and chanting the chorus, I glanced at the rearview and watched Ft.

Bragg vanish into nothingness. "So, dreams do come true after all," I reflected, understanding the image I was seeing—mirror and all—was a vision which had played and replayed in my head many times, especially during those cold mornings in Missouri. "I never gave up…and now I'm here." Once I came to this conclusion it was easy to advance to the next step. "I'll never give up—no matter what happens I'll never stop fighting!"

Having made this declaration, I contemplated where this journey called 'life' might take me. And, with a crooked-tooth smile, I shifted into overdrive and steered my way into the future…*Amen!*

THE END

Author's Perspective

Symbolism is used throughout *Gaikokujin – The Story* to represent various aspects of my being. Shortly after releasing Book 1, I began receiving emails criticizing the comparison between my father and a serpent. For those raised with a Judeo-Christian worldview serpents may simply represent evil but in the ancient world they meant so much more. One of the oldest, most universal symbols, the serpent was associated with wisdom, fertility, enlightenment, healing, immortality, and even magic, itself. However, my idea for the comparison also includes *Quetzacoatl*, the 'Plumed Serpent,' who in the Aztec folklore is prophesied as a great teacher. The *Nagas* of Vedic lore, possibly the origin of the infamous term 'Nigger,' were human/serpent beings known to possess high levels of wisdom. And of course, as mentioned in the intro for Book 1, we cannot forget the kundalini energy which is likened to a coiled serpent residing at the base of the spine that rises to the head when it is awakened by discipline and spiritual study. There are other powerful associations such as *Hermes'* caduceus (which is a short staff entwined by two serpents), the *Rod of Asclepius* used by the medical association, as well as the Greek Goddess of Wisdom, *Athena*, who has a serpent on her shield. In fact, 'Amaru' is an ancient Andean snake spirit who is the guardian deity of the Incas and their predecessors.

Here is wisdom. Let him who has understanding calculate the number of the beast, for it is the number of a man: His number is 666 ∽ *Revelations 13:18*

The Beast stands for the primal instinct of savagery

that exists within all human beings. To many readers, it may seem to be a product of my imagination. But I do not agree. In fact, superhuman abilities—including strength well beyond normal—have been reported so much that common anecdotal incidents such as mothers lifting cars to rescue their children have been coined with its own terminology: 'Hysterical Strength.' Usually occurring when people are in a life-and-death situation, its only predictable attribute is it cannot be turned on or off consciously (i.e. by the ego). The Beast is the dark side of my personality. We all know that from the darkness comes light so before there was any light, by definition, there must have been perpetual darkness. Western society teaches that darkness is synonymous with evil and, of course, that evil is bad. But what if, let's imagine, 'good' and 'evil' were not what we thought they were. What if, instead, they represented nothing more than *basicity* and *acidity* on a Morality-Ph scale?

The Number of the Beast = 6-6-6 = Melanin

Composed of 6 protons, 6 electrons and 6 neutrons, carbon-12 is one of the five elements in the human DNA. Carbon-12 is the most abundant of the two stable isotopes comprising the element carbon, accounting for almost 99% of carbon. In addition to providing its black color, carbon is the organizing molecule that structures melanin and gives it the ability to absorb energy and combine with other molecules while retaining its stability and coherence. Called the 'chemical key to the brain—and to life itself—the numerous physical benefits of melanin have been well documented; but it is the mental and spiritual characteristics that are emphasized throughout the story. Researchers such as Dr. Richard King, Dr. Carol Barnes, Dr. Ann Brown, Anthony

Browder, as well as many others have written on this topic, explaining how melanin and an activated pineal gland are indispensable components for connecting to higher levels of consciousness.

"Melanin is an ancient substance that links us to previous worlds…and, in movies, previous worlds and underworlds are usually evil" ~ Occultist Brother Panic

Understanding that *God* and the *Devil*, just like *Horus* and *Set*, *up* and *down*, *yes* and *no* are merely opposite polarities in our world of duality, allowed me to grasp why melanin-rich people are viewed as 'public enemy number 1.' Just as the evil spirits in horror movies are from 'hell' or some other world in the past (or present) melanin, likewise, links us to something which is beyond this existence. Bobby Hemmitt, teaches that 'demon' in ancient texts can be translated as both 'genius' and 'melanin' before saying: "In your blood are these microscopic, demonic substances…so you're scared of your own damn substance!"

Once I released this irrational fear, I was able to decipher the roles of demons and other evil entities in movies or books. In addition, I understood the origin of the *haves* vs. the *have nots*, *developed* vs. *developing* countries, even the difference between a *terrorist* (on the news) and a *freedom-fighter*. I began to realize what it meant to be melanin-rich and what the symbols are for a melanin-rich person. This enabled me to watch TV shows and other forms of western entertainment without becoming emotionally wrapped up in racist or other subliminal messages.

Final Note:

Any conversation about melanin must include black people. That said, my use of melanin-rich does not emphasize race but rather the highest state of being. It is about Christ Consciousness. Please keep in mind that in spite of Christianity being a featured topic, *Gaikokujin – The Story* is not a religious novel. The Serpent, the Beast, Melanin-Richness, and Christ Consciousness all represent unlimited power.

Acknowledgements

To my 7th grade English teacher, Ms. Eldred. You called me a "gifted writer," and I made you promise to never tell anyone because I was embarrassed. Back then, I wish I could have explained to you about "being black." Thank you for inspiring me…and for keeping the secret!

To John, Carl, Kelly, Sam, Dennis, Ralph, Rob & Rose, Sanford, Chill, James, Noguera, and everyone who attended a service at the Door during that era. So much investigation, teamwork and learning…*what a blessing indeed!*

Trainers: A big thanks to Carl Crawford for not only being my elder brother in Christ but also my training buddy. We did some work and achieved the impossible…many times over! To my homie, Carrington. I'll never forget those intense work-outs at the gym on Smoke Bomb Hill…you taught me much and, yes, I did fake it in that final round. Respect bruh! And I cannot leave out the 100-yard-dash champion, Johnson. You made me learn how to run with good form; I was so tired of getting dusted by you. I don't know if I ever told you this but on the day I finally beat you I had my eyes closed for the final eighty yards in order to ensure I maintained proper technique. *But I finally got you!* On another note: I still can't believe you're gay.

To the officers and warrant officers that hooked a brutha up – thank you! A special thanks to Captain Price for supporting a young man trying to do something right with his life—*plus, that was a helluva ride in that Chinook!* That also goes for the Sergeant First Class (I cannot remember your name) who let me off the hook from the charges at the replacement center. Black men looking-out for younger black men are never shown in the media; so I wanted to make sure I did.

Air-Assault School was a blast! To every Air-Assault Instructor who was present that day at lunch; I appreciate your understanding. Stockert, Buswell, Frank, and the guy from the 10th Mountain Division (who got recycled): it was hell but we had fun! Frank, I still say had it not been for the muscles in both my legs cramping up, it would have been me (instead of you) who won that 12-mile ruck-race.

To Dean Reed, Coach Anderson, Bill & Jennifer, the E.O.F. Program, and anyone who witnessed the uncanny events which transpired on Livingston Campus in April 1989.

There are a few events mentioned in the book which really stand out in my mind. One is when I ran into Jerry Guzman's little brother, Eddie, and he refused to believe I was the same guy who used to sell weed at the courts. In addition to repeating over and over how healthy I looked, he also claimed there was a light emanating from me (or surrounding me, I wasn't quite sure). The second one is the righteous example my sister-in-law demonstrated concerning the whole fiasco about my car. The way she put her foot down and took a stance cannot be emphasized enough. Thank you, Kathy! And last but certainly not least, I'd like to extend my final shout-out to the guy who symbolized everything I couldn't stand about the Army: Staff Sergeant Queen. To you,

I only have one thing to say: All the Way! *Hahahahahahaha!*

〜Tak Amaru, May 2018

ABOUT THE AUTHOR

Takuan Amaru is an accomplished writer, teacher, and youth advocate. He is the author of over 100 articles ranging on diverse topics such as popular culture, music, history, and ancient spirituality / philosophy. Takuan borrows from his former occupations as a soldier, social worker, mental-health specialist, athlete, music artist, and high school teacher / coach to connect with readers on an intimate level. He makes his home in Nagoya, Japan. For more information, please email him at: takuanamaru@gmail.com. Or, connect via Facebook.

Glossary of Terms, Historical Figures, and Events
(3 Volumes)

A – B

ACAP is the abbreviation for: Army Career and Alumni Program

Affirmative Action is a policy that seeks to redress past discrimination practices through measures to ensure equal opportunity in education and employment

Air Jordan is a nickname for Michael Jeffery Jordan (1963 -), who is considered by many to be the greatest basketball player of all time

Air-ball is a shot attempt in basketball that misses both the backboard and rim *(see Brick)*

Akashic Records: According to *Robert Bruce* (2009), it is a frequency that permeates all dimensions. An interdimensional broadcast containing records of all past events and future probabilities (pg. 277)

Akitu (or *Akītum*) means: cutting of barley; it was the Sumerian spring festival in ancient Mesopotamia

Albert Hofmann (1906 – 2008) was the Swiss scientist credited for synthesizing the psychedelic effects of LSD

Alfred is the butler and father-figure to the famed Marvel Comics super-hero, *Batman*

All the Way Live! Refers to: an exceptionally cool vibe at a party; popularized by a 1978 single by Lakeside

Alvin Ailey (1931 – 1989) is the choreographer who is credited with popularizing modern dance

Amazing Grace is a Christian hymn written by poet and clergyman John Newton in 1779

Amazon Warriors were called *Oiorpata* in the Scythian lexicon. According to Greek mythology, they were a nation of all-female warriors

Amen (also *Amon, Amun*) is an ancient Egyptian god who, together with his spouse Amaunet, rose to the position of patron deity of Thebes during the 11th dynasty of the Old Kingdom (c. 21st century BC). The name itself signifies the 'hidden one,' and according to Dr. Muata Ashby (2000-2001), the concept of Amun is the central theme of every world religion – and of modern physics as well (p. 77)

American: Until the 19th century, *Negro, Indian, Colored, Black,* and

344

Moor were used interchangeably with *American;* Caucasians were referred to as 'Europeans' or 'settlers' (in their history texts)

Amos 'n' Andy: In the 1920s - 1950s, two Caucasians in *black-face* portrayed 19th century, racist stereotypes on radio and television shows

Angkor Wat [អង្គរវត្ត] is a vast temple complex built by Suryavarman II, the Khmer King. It was dedicated to the god, Vishnu. It is still the symbol of Cambodia and appears on its present day national flag

Anomaly: Deviating from what is standard, normal, or expected; i.e. an inconsistency

Anubis is also known as *Anpu.* This ancient Egyptian god is the 'opener of the way' into the Underworld

Apollo Theater: Reference to: the *World Famous Apollo Theater;* located on historical 125th Street in Harlem, NYC

Apostle-hood: In classical Greek, *Apostle* means: one who is sent away; this is what the disciples were called after Jesus' death

ARCOM is an acronym for: Army Commendation Medal

Area J: A rugged training area located on Fort Bragg, NC

Aretha Louise Franklin (1942 -) is one of the best-selling female artists of all time; known as the 'Queen of Soul'

Arizona Brown is marijuana from Mexico that is rumored to be smuggled into the US through Arizona

Arms Room: a secure area for stocking military armaments

Army Slogan: "Be All You Can Be!" was the official Army slogan from 1980 – 2001. It was featured on a commercial with another popular phrase: *"We do more before 9 am than most people do all day!"*

As the sound of many waters is a quote in Revelation 1:14-15. It states: *His head and his hairs were white like wool as white as snow; and His eyes were as a flame of fire; His feet like unto fine brass as if they burned in a furnace; and His voice as the sound of many waters*

Asiatic: the Original Man; we have existed for aeons preceding anything documented in western history books. The Noble Prophet, Drew Ali, referred to black, brown, red, and yellow people as *Asiatics*

Assata Olugbala Shakur (also known as JoAnne Chesimard) (1947 -) is a former member of the Black Panther Party and Black Liberation Army. Between 1971 and 1973, Shakur was accused of several crimes and was the subject of a multi-state manhunt. In May 1973, Shakur was involved in a shootout on the New Jersey Turnpike. She was wounded while BLA member, Zayd Malik Shakur, and New Jersey State Trooper, Werner Foerster, were both killed in the incident. Assata was accused of murdering the officer and assaulting fellow Trooper, James Harper. Between 1973 and 1977, Shakur was indicted on many charges. Some of which included: murder, attempted murder, armed robbery, bank robbery, and kidnapping. (Note: it is documented fact that many of these crimes occurred while Shakur was in legal custody. Many claim this illustrates she was being framed by the state of NJ). The charges resulted in three acquittals and three dismissals. However, in 1977, she was convicted of the first-degree murder of Officer Foerster, and of seven other felonies related to the shootout. Shakur was incarcerated in several prisons in the '70s. This includes serving time in a men's prison where, as a "cop killer", she was subjected to regular vaginal-and-anal strip searches. *Is this equivalent to saying she was repeatedly raped?* In 1979, she escaped from prison, and is now in Cuba, where she has been living in political asylum since 1984. Since 2005, the FBI has classified her as a 'domestic terrorist' and offered a $1 million reward for assistance in her capture. In 2013, the New Jersey Attorney General doubled the reward for her capture to $2 million. Shakur is the first woman on the FBI's Most Wanted Terrorist List. According to Ms. Shakur herself, she is a "20th century escaped slave"

ASVAB is the initials for the Armed Services Vocational Aptitude Battery. This entry test is administered by the United States Military Entrance Processing Command. It is used to determine qualification for enlistment in the US Armed Forces

Ate up is military slang meaning: far below the accepted standard; i.e. bad, terrible, fucked up

Awesome God is a contemporary worship song by Rich Mullins on his 1988 album, *Winds of Heaven, Stuff of Earth*

AWOL is a military acronym for: Absent Without Official Leave; i.e. a deserter

Baba Dwame Ishangi (1934-2003) the artistic director of the world renowned Ishangi African Dancers is also an accomplished African folklorist, dancer, percussionist, choreographer, lecturer, storyteller, sculptor, yoga instructor, nutritionist, poet, family counselor, spiritual advisor, and teacher

Babbit is marijuana with very low levels of THC; i.e. bad weed

Back Slide is Christian term meaning: to return to a prior state of sinful living; i.e. to regress

Baller is slang for: basketball player; it later adopted attributes of street hustling and womanizing

Balls: This term makes reference to the testis. It means: courage, brashness, boldness. "Having balls' is military slang for: having the nerve to do something

Bama means a southerner (from Alabama) trying to blend in up north, but is so obviously 'country'

Bar-Mitzvah is a Jewish coming-of-age ritual. It is akin to the female version, *Bat Mitzvah*

Barrio is a Spanish term for the *Hood*. In the US it is the Latino equivalent of *Ghetto*

346

Battle Creek, MI is the home of *Kelloggs;* a multinational manufacturer specializing in breakfast cereal products

B-Boys is terminology for: a participant in the Hip Hop culture of the early '80s; there were also *B-girls*

BDU is the initials for: Battle Dress Uniform. It is the olive-drab, camouflage uniform

Be Down: This phrase is questioning if a person is worthy to be included. It's a shortened form of 'down by law'

Bean Pie: A pie often sold by representatives of the Nation of Islam

Beating Meat is slang for: masturbating, i.e. jerking off, choking the chicken, etc.

Beef: 'Having a beef' is slang for: holding a grudge against someone and wanting to fight them

Beemer is a nickname for: Bavarian Motor Works; BMW

Beethoven: [ˈluːtvɪç fan ˈbeːt.hoːfən] (1770 – 1827) was the son of a Moorish woman. Most people have no idea that one of the most famous composers of all-time was, in fact, a 'black-a-moor'

Benjamin Banneker (1731 – 1806) was an astronomer, mathematician, inventor, author, farmer, engineer, and social critic. This African man was an internationally known polymath who lived as a 'free man' during the chattel-slave era of the Americas. A few of his many contributions include being the original publisher of the *Farmer's Almanac,* the architect who laid the plans for Washington DC, and inventing the modern clock. For this reason, according to Dr. Booker T. Coleman, the clock in London is called 'Big Ben'

Bensonhurst: This section of southwest Brooklyn is predominantly populated by the descendants of Italian immigrants

Bent: 'To get bent' is street terminology for: getting intoxicated / high

Bento [弁当]: refers to: a lunchbox

Big Gulp: A super-sized 20-64 ounce soft-drink introduced in 1980

Billy Bad-Ass was my shit-talking alter-ego. He is not to be confused with the Beast, who rarely spoke

Binghi: The *Nyahbinghi Order* is the oldest of all the Rastafari mansions and was named after Queen Nyahbinghi of Uganda, who fought against European invaders in the 19th century

Bite or Bitin' is the act of intentionally trying to pass another artist's lyrics off as one's own in a plagiaristic context

Bite out (someone's) Back is a phrase meaning: talking negatively about someone in secret; i.e. talking behind someone's back

Black: Beyond denoting a race or color, this term symbolizes many things (see Melanin, Moors, Negro)

Black Hawk is a nickname for the UH 60 series of military, utility helicopters

Black History Month is held annually in February to celebrate important people and events in the history of the African diaspora

Black Man's World is another reference to BMW

Black Ops is a loose reference to government, covert operations with negative overtones

Black Panther Party (for Self-Defense) was a revolutionary socialist organization promoting the Black Power movement in the US from 1966 to 1982

Black Sheep is an idiom for: an odd or disreputable member of a group; especially within a family unit

Black-and-White is slang for: police car

Blazing is street slang for: high-level; it can refer to anything from a beautiful woman to very potent cannabis

Blessed are the pure of heart, for they shall see God is a quote from Matthew 5:8 of the New Testament

Blow is one the various street-names for cocaine; i.e. *yayo, nose-candy, snow white, etc.*

Blue Devils is the nickname for: Duke University athletic teams

Blue Light Special: In a US department store named *Kmart*, a flashing blue light is turned on to indicate a short-term discount

Blues (or Dress Blues) are the Air Force dress uniform; i.e. their version of the Army's Class A uniform

BMO is the abbreviation for: Battalion Maintenance Officer

B-More is the nickname for: Baltimore, Maryland

Body-Boxing is a brutal form of boxing wherein punches to the legs, abdomen, and chest are thrown as hard as possible

Bogart: 1. The act of shoving someone out the way. 2. Cutting in front of someone. 3. Taking more than one's fair share

Bokuto [木刀] is a wooden sword commonly used in *Kendo*

Bon-odori[盆踊り] is a dance commemorating the Buddhist custom of honoring the spirits of one's ancestors

Bonaparte: A comical reference to Napoleon Bonaparte becoming a tyrant due to his 'short man' complex

Bones is slang for 'dollars'

Box is a street name for: a large portable radio/cassette player; whites labeled them "ghetto blasters"

Brainiac is a term for: studious individuals

Brick: In basketball, this is a bad shot that bounces hard off the backboard or the rim

Brickhouse is jargon for: an irresistibly sexy woman; made famous in a song by the Commodores

BRM are the initials for: Basic Rifle Marksmanship

Broomhilda is a comic strip by Russell Myers depicting a man-crazy, cigar-smoking, beer-guzzling, 1,500-year-old witch. In ancient times, the

348

Celtic people had an entirely different image of the witch, or 'crone'. She was revered as the 'dark mother', the healer, the wise woman. The buffoonish images of women, or those of the 'wicked witch', are wholly concepts created by western society

Brother: Many ethnicities and groups use 'brother' to address its male members. However, 'a brother' or 'a sister' typically refers to melanin-rich people

Brown-Round is the Army's nickname for: a drill sergeant's hat

Brown-nose is Army slang for: ass kisser; supposedly, these individuals 'kiss ass' so often, they have brown, fecal residue on the tips of their noses

Brown People are generally Latinos, Indians, and dark-skinned Asians

Bruce Lee: [李小龍] *Lee Jun-fan* (1940 – 1973) this Hong Kong fighter and filmmaker, who founded *Jeet Kune Do,* is perhaps the most influential martial artist of modern times. Bruce Lee's widow, Linda Lee Cadwell, asserts that Bruce created the concept for *Kung-Fu* (with himself as the star) before Warner Brothers outright stole the idea. It is believed that David Carradine was inserted because of opposition to a Chinese man being cast in the role of a hero

Brut is a brand name by *Fabergé* for a line of men's cologne

Buck is slang for: firing a gun

Buddah is a nickname for marijuana because THC is known to cause a deep level of meditation

Buggin' out is slang for: having fun or acting crazy; popularized by a 1985 song by Whistle entitled *Just Buggin*

Bumming (something) is slang for: receiving something for free

Bumple-stiltskin is a comical reference to the imp-like creature in the German fairy tale, *Rumplestiltskin*

Burner is another reference to a handgun

Bushido [武士道]: is the samurai's moral code emphasizing frugality, loyalty, and honor unto death

Bust (someone's) Balls is Army slang for: to embarrass or humiliate

Bust a Nut means: male ejaculation; i.e. to cum

Busta is slang for: an uncool person; i.e. a nerd

Buster Brown is a comic strip character created in 1902 by the *Brown Shoe Company*

BX is an acronym for: Base Exchange; these are huge retail stores for Air Force personnel and their families (similar to PX)

C – D

Cadre means: the military personnel in charge

Cammied-up is the act of using camouflage paint and clothing in order to blend into the surrounding environment; i.e. a guerilla

Candy Shop: A metaphor for: a place where illegal drugs are sold

Carl Wade Stiner (1936 -) is a retired US Army, four-star general

Caught Out There is slang for: getting caught doing something wrong plus the consequences that go along with it

Chakra is a *Sanskrit* term. Often thought of as 'spinning wheels of energy', they represent the seven subtle energy centers aligned from the base of the spine to the top of the head. In Hindu metaphysical and tantric/yogic traditions, it is believed that when all seven chakras are in alignment, a person's life force *(kundalini)* can travel up the spine to the crown of the head

Challenge-Password is Guard Protocol. A question is posed to the oncoming party who must provide a valid answer to be authenticated

Chaptered (Out): Army Regulation manual 635-200 covers all types of less-than-honorable discharges

Charlie Chan: This Chinese-American detective, created by Earl Derr Biggers, is viewed as a racist stereotype by many Asians

Charlton Heston: John Charles Carter (1923 – 2008) was an actor known for his portrayal of *Moses* in *The Ten Commandments*

Cheeba is a street name for: cannabis or marijuana

Cherry Blast: is the nickname for the first parachute jump after Airborne school; i.e. the sixth jump

Chi; or *Qi* [氣] is an active principle forming part of any living thing; frequently translated as 'natural energy', 'life force', or 'energy flow', it is the central underlying principle in traditional Chinese medicine and martial arts

Chicken George: A reference to the subservient, fearful character in *Roots,* played by Ben Vereen

Chill-Guill was my nickname for Perez. It was also to honor one of *Doug E. Fresh's* deejays named *Chill Will*

Chink was originally a British slur for Chinese. Nowadays, this pejorative refers to Asians in general

CIA: On August 18, 1996, the *San Jose Mercury News* published the first installment of a three-part series of articles concerning crack cocaine, the Central Intelligence Agency, and the Nicaraguan Contra Army

CID are the initials for the Criminal Investigation Command. This unit investigates crimes within the US Army; akin to Internal Affairs

City of Brotherly Love is a nickname for Philadelphia; i.e. Philly

Civvies is military slang for: civilian clothes

Clap is a nickname for: Gonorrhea; a sexually transmitted infection (STD)

Clinton Eastwood, Jr. (1930 -) is another icon actor for white masculinity

Clockin' Dollars is a euphemism for: making money; i.e. working around the clock

Cloud 9 is an idiom meaning: a feeling of euphoria; i.e. floating on clouds

Clowning (someone) is slang for: making fun of; to ridicule someone

CO are the initials for: Commanding Officer

Coca-cola: Prior to the 20th century, cocaine was a legal ingredient used in this popular, carbonated soft drink

Cold Lamping is an alternate form of *chilling* or *cold-chilling*

Colored: An outdated Jim Crow reference meaning: black or African-American

Colt: A horse in its infancy stage is actually called a 'foal'

Columbian Gold is a a native strand of marijuana grown in Columbia. It is known for its golden hairs and powerful psychedelic effects

Commie is short for 'communist', but really meant anyone not agreeing with US policy during the Cold War. This code word for 'the enemy' was changed in the 21st century to *Terrorist*

COMMO is the Army abbreviation for: the communications platoon

Conan the Cimmerian is a sword and sorcery hero created in 1932 by Robert E. Howard

Concertina Wire is sharp, barbed wire that is formed in large coils. Also called 'Dannert Wire'

Confucius [孔子] (551 – 479? BC) was a teacher and philosopher who emphasized human morality; he is credited with being the first to write the *Golden Rule* and is the author of many famous texts including the *Five Classics*

Cool Jay is a shortened form of LL Cool Jay

Cop is slang for: a police officer. Or a verb meaning: to receive something by either purchasing or stealing it

Coqui 900 is a malt liquor brew by *Pabst Brewing Company.* It was popular in Philly for its potency

Cowardly Lion is a reference to the timidly fearful character in the 1939 musical-film, *The Wizard of Oz*

Cowboys and Indians: In this make-believe ritualistic role-play, children re-create the massacre of the original Americans

CPA: Certified Public Accountant

CQ is an abbreviation for: Charge of Quarters; the NCO in charge overnight

Cracka is a term used to identify the class of societal slave drivers; i.e. the foreman who *cracks* his whip

Cracka Theology is my way to express the system of white supremacy. Dr. Neely Fuller and **Crackhead** is slang for: a person addicted to crack-cocaine; it also suggests poor personal hygiene and kleptomaniac behavior

Crazy Horse: Thašúŋke Witkó (1840? - 1877) was an American hero who defended the territories and way of life of the Oglala-Lakota branch of the Sioux Nation; he earned a reputation for being 'untouchable – unkillable' amongst the invading 'pale-face' soldiers

Crib is slang for: a person's house. According to Dr. Francis Cress Welsing, we unconsciously equate the bed of an infant with our home due to being reduced to 'child status' (minority) by white supremacy

Cum is slang for: semen

Curious George: Comical reference to the monkey in a popular children's book by Hans Augusto Rey and Margret Rey

Dap: Slapping hands or exchanging pounds (bumping fists); it is a sign of respect or group solidarity

Darth Vader is the main villain in George Lucas' *Star Wars* saga. After turning to the 'dark side', he evolves into a menacing character known for punishing his subordinates' mistakes with death

Daruma: *Bodhidharma* was a dark-skinned man born in the Indian state of Tamil Nadu during the $5^{th}/6^{th}$ century CE. Credited as being the transmitter of *Ch'an* to China, he also began the physical training of the *Shaolin* monks that led to the creation of *Shaolinquan*

Debarge: A family, music group that was revered by females who adored the light-skinned, wavy hair type of guy

D-Day refers to the Normandy landings of the Allied invasion. It occurred on June 6, 1944

Delta Force: 1st Special Forces Operational Detachment-Delta (1st SFOD-D) is one of the four secretive, tier-one counter-terrorism and special mission units

Deuce and a Half: The M35 series of trucks are large utility vehicles in the 2 ½ ton weight class

Dick-down is slang for: having sex

Diesel is short for *cock-diesel,* which is slang for: an extremely muscular physique; i.e. like a body-builder

Dime-piece or Dime is a metaphor for: a rating of 10. It is used to describe a good-looking female. Or, it is $10 worth of marijuana

Dimples Dee is the emcee moniker for Crystal Smith

Dissed is Hip Hop terminology for: being disrespectful toward someone

Dixie is the brand name of a line of disposable paper cups

Dizzy Gillespie: John Birks Gillespie (1917-1993), is one of the jazz pioneers credited with ushering in the 'Be-Bop' era

DJ Cash Money: Jerome Hewlett is a Philadelphia-based *turntablist* who is well-known for winning deejay contests worldwide

DJ Chuck Chillout: Charles Turner (1962 -) was a featured deejay on NYC's 98.7 *Kiss FM*

DJ Debonair & Tricky D are two progenitors of Miami Bass music in the late '80s

DMZ are the initials for: Demilitarized Zone. In spite its name, this area, which runs across the Korean peninsula, is the most heavily militarized border in the world

Dog Star is the brightest star in the night sky. Many believe *Sirius* is the original home of melanin-rich people

Don is loosely derived from Italian and Spanish; we used it to mean a cool guy with the girls – i.e. a playboy

Dove Sack is drug-dealing terminology for: a bag of marijuana or cocaine

Down by Law is slang for: having respect in the streets. It was popularized by MC Shan's 1987 album entitled, *Down by Law*. In the '90s, this expression was eclipsed by *Keep it Real* as the preferred catchphrase in Hip Hop

Dr. Dunkenstein is a moniker created by Darryl Dawkins to describe his thunderous, backboard-shattering dunks

DRF are the initials for: Division Ready Force. Combat brigades rotate in the planned deployment sequence of readiness

Dr. Ben: Dr. Yosef A.A. Ben-jochannan (1918 – 2015) taught us about many of Africa's ancient civilizations as a professor at numerous institutions including Cairo's University of Al-Azhar and Cornell University. A fellow historian and contemporary, Dr. Asa Hilliard III, described him as "fearless, audacious, and driven." He claimed that *Dr. Ben* did not "merely ask us to accept his testimony" but rather "put the primary evidence for his conclusions before us."

Dr. Frances Cress Welsing state that a system is practiced by the global white minority, on both conscious and unconscious levels, to ensure their genetic survival by any means necessary. Accordingly, this system attacks people of color (particularly people of African descent) in nine major areas: economics, education, entertainment, labor, law, politics, religion, sex, and war

Dr. J: Julius Winfield Erving II (1950 -) is the player credited with launching the modern style of playing 'above the rim'; the *Doctor* is considered one of the best dunkers of all-time

Dr. John Henrik Clarke (1915 – 1998) was a pioneer at Cornell University and Hunter College. Beyond revealing the truth about black people's history, he was famous for confronting and defeating western historians in public debates, most notably Wellesley College European classics professor Mary Lefkowitz. According to Dr. Clarke: "the first light of human consciousness and the world's first civilizations were in Africa." He taught us that the so called Dark Ages were dark only for Europe

Dravidian: Due to their dark skin, the original descendants of India have been relegated to a low-caste called *Untouchables*

Drop: the command to get down and do push-ups. Or, it means: a knockout (KO) in boxing

Drop Dime is street vernacular for: snitching or ratting

Dropping Knowledge is terminology for: teaching; usually by lecturing

Dumbed Down: This form of mental exploitation contains elements of *misinformation* and *disinformation*

Dun is a Moorish title; similar to El, Bey, Ali, AL, Dey, etc.

E – G

Earth, Wind, and Fire is one of the most successful bands of the twentieth century; *EWF* was one of the first black groups to claim a spiritual lineage in ancient Egypt

Eating out the palm of your hand is an idiom meaning: to have someone under a spell which leaves them helplessly gullible

Edward Leo Peter McMahon Jr. (1923 - 2009) was famous for being the set-up man for Johnny Carson

Egg McMuffin is the signature breakfast sandwich sold by McDonalds

EIB are the initials for: Expert Infantryman Badge

Elaine Brown (1943 -) the former Black Panther Party chairperson (and mistress of Huey Newton) is a prison activist, writer, and singer

Elvira: *Elvira, Mistress of the Dark* is a comedy horror character created by James Signorelli

Embed Miltarism: Since the 1980s, embed militarism in movies has been funded by a taxpayer subsidy through the military and its contractors. This process of Pentagon-Hollywood collusion includes military officials producing, collaborating on screenplays, line-editing scripts, and even changing plot and dialogue in order to guarantee the film is pro-military (Sirota, 2011)

Emotional Pain Body: As explained by Dr. Umar Johnson: an EPB is a "chip of self-hatred" that is suppressed in the subconscious of a person and can be activated suddenly and without warning if she/he is put in a stressful situation

End of Cycle Test (EOCT): is the final examination in basic training

Enquiring Minds is a reference to: the gossip tabloid newspaper, the *National Enquirer*

Enterprise is a reference to a spacecraft commandeered by *Captain Kirk* in *Star Trek*; i.e. the USS Enterprise

Ernest "Ernie" Eugene Barnes, Jr. (1938 – 2009) was an artist. His piece entitled *Sugar Shack* became famous on the sitcom, *Good Times*

Ernesto 'Che' Guevara (1928 - 1967) was an Argentine rcvolutionary, physician, guerrilla leader and author

ETS is the military abbreviation for: Expiration Term of Service

Everclear is a brand of rectified alcohol distilled from grains; it is bottled at 190-proof (95% ABV)

Extra Sensory Connection was a classic 'slow-jam' radio program broadcast on WDAS

Eye for an Eye: In Exodus 21:23-24, it is written: *And if any mischief follow, then thou shalt give life for life, eye for eye, tooth for tooth, hand for hand, foot for foot*

Failure to Adapt: AR 635-200, chapter 11, states the measures for dismissing personnel due to 'failure to adapt to the military environment'

Fart is slang for: flatulence; i.e. breaking wind

Fayette-nam was a nickname given to Fayetteville in the '60s by protesters of the Vietnam war

Field Negro: As explained by Malcolm X, in slavery, the 'house negroes' worked inside as butlers and maids while the others performed manual labor outside (see House Negro)

Fire Guard is a night guard-duty for trainees only; i.e. the soldier must stay awake and patrol the barracks while others sleep

Fireman's Carry is a technique for a person to carry another person without assistance by placing the body across their shoulders

First Call signals the start of the day; i.e. wake up

Fishers of Men and Women is written in Mark 1:17 in the New Testament

Five-O is slang for: police; it is derived from the TV drama, *Hawaii 5-0,* which aired from 1968-1980

Flat-line: To register as having no brain waves or heartbeat on an electronic monitor; i.e. dead

Flower Child was a nickname for idealistic young people during the 1967 Summer of Love

Fly Girl is Hip Hop slang for: a fashionably sexy female

Forties (40s) is terminology for: a 40-ounce bottle of malt liquor

Fortune 500 is a magazine which annually lists the top ranking corporations by their gross revenue

Foxy 99 FM: WZFX is a radio station in Fayetteville, NC

Fresh Fest: The first major Hip Hop tour; it featured the hottest names of '80s Rap

Frogmen was a nickname for the SEAL trainees

Front or Frontin' is Hip Hop jargon meaning: to assume a phony or disingenuous stance

Front-Leaning Rest is Army terminology for: the push-up position

FSU are the initials for: Fayetteville State University

Ft. Leavenworth is the US Army installation which serves as the military's corrections complex. The Department of Defense's only maximum security prison is located in Kansas

FTX: is the abbreviation for: Field Training Exercise

Furious Five: Joseph 'Grandmaster Flash' Saddler (1958 -) is the pioneering deejay who is credited with inventing the 'cross-fader.' His five emcees: *Melle-Mel, Mr. Ness, Raheim, Kid Creole* and *Cowboy* formed this pioneering Hip Hop group from the South Bronx

Gaijin [外人] is a bigoted word originally reserved for Portuguese, Dutch, and other Europeans sailors; i.e. non-human, barbarian, savage. In modern Japan, it has become a pejorative to signify any non-Japanese person

Ganja is slang for: marijuana; derives from *Ganjika* in Sanskrit

Gasface is 80s slang meaning: to make a stupid face to show disrespect toward someone you don't like. It was popularized in a song by *3rd Bass*

General Order: Orders to Sentry is the official code of conduct governing guard duty in the US armed forces

Gentrification: the Urban renewal (1949 Housing Act), or 'slum elimination,' is a mechanism of racial discrimination used to force a change of residence upon people who lack resources to cope in a biased housing or business market. Once the people are removed, upscale neighborhoods, resorts, freeways, or golf courses are erected. According to James Baldwin (1963): "Urban renewal means Negro removal" (Standley, 1989, pg. 42)

Get Ghost is slang for: disappearing from the scene, i.e. to leave

Get Jacked means being a victim of a car-jack or a strong-arm robbery

Gettin' New is the act of being two-faced or phony in a new environment or social situation

Gettin' Nice: Slang for the 'high' feeling one gets from marijuana or liquor; i.e. a mild euphoric state Gettin' Puffed is slang for: getting high on marijuana

GI is the abbreviation for: Government Issue; sometimes it is short for GI Party

GI Bill: A range of benefits including cash for college. GI's in the program donated $100 bucks a month and received payments after being honorably discharged and enrolled at an approved institution

GI Party: Soldiers collectively cleaning the barracks on the weekends or before an inspection

Globe Trotterish is a reference to the *World Famous Harlem Globetrotters* – most notably Marques Haynes

Go [围棋; 圍棋; 囲碁; 바둑]: literally means: encircling game. It is a board game involving two players that originated in ancient China more than 2,500 years ago. In antiquity, it was considered one of the four essential arts of a cultured scholar.

Golden Rule: The traditional maxim stated: 'One should treat others as they would like to be treated'; however, the contemporary version has become: 'The man with the gold makes the rules!'

Goliath: In 1ˢᵗ Samuel 17, *Goliath of Gath* was a giant Philistine warrior who was defeated by *David*

Good Times is a popular sitcom portraying the projects of Chicago, Illinois; it aired from 1974 - 1979

Good Hair: Part of the *Willie Lynch Doctrine* states that non-Caucasian hair textures are 'bad hair.' A documentary by Regina Belle, entitled: *My Nappy Roots: A Journey through Black Hair-itage* explores this subject in detail

GP Mediums have been the most used 'general purpose', canvas tent in the US armed forces since World War II

Grapevine: An unofficial source of rumors, news, or gossip spread by spoken communication

GrandMixer D.ST: Derek Showard is the deejay credited for establishing the turntable as a fully improvisational music instrument

Grasshopper refers to a *Kung Fu* flashback scene in which *Master Kan* says to Caine as a boy: "Grasshopper, quickly as you can, snatch the pebble from my hand". After Caine tries and is unable to do so, the master replies, "When you can take the pebble from my hand, it will be time for you to leave".

Great White Hope: John Arthur "Jack" Johnson (1878 – 1946), nicknamed the 'Galveston Giant,' became the first 'colored' champion in 1908. This was at the height of the Jim Crow era. Ever since then, every few years, a new 'great white hope' (i.e. a white man or group who can defeat the 'black threat') surfaces in the media

Grimace is a large, purple character in a fantasy world used by McDonald's to attract children, called *McDonaldland*

Grinch refers to the comically heartless character created by Dr. Seuss in 1957

Gringo: Similar to *Gaijin* and *Toubob (West Africa),* this is the pejorative term used by Latinos to describe the melanin-deficient invaders of their country

Grittin' on (someone) is the act of staring at a person with the intention of provoking a fight

Grizzly Adams is the main character in a movie about a California mountain man / trainer of wild animals; i.e. an updated *Tarzan*

GURU: Keith Edward Elam (1961 – 2010) became known as *Gifted Unlimited Rhymes Universal* with his partner, DJ Premiere

Guy-Smiley: A game-show host character on *Sesame Street* who is known for his broad smile

H – K

Haile Selassie I (1892 – 1975) was the Emperor of Ethiopia from 1930 to

1974. He was the heir to a dynasty that traced its origins by tradition from *King Solomon* and *Queen Makeda (also known as the Queen of Sheba)*

Half-Klick is an Army slang for: half of a kilometer. One klick equals a kilometer

Hanafuda [花札] are Japanese playing cards used for a number of games; it literally translates as 'flower cards'

Happy Face: A popular picture-design used on blotter sheets of LSD

Hard Rocks: tough guy or hoodlum; this term evolved into *thug* in the '90s and was popularized by Tupac Shakur

Harriet Tubman (1820 - 1913) Nicknamed *Moses* due her role in orchestrating rescue missions to free people from slavery, ironically, she actually had to threaten many 'dumbed-down' negroes to get them to leave their bondage. *"Live North or die here!"* This was the phrase she used while pointing her double-barreled shotgun in their faces

Heat Miser's Lyrics: The actual lyrics are: *"He's Mr. Heat Miser, he's Mr. Sun..."*

Hee Haw is a reference to a 1970s television show featuring country music; *i.e. redneck, hillbilly, or honky*

Heisman Trophy: the annual award given to the most outstanding player in collegiate football; i.e. college football's MVP

Hi-C is a neighborhood emcee

High Speed is Army slang to describe extreme people or situations. It can be either positive or negative. It is also used for cool stuff in order to express the cutting-edge greatness of it

Hitting the Pipe is street terminology for: smoking crack

Hoagies are a popular torpedo-shaped sandwich in northeast US cities; also known as a *submarine*

Hombres is Spanish for: men

Homegirl: In '80s Hip Hop slang, it means: a female friend who is almost like a sister; there were also *homeboys*

Honkie is a nickname earned by Caucasians in the early 1900s. Especially during the 'depression', many melanin-rich women were forced into prostitution. This is what the families of these women called the European men outside their homes honking their horns at all hours of the night

Hood is short for: neighborhood. However, since black people don't live in actual communities, the result is a *hood*. And according to Dick Gregory, "a hood is something you put over your head to hide something you're ashamed of"

Hood Ethics: The dictated customs which are created in a volatile, aggressive environment in order to survive

Hoopty is slang for: a car in poor condition; i.e. beat up, busted, etc.

Hoosiers is the nickname for: Indiana University athletic teams

Houdini: Erik 'Harry Houdini' Weisz (1874 – 1926) was a Hungarian

358

stunt performer billed as an Escape Artist

House Negro: this label refers to people who disown their own racial identity to please Caucasians

House Nigger: The slave who imagines himself as being closer to his master than the field hands because he lives inside the house

Housing: Military service members with a spouse receive extra money as part of their allowance for living quarters

Howitzer is a type of 105 mm, anti-aircraft cannon

Huey Percy Newton (1942 – 1989) Dr. Newton formed the BPP along with co-founder, Bobby Seale

Hustle: This popular disco dance became the name of its own song in 1975

Hustler is a pornographic magazine published by Larry Flint

ICU is an abbreviation for: Intensive Care Unit at a hospital

Ijime [苛め] is a form of bullying someone deemed different from the group; it is very popular in Japan

Iron Mike: 1. A statue of a paratrooper. 2. A forward lunge exercise. With legs shoulder-length apart and hands on hips, a person steps forward with one leg at a 90 degree angle, then pushes back to the start position and repeats the process with the other leg

Iron Mike Tyson: Michael Gerard Tyson (1966 -) was perhaps the most dynamic KO artist of all-time. He dominated the heavyweight division similar to how Jack Johnson, Joe Louis, and Muhammad Ali reigned during their time as champion

Jabber Jaw is an idiom for: a person who talks too much

Jack Frost was an actual baller from my hood. This guy's reputation for dunking on people rivaled Jo-Jo's KO fame

Jackie Robinson (1919 – 1972) Jack Roosevelt Robinson was NOT the first African / Black to play professional baseball alongside white players. He wasn't even close. Blacks played for decades following the Civil War. Incidentally, in 1944, 2nd Lieutenant Robinson was assigned to the *761st Tank Battalion (nicknamed the "Black Panthers")* at Camp Hood, Texas. He was court-martialed for refusing to move to the back of the bus after being ordered to do so by a Caucasian bus driver

Jack is short for 'jack shit', it's slang for: nothing; i.e. diddly

Jam is street terminology for: a party

James Arthur Boehcim (1944 -) is the head coach of the men's basketball team at Syracuse University

James Clavell: Charles Edmund DuMaresq Clavell (1924 – 1994) was a novelist best known for his Asian Saga series

Jammy: Slang for: gun

J'd: Street terminology for: smoking a joint

Jegna is an Amharic (Ethiopian) word meaning: a brave person, elder. Note: Jon instructed me to *never* refer to him or Curt as a 'mentor'. This was because the duties of a 'mentor' were derived from the mythical Greek character who educated *Odysseus'* son, *Telemachus.* Jon said that a significant part of *Mentor's* role was to introduce the boy to a pederasty lifestyle (i.e. men raping children)

Jehovah's Witness are a modern spin-off Christian denomination created by Charles Taze Russell

Jenny Craig is the name of a weight loss, weight management company founded in 1983 in Melbourne, Australia

Jesus Christ Superstar was a musical staged on Broadway in 1971

Jewish American Princess is a Jewish girl. The term sometimes incorporates a stereotype implying materialistic, selfish behavior

Jim Crow are laws that mandated de jure racial segregation in all public facilities; i.e. apartheid, open racism

Jimmy is short for 'Jimbrowski'. This is a comical euphemism for 'penis' made popular by the *Jungle Brothers, KRS-1,* and *De La Soul*

John Brown (1800 – 1859) electrified the nation after he and his gang of 21 killed several Caucasians – including Mayor Fontaine Beckham. Believing he was the instrument of God's wrath for the sin of owning slaves, he was a heroic martyr and a visionary. His response to being sentenced to death: "Had I so interfered in behalf of the rich, the powerful, it would have been all right".

John Wayne: Marion Mitchell Morrison (1907 – 1979) was an actor who epitomized white masculinity in his movies

Johnnie Law is slang for: the police

Judas is a reference to *Judas Iscariot* (Hebrew: יהודה איש־קריות). One of the twelve disciples of Christ, he is infamously known for his kiss and betrayal of Jesus, for a payment of 30 silver coins

Juice: 'Having Juice' is equivalent to being respected; i.e. down by law

Jump Street is slang for: the beginning of any sequence; i.e. the starting point

Kata: is a fundamental martial arts stance with the feet placed shoulder-width apart. Also called a 'horse stance'

Kayumanggi: In *Tagalog,* this means: brown

Kelloggs Sugar Smacks is the name of a children's breakfast cereal by the Kellogg's Company

Kent State University: On May 4, 1970, the Army National Guard opened fire on this campus at an anti-war protest killing 4 students and wounding 9 others

Kick Game is slang for: to woo; i.e. to enchant or seduce

Kickin' it is a phrase meaning: to hang out with, or spend time with. Or, it is synonymous to 'Kick Game'

King David: According to the bible, he was the second king of Israel, and an ancestor of Jesus

360

Kissing the Sky: This phrase is taken from the lyrics of Jimi Hendrix's song, *Purple Haze*

Kiwi is a brand of shoe polish commonly used by US Army personnel

Knight's Creed: The Code of the Knights is: *'Protect the weak, defenseless, helpless, and fight for the general welfare of all'*

Knock It Down is street vernacular for: having non-romantic sex with a girl; i.e. hit it

Kodak Moment: A priceless moment that is captured by a photo, or should have been. This phrase is attributed to the Eastman Kodak Company

Kool Herc refers to: Clive Campbell (1955 -) This Jamaican-born deejay is the first in the recognized 'Trinity of Hip Hop Architects' along with *Afrika Bambaataa* and *Grandmaster Flash.* Note: it is debatable as to whether other deejays such as *Grandmaster Flowers, DJ Hollywood, Pete DJ Jones,* and others preceded them

Kool-Aid is the name of a soft drink known for its mascot: an anthropomorphic grinning pitcher

Ku Klux Klan: A highly advanced secret society. Although the KKK is infamous for 'rednecks' and public lynchings known as *pick-a-niggers* (which later became *picnic),* many people fail to realize this white supremacist group has its roots in Moorish science. Nowadays, it is believed by many the Klan has disrobed to become the *Tea Party* (Booker T. Coleman, *Hidden Colors 2*, 2012)

Kumbaya is a reference to a children's spiritual hymn from the 1930s

Kundalini: Literally meaning 'coiled power,' it is believed that awakening this primeval energy results in evolving to higher levels of consciousness

Kurombo [くろんぼ] is a racial slur for: dark-skinned peoples; akin to the word *nigger* or *sambo*

Kwai Chang Caine is the main character in the television series, *Kung Fu*

L – M

Laid: 'Getting Laid' is slang for: having sex

Land Speeder: An anti-gravity craft featured in *Star Wars*

Land of Make-Believe refers to the *Neighborhood of Make-believe,* which is an imaginary town for puppets on the show, *Mr. Rogers' Neighborhood*

Larry Davis (1966 – 2008) later changed his name to Adam Abdul-Hakeem. He gained nation-wide notoriety after winning a shootout with NYC Police officers in November 1986. Davis's defense attorneys claimed that the police were trying to murder him because of his knowledge of the involvement of corrupt police in the drug business.

After escaping unscathed, Davis was the target of a 17-day manhunt. *The Larry Davis Story,* a documentary directed by Troy Reed, alleges the NYPD was involved in narcotics trafficking, and claims that the shootout came after Davis backed-out of a drug deal. Incidentally, Adam Abdul-Hakeem was the first person in US judicial history to be found innocent by reason of self-defense in a police-shooting case

Larry, Moe, and Curly: are known as 'the Three Stooges'. This are a famous 20th century, American vaudeville, slapstick comedy team

Latin Rascals: In 1981, Tony Moran & Albert Cabrera began splicing together hit songs on a NYC dance radio station, WKTU

LEG: This condescending term is used by paratroopers to describe non-Airborne personnel. The letters stand for: Lacking Enough Guts (similar to POG)

Lemon is an idiom meaning: unsatisfactory or defective; i.e. a hoopty or a piece of junk

Len Bias: Leonard Kevin Bias (1963 – 1986) was a basketball player drafted in 1986. He died two days later from cardiac arrhythmia induced by a cocaine overdose

Lone Wolf McQuade: In this 1983 film, J.J. McQuade is a tough-guy who prefers to work alone; he lives in a dirty trailer with a wolf

Lotta-Mo: 'I got a lotta-mo' is a phrase popularized by Mr.T in the movie *Rocky III*

LSD: Lysergic Acid Diethylamide

Lunch is modified terminology for: missing a sure opportunity; i.e. out to lunch

Lyndon B. Johnson (1908 – 1973) was President of the US from 1963–1969

Mac and Tosh are an animated cartoon duo created by Warner Bros. They are known for their over-exaggerated, polite gestures

Make Money was Curt's way of saying: to make significant gains in a chosen endeavour

Make Way for the Bad Guy is a *Scarface* quote by the character *Tony Montana,* played by Al Pacino

Malcolm X (1925 – 1965) changed his name to **Al-Hajj Malik El-Shabazz (الحاج مالك الشباز).** He was a Muslim minister and spokesman for Black Nationalism; he is noted as one of the greatest Americans in history

Man's man: A rugged leader; according to some, what all men should aspire to be; akin to the concept of the *Alpha Male*

Manzai [漫才] is a traditional style of Japanese, stand-up comedy involving two performers

March Madness is the official nickname for: the Division I college basketball tournament held each spring

Mark: A person identified as an easy target; i.e. a sucker

Mason-Dixon Line: Surveyed by Charles Mason and Jeremiah Dixon in the 1760s, it became the border between the North and South

Master Jay is a deejay moniker. He spun rap on WKDU long before it was accepted on mainstream, Philly airwaves (not to be confused with *Jam Master Jay,* of *Run-DMC)*

Mayari: In *Tagalog* mythology, she is the lunar goddess. The daughter of *Bathala,* the king of the gods, she is revered as the most beautiful deity in Bathala's court

McGuire Air Force Base is located in South Jersey, near Wrightstown and New Hanover Township

Medal of Honor is the USA's highest military honor. It is awarded for personal acts of valor, above and beyond the call of duty

Melanin: Derived from the Greek *melanos,* which means 'black', this is the most important, the most complex, and the most perfect molecule in the human body. This biological living light-source, which connects organisms to the universe, is influenced by the electro-magnetic field, light waves, and sound vibrations. Because of its magnetic properties, according to Anthony Browder (1989), "People with higher concentrations of melanin in their bodies are more in tune with nature...more spiritual".

Melanin Challenged: Scientific research has shown that some 85% of people with high concentrations of melanin in their skin produce 'melatonin', while only 15 percent of people lacking melanin cannot produce this spiritually inducing substance (Browder, 1989, pg. 94)

Melanin-Deficient refers to the state of lacking a functioning pineal gland; in scientific terms: the absence of the polymerization of oxidation products of tyrosine and dihydroxyphenol compounds. Note: Melanin deficiency has been connected with various genetic abnormalities and disease states

Melanin-Rich: In this book, this term is synonymous with 'black' or 'brown' people. Popularized Dr. Frances Cress Welsing and Yaffa Bey, it represents the condition of a healthy, functioning pineal gland; i.e. uncalcified

Melle Mel: Melvin Glover (1961 -) is an original member of the Furious Five. He is credited with coining the term 'MC' for 'Master of Ceremony'. Simply put, he is one of the greatest of all-time.

Messy Marvin is a reference to a sloppy boy in a popular, *Hersey's Chocolate* syrup commerical

Miami Vice was a television crime-detective series that aired from 1984 - 1989

Michael Joseph Jackson (1958 – 2009) is recognized as the most successful entertainer of all time. A global figure in popular culture virtually his entire life, he is often referred to as the 'King of Pop'

Mickey: 'To slip someone a mickey' describes surreptitiously slipping drugs into a person's drink

Midas Touch: In Greek mythology, the God *Dionysus* granted *King Midas of Phrygia (modern day Turkey)* the power to transmute whatever he touched into gold

Midnight Oil is an idiom referring to: studying late into the night; i.e. pull an all-nighter

Mighty Mouse is an anthropomorphic, superhero character created by the Terrytoons Studio in 1942

Miles Dewey Davis III (1926 – 1991) was a jazz musician, trumpeter, bandleader, and composer; widely considered one of the most influential musicians of the 20th century

Military-Industrial Complex: The aggregate of a nation's armed forces and the industries that supply their weapons and materials

Mind-Control is a systematic method to manipulate others' thought patterns

Money Mike is where my street-ball moniker came from

Monie-Love: was my nickname for Monica. Coincidentally, the identical moniker was made famous by Simon Gooden a couple years later

Moolie: Derived from Italian for *eggplant,* it's a pejorative for a dark-skinned person; akin to *nigger*

Moor / Moors / Moorish: Until the 19th century, *Negro, Indian, Colored, Black,* and *Moor* were used interchangeably with *American;* Caucasians were referred to as 'Europeans' or 'settlers' (in their history texts). Many people know the Moors ruled Spain from 711 to 1492, and are credited with bringing Europe out of the Dark Ages. However, there's much more. According to Hakim Bey, the Moors are the aboriginal / indigenous inhabitants of North, Central, and South America, including all of the adjoining islands. The Moorish empire extended from Africa & Europe to the Americas; which was known in ancient times as *Amexem*

MOS is an acronym for: Military Occupation Specialty

Moses: Arabic [موسى] Hebrew [1 [מֹשֶׁה. According to the Qur'an, Baha'i scripture, and the Hebrew Bible, he was a religious leader, lawgiver, and prophet. 2. Nickname for: Harriet Tubman

Mozart: ['vɔlfgaŋ amaˈdeus ˈmoːtsaʁt] (1756 – 1791) *Is it possible the most prolific composer of the Classical era was taught by an Austrian Moor?* Angelo Soliman (1720-1796) was a native of Central Africa. Kidnapped as a child, he was presented to the imperial governor of Sicily in 1734. By adulthood, Soliman was known to be an expert in many fields. As a renowned musical-composer, it is said he had a large influence on the young prodigy while serving as Prince Georg Christian's confidant

MRE are the initials for: Meal Ready to Eat; they are self-contained field rations

Mr. Magic was the moniker for John Rivas (1956 – 2009). He hosted the

Disco Showcase on WHBI, which later had its 'world premiere' as the *Rap Attack* on WBLS. Marley Marl was his deejay, and the first member of the legendary *Juice Crew*

Mr. Magoo is a near-sighted cartoon character created in 1949 that, by luck, avoids disaster after disaster

Ms. Piggy is an animated pig-like puppet played by Frank Oz on *The Muppet Show*

MTV is a popular US cable and satellite music video channel

Muhammad Ali (1942 -) was known as Cassius Marcellus Clay before he embraced Islam and changed his name. Recognized as 'The Greatest', he'll always be remembered for his famous quote when he refused to fight in the Vietnam War: "Ain't no VietCong never called me 'nigger'. They ain't my enemy – *you* my enemy!"

Mushroom: Psilocybin or "magic" mushrooms are fungi that contain psychoactive indole alkaloids

Musk: The aroma obtained from a gland of a musk deer. Believed to have originated in ancient Egypt, Queen Cleopatra was known to wear this oil

Mustangs are one of the first-generation Ford Mustangs; known as a 'pony car'

N – P

NCAA Championship: The 1987 NCAA Finals was held on March 30, 1987, at the Louisiana Superdome in New Orleans. The Finals are the culmination of March Madness

Noriega: Manuel Antonio Noriega Moreno (1934 -) This Panamanian leader is one of the many publicized enemies who was either inserted into the leadership position by the US, or was known to be a collaborator of the CIA. Noriega has been serving sentences in various prisons since surrendering to US troops in 1990. Other notable 'public enemy' types fitting this criteria are: *Mohammed Reza Pahlavi (the Shah of Iran), Saddam Hussein,* and *Osama bin Laden*

Nappy is a description of: natural African-textured hair

Nathaniel Turner (1800 - 1831) was a prophet who saw visions that prompted him to lead one of the most effective rebellions in US history. Stating he was "Intended for some great purpose", although there were many such revolts, his ignited a culture of fear amongst Caucasians which still exists today

Nature: It is reported that many indigenous people called the planet 'mother'. However, the ancient Egyptians referred to the land as a male deity, *Geb.* His wife, *Nut,* was the goddess of the sky

NCO is the initials for: Non-Commissioned Officer

NCOIC are the initials designating the Non-Commissioned Officer in

Charge

Negro denotes 'black' in Spanish. In contemporary usage, it means: a dark-skinned person manufactured in the likeness of a European (see Black)

Neo-Colonialism is a policy whereby a major, world power uses economic and political means to continue ruling its former colony from behind the scenes; i.e. the puppet master

New Yorkers are very thick, stylish laces made popular in NYC Hip Hop culture in the early '80s

Newbie means an inexperienced newcomer; i.e. noob

Nigger: Since colonial times this has been the main ethnic slur directed at peoples of African descent. Most believe it is synonymous with 'ignorant person'. However, the origin of this word is debatable. Some claim it derives from the Sanskrit and Pāli word: *Nāga.* This is a god taking the form of a great snake; specifically the king cobra. It is found in Hinduism, Buddhism and Jainism. Still, others believe it comes from *Negus;* meaning King, or Ruler in Amharic. The scholar, Taj Tarik Bey, teaches that Caucasians were the original niggers, in the form of the *Troglodyte Niger.* This is a type of pale-face chimpanzee

Nippon [大日本帝國] was a world power before the inhabitants of the *Land of the Rising Sun* became *Japanese* in 1947

Non-Commissioned Officers (NCO) are military personnel in positions of authority (E-5 – E-9), but not in positions of 'command' per-se. All commanders must be commissioned officers (O-1 – O-10)

Nori [海苔]: refers to: seaweed

North Cackalackee is a nickname for North Carolina

Northern Lights is a pure *indica* strain of weed with bud crystals that glimmer, i.e. the resemblance to the northern lights sky

Nose Wide Open is a term usually for a male who is crazy in love or lust over a girl, and as a result will focus his total attention on her, ignoring his friends; maybe a hint she is exploiting him

Nubia: The Kingdom of Kush (the Land of Gold) was located on the Nile River, to the south of *Kemet* (ancient Egypt)

NVG is the initials for: Night Vision Goggles

NWA: This group from Compton, California is considered one of the seminal acts of 'Gangsta Rap'. The original group also featured *Arabian Prince*

Nyquil is a brand of cold medication containing alcohol

Occipital Lobe: Located at the rear of the brain, it is the main visual processing center

OCS are the initials for: Officer Candidate School

OG are the initials for: Original Gangster; this street terminology shows respect for an older hustler

Ol' E is an abbreviation for: a 40 ounce bottle of *Old English 800* malt liquor

OPFOR is an acronym for: Opposing Force; this unit represents the enemy during war-game scenarios

Orangemen is the nickname for: Syracuse University athletic teams

Orgone Energy is a hypothetical universal life force closely associated with sexuality. It was proposed in the 1930s by Wilhelm Reich

Original People is a reference to: the indigenous people of the planet; i.e. Asiatics

Othello is a tragedy about the *Moor of Venice,* by William Shakespeare. It is based on *Un Capitano Moro,* by Cinthio

Oxy 10 is a skin cream for acne

PAC is an acronym for: Personnel Actions Command

PAL is an acronym for: Police Athletic League

Parris Island is a military installation used for the Marines' basic training. It is located in Port Royal, South Carolina

Pathfinders are covert soldiers who set up helicopter landing sites in hostile territory

PATS is an acronym for: Program for Academically Talented Students

PCS is the abbreviation for: Permanent Change of Station

Peeping Tom is a person who gets pleasure (usually sexually related) from secretly watching others; i.e. a voyeur

Perpetrating means: the act of faking something or being phony; it was a popular idiom in '80s Hip Hop

Peter Brian Gabriel (1950 -) is a musician most known as the lead vocalist of the rock band, Genesis

Peter Edward Rose (1941 -) Nicknamed 'Charlie Hustle', Rose is the MLB all-time leader in hits. Ironically, he is not in their hall of fame due to being accused of illegally betting on games

Peter Tosh (1944 – 1987) was a Jamaican reggae musician; he was a core member of *The Wailers*

PHAT is an acronym for: Pretty, Hot, And Tantalizing

Phenom is short for: phenomenon. It is slang for: a person or thing of outstanding abilities or qualities

Pig: Derogatory slang for: police; it was commonly used in the '60s and '70s

Pinocchio: is a fictional protagonist in the children's novel *The Adventures of Pinocchio* (1883), by Carlo Collodi. This animated wooden-puppet's nose grew longer whenever he told a lie

Pirates is the nickname for: Seton Hall University athletic teams

PLF is the abbreviation for: Parachute Landing Fall. This is the landing technique taught at Airborne School. Properly executed, it allows a paratrooper to land without sustaining injury

PLL are the initials for: Prescribed Load List

POG, or Pogue, is an acronym for: Personnel Other than Grunts. This condescending term is used to describe weak soldiers

Po-Po is an acronym for: Police Officer

Point-Man: means to assume the first and most exposed position in an advancing combat formation

Police Call is a brief reconaissance / clean-up mission

Popeye: *Popeye the Sailor* was a comic strip character created by Elzie Crisler Segar in the 1920s

Post Traumatic Stress Disorder (PTSD) is a severe anxiety disorder that develops after being exposed to extreme psychological trauma

Postwar Japan refers to: the period immediately following the end of World War II in 1945 to the present day

Pothead is slang for: a habitual cannabis smoker

Pound: Also called *dap* or a *fist pound;* Caucasians later adopted it and called it a *fist bump,* and by many other names. This hand-gesture, which is a symbol of respect, is commonly used by athletes to celebrate with teammates

POV is a military acronym for: Privately Owned Vehicle

Predator: Also called 'Yautja,' these extraterrestrial hunters use advanced technological weaponry to hunt any being they consider a worthy opponent

Presidential Unit Citation is awarded to units of the US Armed Forces for extraordinary heroism. It's on par with the Medal of Honor

Prima donna means: the leading woman soloist in an opera. However, sports writers adopted it to label vain, star athletes

Prodigal Son: In Luke 15:11–32, a wayward son squanders his inheritance but returns home to find his father has forgiven him

PT is a military acronym for: Physical Training

Pu-tang is slang for: vagina; i.e. pussy

Public Enemy: Consisting of *Chuck D, Professor Griff, Flavor Flav, Terminator X,* and the *S1Ws, PE* is famous for their Black Power charged lyrics and criticism of the establishment

Puerto Rico: The ancient name the *Tainos* used was *Borinquen,* which means 'Land of the Valiant Lord'

Pups was a nickname for the SEAL trainees

PX is an acronym for: Post Exchange; these are huge retail stores for Army personnel and their families (similar to BX)

PYT are the initials for: Pretty, Young, Thing. This is a song by Michael Jackson on the album, *Thriller*

Q – S

Quiet Storm is a nationwide, late-night radio program featuring love songs

Quincy's: A buffet restaurant in Fayetteville, NC

Rainbow Coalition: This is not to be confused with Jesse Jackson's diluted organization. The original coalition was led by Chairman Fred Hampton, and comprised of several extremely radical melanin-rich groups. When Hampton was assassinated by Chicago Police, this multicultural assembly was on the verge of creating a rival to counter the racist ruling class in the Windy City

Rangers are the elite infantry unit of the US Army

Rastaman is terminology meaning: an adherent of *Rastafari*

Ray Charles Leonard (1956 -) this 1976 gold-medalist was named *Boxer of the 1980s*

Ready Rock is street terminology for: crack rock; i.e. cocaine that is ready to smoke

Red Alert: Fred Crute (1956 -) was a deejay for the *Almighty Zulu Nation* before gaining popularity on KISS FM; he is credited with popularizing dance hall music on the radio

Redneck is a nickname for: Caucasian slaves who spent an extended amount of time working in the sun

Red Wolf: This North American canid was once the alpha-predator in the woods throughout the Southeastern states

REM 4: Rapid Eye Movement is the deepest stage of delta sleep

Replacement Centers are temporary living quarters for personnel until they process into their new unit; i.e. a reception station

Rev. Albert Greene (1946 -) is famous for singing both gospel and (secular) soul music

Rev. Dr. James Cleveland (1931 - 1991) Crowned as the 'King of Gospel', this singer/composer popularized the modern gospel sound

Richard Franklin Lennox Thomas Pryor (1940 – 2005) Perhaps the funniest stand-up comedian of all-time, he was known for his social examinations of racism while consciously probing history; most notably, ancient Egypt

Richie Cunningham is a character from the sitcom *Happy Days.* He was a pip-squeak, redhead with freckles

Richie Rich is slang for: a person who grows up in a wealthy family. It originates from the 1950s cartoon

Rick James: James Ambrose Johnson (1948 - 2004) popularized funk music in the late 1970s and '80s

Riddler: is a comic book super-villain appearing in *Batman* comic books, published by DC Comics

Roach: the remains of a joint, blunt, or rolled-up cigarette after most of it has been smoked

Robert Ludlum (1927 – 2001) was an author of suspense novels about governmental conspiracy theories

Robert Montgomery Knight (1940 -) is a retired Indiana University basketball coach

Roberto Clemente (1934 - 1972) was a pro baseball player from Puerto Rico. Arguably the best right-fielder of all-time, he died in a plane crash on New Year's eve while delivering aid to earthquake victims in Nicaragua

Rock is street slang for: a basketball. Or, a cluster of cocaine

Rockin' the Cradle is a crass reference for: having sexual relations with a person deemed too young; i.e. statutory rape

ROK is the abbreviation for: Republic of Korea; i.e. South Korea

Roody-poo is a combination of the word 'rude' and 'poo'; i.e. a lame, easy, soft, cowardly, etc.

Roots is a best-selling novel by author Alex Haley; it was later aired as a historical TV drama in 1976

Roscoe is a nickname for: handgun; i.e. gat, heater, etc.

ROTC: The Reserve Officer Training Corps prepares students to be a commissioned officer

Rubber to hit the Road is an idiom meaning: the most important point; i.e. the moment of truth

Rumble in the Jungle is a reference to: the *Rumble in the Jungle* boxing match on October 30, 1974, in the Democratic Republic of Congo, between George Foreman and Muhammad Ali

Run-DMC: Joseph 'Run' Simmons, Darryl 'DMC' McDaniels, and Jason 'Jam Master Jay' Mizell comprised this influential rap group

Running a Train is a ritualistic re-enactment of slave owners raping one slave; i.e. post-traumatic slave behavior

R&R is an abbreviation for: Rest and Relaxation

Sakura [桜] means: cherry blossoms

Salem Witch Trials: In Massachusetts, between February 1692 – May 1693, 14 women and 5 men were executed after being accused of doing witchcraft; i.e. the "devil's magic". Hundreds more were imprisoned resulting in many more deaths

SAT: The Standardized Admissions Test was the most widely accepted college admissions test in the US

Sayonara [さようなら] means: Good-bye

Scared Straight: The act of abandoning a life of crime due to stark fear. This phrase was popularized by a 1978 documentary

Scarface was originally a 1932 film portraying the life of gangster Al Capone. The 1983 remake about a Cuban immigrant turned drug dealer is more well-known

Scarlet Letter: In this 1850 sadistic work by Nathaniel Hawthorne, a European community humiliates a woman by forcing her to wear a scarlet

370

'A' on her dress as a punishment for allegedly committing adultery

School Boy: This belittling term meaning *nerd* is also the name of a style of frames

S-Curl: Reference to the *Luster* hair-care product that slightly straightens 'nappy' hair into curls and waves

SEAL is an acronym for Sea, Air, and Land Teams; they are the special operations force of the US Navy

Sell-out is slang for: A person who betrays his people to promote his own personal advancement

Seminoles is the nickname for: Florida State University athletic teams

Senioritis is an informal term referring to a reduction of academic focus characteristic of some high-school seniors, especially after they've been accepted into a university

Sensei [先生] is defined as: teacher; literally, it means a 'a life before another'

Sent-up is street terminology for: getting sent to prison

Separate Rats is short for separate rations. Service members with a spouse receive extra money as part of their allowance for meals

Serpentine Fire is an indirect reference to a song by Earth Wind and Fire. In Sanskrit, *Prana* [प्राण] means *Kundalini Energy*

Sess: Meaning high-quality, female cannabis; this is a shortened form of the Spanish word, *Sensimilia*

Setting-Up Camp is slang for: the act of preparing for rulership or leadership in any significant venture

Sev is an abbreviated form of *7- Eleven*. It was also Takuan's street-hustling moniker. Tak's friends called him this due to his proclivity for shoplifting

Seventh Heaven means: a state of intense happiness or bliss. The number 7 is prevalent all throughout Creation. From the number of notes, the days of the week, to the number of orifices on the human body, there are numerous examples. Accordingly, many spiritual systems profess there are 7 heavens, with the 7th being the highest

Shakespeare, William (1564-1616): It is rumoured the famed poet either assisted in the compilation of the King James version. Or, he and the king are the same person

Shammer is military slang for: a person who shirks his duty; i.e. lazy or shiftless

Shibumi: This novel, by *Trevanian,* incorporates the philosophy of the Japanese game *Go* to create the 'perfect assassin'

Shirley Ann Caesar (1938 -) is the gospel singer nicknamed the 'First Lady of Gospel Music'

Shit on Lock is slang for: having a situation under control

Shittin' Bricks is slang for: being extremely petrified, nervous, or upset

Shock and Awe is a US military doctrine utilizing the use of overwhelming power to paralyze an adversary's will to fight

Shogun: [征夷大将軍] *Sei-i Tai-Shogun* means: 'Barbarian-subduing Genralissimo'. This was the most sought after military rank in *Nippon* for over a thousand years. A Samurai named *Sakanoue no Tamuramaro [坂上田村麻呂] (758? – 811?)* was the first to assume this exalted position. Depicted as a "paragon of military virtues," according to historian, Dr. Alexander Francis Chamberlain, he was a "Negro." This warrior is venerated at *Kiyomizudera* [清水寺], which is the temple Sakanoue established in Kyoto City

Shook and Shook-Daddy are slang for:being scared; i.e. petrified

Shorty is slang for: either a child or a young lady

Shuckin' and Jivin' is slang referring to: deceit, mischief, or involving lies

Sitting Bull: Tȟatȟáŋka Íyotake (1834? – 1890) was a Hunkpapa-Lakota Sioux holy man who, in June of 1876, led a united coalition of American tribes in the *Black Hills* to massacre Gen. **George A. Custer** and his 7th Calvary

Skeezer is '80s slang for: a girl who is known to be sexually promiscuous; i.e. a whore

Skunk: Perhaps the most fragrant strain of cannabis in the world, it is also known for its sweet flavor and pleasant high

Slap-boxing was a contest using open hands to penetrate an opponent's defense and smack him in the face

Slow Jams: In modern America, with the exception of the Latin dances (salsa, merengue, etc.), melanin-rich men and women rarely dance in each other's arms. However, back in the day, it was an essential segment of every party

Sneak is slang for: punching someone in the face when they aren't expecting it; i.e. a sucker-punch

Sole Survivor Policy: see DD 1315.15

Soror is Latin for: sister

SOCOM: US Special Operations Command (USSOCOM); i.e. the Special Forces

SOS is the abbreviation for: *Scientists of Sound.* They were deejay crew in my town.

Soul Train was created and hosted by Don Cornelius. The "hippest trip in America" aired in syndication from 1971 until 1993

Soul to Soul is a British music group comprised of: Jazzie B, Caron Wheeler, Simon Law, Daddae, and Nellee Hooper

Spades is a card game played in pairs. It is very popular in black and brown communities

Special Forces: US Special Operations Command (USSOCOM)

Spicoli: *Jeff Spicoli* is a character from the comedy film, *Fast Times at Ridgemont High,* played by Sean Penn. He is depicted as a 'surfer-dude' who enjoys smoking marijuana

Spike Lee: Shelton Jackson Lee (1957 -) is a film director well known for examining race relations

Spit-shine: A meticulous method for polishing boots which leaves the surface of the leather as reflective as a mirror

Spliff is slang for: a cone-shaped marijuana cigarette

Sports Center is a daily sports, news program on ESPN

Steady B: Warren Sabir McGlone (1969 -) is infamous for being an emcee who actually lived the life of a 'hustla' – not just rapped about it. *Steady B* is currently serving a life sentence for his part in the murder of a police officer during a botched bank robbery in 1996

Steatopygia means an extreme amount of fat on the buttocks region

Stevie Gee is a neighborhood emcee

Stick is a designated group of paratroopers jumping together from an aircraft during an Airborne mission

Stick Ball is a street version of baseball. This game was popular in US cities because it only required a stick, a ball, and some space

Stogie is slang for: a cheap cigar

Straw Man: According to the Redemption Theory, the US government creates a fictitious person corresponding to each newborn citizen and pledges them as collateral to borrow money; i.e. foundation of slavery

Street Entrepreneurship is the ability to hustle or make money; sometimes by selling illegal merchandise

Super Six: This was the name of an actual posse in my hood. Comprised of six members, they were known for their various shades of sheepskin coats and stomping kids in the ground

Sun Tzu [孫武] (544?–496 BC) was a high-ranking Chinese general during the Zhou dynasty's Spring and Autumn Period

Survival of the Fittest: According to Wayne Chandler, Darwin's theory of evolution contradicts every ancient codex on how humans and animals evolved. Claiming it "lacks convincing evidence", Chandler also talks about a "pervasive genius" which encompassed the ancient world. He goes on to describe a time "when humans were truly advanced beings" and "walked in harmony with God and Nature" (pg. 215)

SWAT is an acronym for: Special Weapons and Tactics; it is an elite paramilitary unit that was created to combat 'radical' organizations like the Black Panthers

Sweating is slang for: obsessing over a person

Synagogue of Satan: Revelation 3:9 states: "Behold, I will make them of the synagogue of Satan, which say they are Jews, and are not, but do lie; behold, I will make them to come and worship before thy feet, and to know that I have loved thee"

S-2 is Military Intelligence; they collect data on enemy movement, strengths, and battlefield deployments

T – Z

T-10: The most common static line-deployed parachute used for combat, mass-assault, Airborne operations

TA-50: Table of Allowances is the standard issued gear; i.e. kevlar helmet, ruck sack, canteens, etc.

Taino-Arawak are the indigenous peoples of the Caribbean Isles

Takuan is the first name of Soho Takuan [宗彭沢庵] (1573-1645) He was a Zen monk, calligrapher, painter, poet, gardener, tea master, and author. His collected writings total six volumes and over 100 published poems, including his best known treatise, *The Unfettered Mind*. A central figure in the Rinzai School of Zen Buddhism, his list of accomplishments include being the inventor of the pickled, *daikon* radish that was named after him. At the moment before his death, it is said he painted the Chinese character [夢] 'dream', laid down his brush, and died

Tall, Young, Legend in Leather is a title used by LL Cool J in his lyrics to describe himself

Tamahu: The ancient Egyptians spoke of a group of uncouth nomads that were described as having pale skin, red to blond hair, and blue eyes.

Tarzan is a *very* fictional character who rules the "African jungles" all by himself. This icon has been a tool for white supremacist imagery since the early-1900s

Tet Offensive: At 3 am on Jan. 31, 1968, North Vietnamese and Vietcong forces launched simultaneous attacks on South Vietnamese and American forces all throughout South Vietnam. The fighting, the heaviest of the Vietnam War, coincided with the Lunar New Year, or *Tet*. It was the military turning point in the war and a political and media disaster for the US

The Christ is a title for Jesus in the New Testament. It is Hebrew for 'Messiah'[מָשִׁיחַ], meaning: the Anointed One

The Clark Sisters are comprised of Jacky, Elbernita, Dorinda, Denise and Karen. They are credited as being pioneers in bringing gospel music to the mainstream

The Doors: Led by Jim Morrison, this rock group took its name from Aldous Huxley's book *The Doors of Perception*

The System is a government structure imposing biased inequality. The discrimination is viewed as 'normal', or even 'ethical', by the law / media simply because they are part and parcel of the very same infrastructure

374

The Winans are a family, gospel quartet from Detroit, Michigan. The members consist of four brothers: Marvin, Carvin, Michael, and Ronald

Thrasher is someone who listens to heavy-metal music; i.e. a metal-head or a headbanger.

Timbuktu: This city, in the West African nation of Mali, is just north of the River Niger. In its Golden Age, the city's extensive trade network along with the *University of Sankore Madrasah* were internationally famous

Timothy Francis Leary (1920 – 1996) was a psychologist known for his advocacy of psychedelic drugs

Titties is slang for: breasts; i.e. jugs, boobs, knockers, etc.

Toby: In a scene in *Roots, Kunta Kinte,* played by LeVar Burton, was whipped into accepting his slave name, Toby

Top is the officially recognized nickname for a US Army 1st Sergeant

Toussaint Louverture: Francois-Dominique Toussaint Louverture (1743 - 1803) led the rebellion at Saint Domingue, in 1791, which led to the Haitian Revolution. A military genius, not only did he outwit Napoleon on the battlefield, he helped found the independent state of Haiti – that to this day, is still being punished for defeating France

Townies: is a condescending term describing the local people; akin to hillbilly

Tramaine Davis (1951 -) is a well-known gospel singer

Triathlons are competitions consisting of a 2.4 mile swim, a 112-mile bicycle ride, and a 26.2-mile marathon

Trim is slang for: vagina

Trippin': Negative terminology meaning: to behave in an irritating way. Or, it means: using LSD

Trips is slang for: tabs of LSD

Tsunami [津波] refers to: tidal wave

Turned-out: is slang related to the sexual act. Usually negative, it can mean raping someone; or satisfying a person to the point they're sexual orientation is altered; i.e. from heterosexual to homosexual

UCMJ is the abbreviation for: Universal Code of Military Justice. It is the military's list of laws and statutes

Ultra Man [ウルトラマン] first aired in 1966, and is still a popular Japanese television series amongst children

Uncle Sam is a popular nickname for the 'US' government

Uncle Tom is the title character in Harriet Beecher Stowe's 1852 novel, *Uncle Tom's Cabin;* it is also an epithet for a person who is slavish and excessively subservient to the ruling class

Underage is a reference to persons who are below the legal age limit to procure or consume alcohol

Undercover Brother is a reference to a movie starring comedian, Eddie Griffin (see bibliography)

Underground Railroad: A secret network of routes and safe houses used by people in the 19th century to escape slavery in the Americas

Unit Colors is the flag identifying the brigade, batallion, company, etc. This practice of marking the location of the commander originated in ancient Egypt

Up North is street terminology for: prison; i.e. up state

Uprock is a soulful type of street-dance consisting of foot shuffles, spins, and freestyle movements

UPS: United Parcel Service is a US-based, global package, shipping company

Up-State is street terminology for: prison; i.e. up north

US Military Installations: The NATO watch committee reveals that the US operates between 700-800 bases in at least 63 countries. There are over 90 in Japan alone

Vapors means: being high in a chemically-poisoned way; this phrase was made famous by Biz Markie in a 1988 song

Vatos is *Calo* slang for 'dude'

Vaya con Dios: In Spanish, this phrase means: to go with God

Venus was the goddess of love and beauty in ancient Rome. She is also known as *Aphrodite*

Vick is street terminology for: robbing or stealing

Video Music Box: Created in 1983 by Ralph McDaniels, it was the first TV show to give mainstream exposure to Hip Hop

Visine is a brand of eye drops that constricts the eye's superficial blood vessels; i.e. "it gets the red out"

Vogue: was a dance imitating super-model poses. Developed in NYC gay clubs, it was later popularized by *Madonna*

WKDU is a Philadelphia college-radio station at Drexel University *(see Master Jay)*

Wack is slang for: something uncool; i.e. corny

Wench is a derogatory word for: an unvirtuous woman; i.e. a bitch or slut

West Point: The preeminent four-year military academy located in West Point, New York

When the Saints go Marching in is a famous gospel hymn often played by Jazz musicians

Whiteboy is a derogatory term meaning: fearful, having no rhythm, or any trait associated with melanin-deficiency

White Devil: Wallace Fard Muhammad was one of the co-founders of the Nation of Islam (NOI). He taught the original humans were melanated and that Caucasians were 'artificial, white devils' created on the Greek island of *Patmos,* by a mad scientist named *Yakub*

White Lie is a diplomatic or well-intentioned untruth; a fib

Who's Zoomin' Who? This phrase means: turning the tables on

376

someone. It was popularized by a 1985 song by Aretha Franklin

Wild Styles is a reference to: the 1983 motion picture produced by Charlie Ahearn

Wile E: Referring to the Warner Brothers character, *Wile E. Coyote*

William Franklin Graham, Jr. (1918 -) is a Christian evangelist, ordained as a southern Baptist minister

Willie Lynch: Allegedly, in 1712, a British slave owner named Willie Lynch delivered a speech in Virginia detailing tactics to pit the indigenous tribes against one another; i.e. the secret to controlling the majority population

"Willie" Wilver Dornell Stargell (1940 – 2001), nicknamed 'Pops', was a left fielder on the Pittsburgh Pirates for 21 years

Wop: the name of a popular dance in the 1980s

Ye are Gods: Psalm 82:6: *I said, 'You are gods, sons of the Most High, all of you';* John 10:34: *Jesus answered them, 'Is it not written in your law, I said, ye are gods?'*

Yeshua [יְשׁוּעַ]: This was a common spelling in many translations amongst Jews of the Second Temple period

Yin-Yang: In Chinese cosmology, *Yin* represents female energy while *Yang* expresses the masculine principle

Yoni [योनि] is a Sanskrit word meaning: vagina or womb; symbolic of the goddess, *Shakti*

Young Boy means: younger kid. However, this label can also be a term of endearment, or an insult toward an actual peer

Your Arms Too Short to Box with God is a Broadway musical based on the biblical book of *Matthew*

Youse is a commonly used phrase meaning 'you guys'. It is used by people of Italian descent in the New Jersey / New York area

Zacchaeus: According to the Gospel of Luke, he was a tax collector in Jericho; his name means 'pure and righteous one'

Zested is slang for: being intoxicated or getting high

Zooted: the state of being overly intoxicated; i.e. fucked-up

Numbers

007 is the codename of author Ian Fleming's legendary MI6 agent, *James Bond*

144,000: In Christianity, this number represents the sum of God's people going to heaven

7-Eleven is the world's largest chain of convenience stores

808: A 3-way speaker system utilizing 5 drivers mounted in a bass-reflex enclosure

Bibliography

Articles

Bishop, J. (1988, Aug. 26). To fend off the sun, researchers are using body's own chemistry. The Wall Street Journal. Retrieved from ProQuest databases.

Chamberlain, A. (1911, Apr) The contribution of the negro to human civilization. Journal of Race Development 1(1). Retrieved from https://archive.org/details/jstor-29737886.

King, R. (1986). Black dot, the black seed of humanity. Ureaus, The Journal of Unconscious Life, 2(1). Los Angeles, California: Aquarian Spiritual Center.

Sirota, D. (2011, March 16). How your taxpayer dollars subsidize pro-war movies and block anti-war movies. The Huffington Post. Retrieved from http://www.huffingtonpost.com/david-sirota/how-your-taxpayer-dollars_b_836574.html.

Blog

The Remix with MsBlue. (2010, October 15). "The psycho-sexual war against black girls!" Bro Umar Johnson [Audio file] Retrieved from http://www.blogtalkradio.com/theremix/2010/10/16/the-psycho-sexual-war-against-black-girls-bro-umar-johnson

Books

Ashby, M. (2005). *The Egyptian Book of the Dead: The Book of Coming Forth by Day*. Atlanta: Sema Institute.

Barnes, C. (1988). *Melanin: The Chemical Key to Black Greatness*. Houston, Texas: Lushena Publishing.

Browder, A. (1989). *From the Browder File, 22 Essays on the African-American Experience.* Washington DC: Institute of Karmic Guidance Publishing.

Bruce, R. (2009). *Astral Dynamics: The Complete Book of Out-of-Body Experiences*. Newburyport, Massachusetts: Hampton Roads Publishing.

Chandler, W. (1999). *Ancient Future: The Teachings and Prophetic Wisdom of the Seven Hermetic Laws of Ancient Egypt.* Baltimore, Maryland: Black Classic Press

Howard, R., Sprague De Camp, L., & Carter, L. (1968). *Conan*. New York: Ace Books.

Kingseed, C. (2006). *Old Glory Stories: American Combat Leadership in World War II*. Maryland: Naval Institute Press.

Muhammad, E. (1965). *Message to the Blackman in America*. Arizona: Secretarius MEMPS Publications.

Rashidi, R. (1985). *African Presence in Early Asia.* Rutgers – The State University of NJ, Piscataway, NJ: Transaction Publishers.

Standley, F. (1989). *Conversations with James Baldwin*. Mississippi: University Press of Mississippi.

Whitaker, R. (1979). *Shibumi*. New York: Crown Publishers.

Music

Baker, A. (1985-1986). Been so long [Recorded by Anita Baker] *Rapture* [Vinyl]. California: Elektra Records. (1986)

Baker, A. (1985). Sweet love [Recorded by Anita Baker] *Rapture* [Vinyl]. California: Elektra Records. (1986)

Barrier, E., Griffen, W. (1986). Eric B. is president [Recorded by Eric B. & Rakim] *Paid in Full* [Vinyl]. New York: 4th & B'way/Island. (1986)

Blackmon, L., Jenkins, T. (1986). Word up! [Recorded by Cameo] *Word up!* [Vinyl]. New York: Atlanta Artist. (1986)

Cameo (1983-1984). She's strange [Recorded by Cameo] *She's Strange* [Vinyl]. Casablanca. (January 16, 1984)

Chandler, J. Bell, F., & McDonald, C. (1981). Silly [Recorded by Denise Williams] *Silly* (single) [Vinyl]. Pennsylvania: Columbia/ARC. (1981)

Dewese, M. (1986). Go see the doctor [Recorded by Kool Moe Dee]. *Go See the Doctor* [Vinyl]. New York: Jive. (1986)

Dixon, M., Murphy, D., Dechalus, L., Withrow, K., Brickell, E., Houser, J., Bush, J., & Aly, A. (1989 -1990). Slow down [Recorded by Brand Nubians] *One for All* [Vinyl]. United States: Elektra Records. (1990)

Edwards, B., Rodgers, N. (1978). Le freak [Recorded by Chic] *Le Freak/Savior Faire* [Vinyl]. Atlantic. (January 1978)

Edwards, B., Rodgers, N. (1978). We are family [Recorded by Sister Sledge] *Easier to Love* [Vinyl]. Cotillion. (1979)

Elam, K., Martin, C. (1990). Just to get a rep [Recorded by Gang Starr] *Step in the Arena* [Vinyl]. New York: Chrysalis/ EMI Records. (1991)

Fekaris, D., Perren, F. (1978). Shake your groove thing [Recorded by Peaches & Herb] *2 Hot* [Vinyl]. Polydor. (1978)

Fequiere, S., Campbell, J., Reeves, F., & Bailey, M. (1985). Roxanne roxanne [Recorded by UTFO]. *UTFO* [Vinyl]. New Jersey: Select Records. (1985)

Gamble K., Huff, L. (1978). Use ta be my girl [Recorded by The O'Jays]. *So Full of Love* [Vinyl]. Philadelphia: Philadelphia International (1977-1988)

Gamble, K, Huff, L., Jackson, A. (1972). Foe the love of money [Recorded by The O'Jays] *Ship Ahoy* [Vinyl]. Philadelphia: Philadelphia International Records. (1973)

Ginyard, R., Bryce, R., Riley, T., & Brown, J. (1988). It takes two [Recorded by Rob Base and DJ E-Z Rock]. *It takes two* [Vinyl]. New York: Profile. (1988)

Green, R., Aleem, T., Aleem. T. (1984). Cosmic blast [Recorded by Captain Rock]. *Captain Rock* [Vinyl]. New York: NIA. (1984)

Greene, S. (1984).Let the music play [Recorded by Shannon]. *Let the Music Play* [Vinyl]. New York: Mirage. (February 1, 1984)

Griffey, D., Sylvers, L. (1978). It's all the way live [Recorded by Lakeside]. *Shot of Love* [Vinyl]. California: Solar Records. (1978)

Hancock, H., Laswell, B., & Beinhorn, M. (1983). Rockit [Recorded by Herbie Hancock]. *Future Shock* [vinyl]. (August 1983)

Hanson, A., Davis, E., Mantronik, K. (1986). Hungry for your love [Recorded by Hanson & Davis] *I'll Take You On/Hungry For Your Love/Hold On To Yesterday EP* [Vinyl]. Fresh Records. (1986)

Hardy, A (1986-1988) Vapors [Recorded by Biz Markie]. *Goin' Off* [Vinyl]. New York: Cold Chillin' Records. (1988)

Hardy, N.S., McDaniels, Jr., Simmons, J., & Smith. (1983). Sucker M.C.'s (Krush Groove 1)[Recorded by Run-D.M.C.] *Run-D.M.C.* [Vinyl]. Profile, Arista. (1984)

Hendrix, J. (1967). Purple haze [Recorded by The Jimi Hendrix Experience] *Are you experienced* [Vinyl]. United Kingdom: Track Records. (1967)

Hutchins, J., Fletcher, J., Carter, D. (1984). Friends [Recorded by Whodini] *Escape* [Vinyl]. Jive/Arista Records (October 17, 1984)

Jabara, P., Shaffer, P. (1979). It's raining men [Recorded by The Weather Girls] *Success* [Vinyl]. New York: Columbia. (1982)

Jackson, M. (1982). Beat it [Recorded by Michael Jackson] *Thriller* [Vinyl]. Epic. (November 30, 1982)

Jackson, M. (1982). Thriller [Recorded by Michael Jackson] *Thriller* [Vinyl]. Epic. (1982)

Johnson, H., Gill, P., O'Toole, M., Nash, B. (1983-1984). The World is my oyster [Recorded by Frankie Goes to Hollywood] *Welcome to the Pleasuredome* [Vinyl]. London: ZTT. (1984)

McCoy, V. (1975). The hustle [Recorded by Van McCoy & the Sould City Symphony]. *Disco Baby* [Vinyl]. New York: Avco Records. (1975)

Moltke, S. (1986). The bridge [Recorded by MC Shan] *Down by Law* [Vinyl]. New York: Cold Chillen/Warner Bros. Records. (1985)

Myers, D., Parrish, G., Dixon, T., & Ferrell, F. (1986-1987). The overweight lover's in the house [Recorded by Heavy D & the Boyz] *Living Large* [Vinyl]. New York: Uptown Records. (1987)

Pryor, R. (1975). That nigger's crazy [Recorded by Richard Pryor]. *That nigger's crazy* [Vinyl]. San Francisco: Warner Bros. Records. (1974)

Richie, L., McClary, T., Williams, M., King, W., La Pread, R., Orange, W., & Dean, C. (1980). Jesus is love [Recorded by The Commodores] *Heroes* [Vinyl]. United States: Motown Records. (1980)

Ridenhour, C., Sadler, E., Boxley, H., & Boxley, K. (1990). *Fear of a black planet* [CD]. United States: Def Jam / Columbia Records.

Ridenhour, C., Sadler, E., Boxley, H., & Boxley, K. (1989). Fight the power [Recorded by Public Enemy] *Fight the power* [Vinyl]. United States: Motown Records. (1989)

Robinson, J., Glover, M., & Robinson, S. (1982). Message II (Survival) [Recorded by Melle Mel & Duke Bootee of Grandmaster Flash & The Furious Five] *Message II (Survival)* [Vinyl]. England: Sugar Hill Records. (1982)

Simmons, J., McDaniels, D. (1983). Jam-master jay [Recorded by Run-D.M.C.] *Run-d.m.c.* [Vinyl]. United States: Profile / Arista Records. (1984)

Simmons, J., McDaniels, D. (1985). My adidas [Recorded by Run-D.M.C.] *Raising hell* [Vinyl]. United States: Profile / Arista Records. (1986)

Smith, C., Williams, Kaye, & Montnegro. (n.d.). Sucker DJ's (I Will Survive) [Recorded by Marley Marl] *Sucker DJ's (I Will Survive)* [Vinyl]. Party Time. (1983)

Smith, J. (1986-1987). I'm Bad [Recorded by LL Cool J] *Bigger and Deffer* [Vinyl]. New York: Def Jam, Columbia, CBS Records. (1987)

Smith, J., Jay, J., & Rubin, R. (1984). I Need a Beat [Recorded by LL Cool J] *Radio* [Vinyl]. New York: Def Jam/Columbia/ CBS Records. (1985)

Tosh, P. (1975). Legalize it [Recorded by Peter Tosh] *Legalize It* [Vinyl]. Jamaica: Columbia Records. (1976)

382

Williams, J. Mantronik, K. (1986). Cold Gettin' Dumb [Recorded by Just-Ice] *Back to the Old School* [Vinyl]. Fresh/Sleeping Bag Records. (1986)

Withers, B., Salter, W., & MacDonald, R. (1981). Just the Two of Us [Recorded by Grover Washington & Bill Withers] *Just the Two of us (B-side: Make Me a Memory)* [Vinyl]. Elektra. (1981)

Movies

Beckerman, S., Feitshans, B. (Producer), & Milius, J. (Director). (1984). *Red dawn* [Motion picture]. United States: MGM/UA Entertainment Co.

Ben-Ami, Y., Carver, S. (Producer), & Carver, S. (Director). (1983). *Lone wolf Mcquade* [Motion picture]. United States: Orion Pictures.

Bregman, M. (Producer), & De Palma, B. (Director). (1983). *Scarface* [Motion picture]. United States: Universal Pictures.

Canton, N., Gale, B. (Producers), Zemeckis, R. (Director). (1985). *Back to the future* [Motion picture]. United States: Universal Pictures.

Chartoff, R., Winkler, I. (Producer). Avildsen, J. (Director). (1976). *Rocky* [Motion picture]. United States: United Artists.

Curtis, K., Harris, T., Ross, D. (Producer), & Murray, D. (Director). (1970). *The cross and the switchblade* [Motion picture]. United States: 20th Century Fox.

Donner, R., Silver, J. (Producers), Donner, R. (Director). (1987). *Lethal weapon* [Motion picture]. United States: Warner Bros. Pictures.

Feitshans, B., Kassar, M., Vajna, A. (Producer), & Kotcheff, T. (Director). (1982). *First blood* [Motion picture]. United States: Orion Pictures.

Fox, T., Henderson, G. (Producers), O'Bannon, D. (Director). (1985). *The Return of the living dead* [Motion picture]. United States: Orion Pictures.

Gordon, L., Silver, J., Davis, J. (Producer), & McTiernan, J. (Director). (1987). *Predator* [Motion picture]. United States: 20th Century Fox.

Grazer, B. (Producer). (2002). *Undercover brother* [Motion picture]. United States: Universal Pictures.

Kennedy, K., Jones, Q., Marshall, F., Spielberg, S. (Producer), Spielberg, S. (Director). (1985). *The color purple* [Motion picture]. United States: Warner Bros. Pictures.

Kopelson, A. (Producer), & Stone, O. (Writer/Director). (1986). *Platoon* [Motion picture]. United States: Orion Pictures.

Lee, S. (Producer/Writer/Director). (1989). *Do the right thing* [Motion picture]. United States: 40 Acres and a Mule Filmworks.

Lester, D., Miller, D., Rappaport, M. (Producer), & Shelton, R. (Director). (1992). *white men can't jump* [Motion Picture]. United States: 20th Century Fox.

Linson, A., Azoff, I., (Producer), & Heckerling, A. (Director). (1982). *fast times at ridgemont high* [Motion picture]. United States: Universal Studios.

Nasheed, T. (Director). (2011). *Hidden colors 1* [Motion picture]. United States: King Flex Entertainment.

Nasheed, T. (Director). (2012). *Hidden colors 2* [Motion picture]. United States: King Flex Entertainment.

Nicolaides, S. (Producer). Singleton, J. (Writer/Director). (1991). *Boyz n the hood* [Motion picture]. United States: Columbia Pictures.

Puttnam, D. (Producer), Hudson, H. (Director). (1981). *Chariots of fire* [Motion picture]. United Kingdom: The Ladd Company.

Raymond, C. (Producer), & Wei, L. (Writer/Director). (1972). *Fist of fury* [Motion picture]. Hong Kong: Golden Harvest Miramax.

Roddenberry, G. (Producer), Wise, R. (Director). (1979). *Star trek: The Motion Picture* [Motion picture]. United States: Paramount Pictures.

Shapiro, A. (Producer), Shapiro, A. (Writer/Director). (1978). *Scared straight!* [Motion picture]. United States: Golden West Television.

Silver, J. (Producer), & Lester, M. (Director). (1985). *Commando* [Motion picture]. United States: 20th Century Fox.

Simpson, D., Bruckheimer, J. (Producer), & Scott, T. (Director). (1986). *Top gun* [Motion picture]. United States: Paramount Pictures.

Solo, R. (Producer), Hopper, D. (Director). (1988). *Colors* [Motion picture]. United States: Orion Pictures.

Spielberg, S., Marshall, F. (Producers), Hooper, T. (Director). (1982). *Poltergeist* [Motion picture]. United States: Metro-Goldwyn-Mayer.

Wachs, R., Wayans, K. (Producers), & Townsend, R. (Director). (1987). *Eddie Murphy raw* [Motion picture]. United States: Paramount Picutres.

Television

Barbera, J., Hanna, W. (Producer). (1977). *Captain caveman and the teen angels* [Television series]. United States: Hanna-Barbera Productions.

Barbera, J., Hanna, W. (Producer). (1980). *Richie Rich* [Television series]. United States: ABC.

Bass, J., Rankin, A. (1974). *The year without a santa claus* [Television animation]. ABC.

Carsey, M., Werner, T., Kukoff, B., Leahy, J. (Producers). (1984). *The Cosby show* [Television series]. United States: Viacom Enterprises; Paramount Domestic Television; Carsey-Werner Distribution.

Cornelius, D. (Producer). (1971). *Soul train* [Television series]. United States: Tribune Entertainment.

Correll, C., Gosden, F. (Creators). (1951). *The Amos 'n' Andy show* [Television series]. United States: WMAQ AM.

Davis, A. (Director). (1947). *The goofy gophers* [Television series]. United States: Warner Bros. Pictures.

Dozier, W., Horwitz, H. (Producer). (1966). *Batman* [Television series]. United States: Greenway Productions/20th Century Fox Television

Freston, T., Pittman, R. (Founders). (1980). *MTV: Music television* [Television series]. United States: Viacom Media Networks.

Healy, T. (Creator). (1925). *The three stooges* [Television series]. United States: Columbia Pictures Corporation.

Levitt, G. (Creator). (1977). *Fantasy island* [Television series]. United States: ABC.

Margulies, S. (Producer). (Jan. 23, 1977 – Jan. 30, 1977). *Roots* [Television miniseries]. United States: ABC.

McDaniels, R. (Creator). (1983). *Video music box* [Television series]. United States: WNYE-TV.

Michaels, L. (Producer). (1975). *Saturday night live* [Television series]. United States: Broadway Video.

Monte, E., Evans, M. (Creators). (1974). *Good times* [Telvision series]. United States: CBS.

Peppiatt, F., Aylesworth, J., Brillstein, B. (Creators). (1969). *Hee haw* [Television series]. United States: CBS-TV.

Ruby, J., Spears, K. (Creators). (1976). *Jabberjaw* [Television series]. United States: Hanna-Barbera Productions.

Takamoto, I., Lovy, A. (Producer). (1973). *Inch high private eye* [Television series]. United States: NBC.

Terry, P. (Creator). (1942). *Mighty mouse* [Television series]. United States: 20th Century Fox.

Tsuburaya, E. (Creator). (1966). *Ultraman* [Television series]. Japan: TBS.

Walsh, J. (Creator). (1979-). *SportsCenter* [Sports news program]. United States: ESPN.

www.ingramcontent.com/pod-product-compliance
Lightning Source LLC
Chambersburg PA
CBHW061549120626
46550CB00004B/1427

* 9 7 8 4 9 0 8 5 5 6 0 5 0 *